Get the eBook FREE!

(PDF, ePub, Kindle, and liveBook all included)

We believe that once you buy a book from us, you should be able to read it in any format we have available. To get electronic versions of this book at no additional cost to you, purchase and then register this book at the Manning website.

Go to https://www.manning.com/freebook and follow the instructions to complete your pBook registration.

That's it!
Thanks from Manning!

The Art
of Unit Testing

THIRD EDITION
WITH EXAMPLES IN JAVASCRIPT

ROY OSHEROVE
WITH VLADIMIR KHORIKOV

MANNING

SHELTER ISLAND

For online information and ordering of this and other Manning books, please visit
www.manning.com. The publisher offers discounts on this book when ordered in quantity.
For more information, please contact

Special Sales Department
Manning Publications Co.
20 Baldwin Road
PO Box 761
Shelter Island, NY 11964
Email: orders@manning.com

Manning Publications Co.   Development editor: Connor O'Brien
20 Baldwin Road   Technical development editor: Mike Shepard
PO Box 761   Review editors: Adriana Sabo and Dunja Nikitović
Shelter Island, NY 11964   Production editor: Kathy Rossland
                                    Copy editor: Andy Carroll
                                    Proofreader: Katie Tennant
                         Technical proofreader: Jean-François Morin
                                    Typesetter: Dennis Dalinnik
                                Cover designer: Marija Tudor

ISBN: 9781617297489
Printed in the United States of America

contents

foreword to the second edition

The year must have been 2009. I was speaking at the Norwegian Developers Conference in Oslo. (Ah, Oslo in June!) The event was held in a huge sports arena. The conference organizers divided the bleachers into sections, built stages in front of them, and draped them with thick black cloth in order to create eight different session "rooms." I remember I was just about finished with my talk, which was about TDD, or SOLID, or astronomy, or something, when suddenly, from the stage next to me, came this loud and raucous singing and guitar playing.

The drapes were such that I was able to peer around them and see the fellow on the stage next to mine, who was making all the noise. Of course, it was Roy Osherove.

Now, those of you who know me know that breaking into song in the middle of a technical talk about software is something that *I* might just do, if the mood struck me. So as I turned back to my audience, I thought to myself that this Osherove fellow was a kindred spirit, and I'd have to get to know him better.

And getting to know him better is just what I did. In fact, he made a significant contribution to my most recent book, *The Clean Coder*, and spent three days with me co-teaching a TDD class. My experiences with Roy have all been very positive, and I hope there are many more.

I predict that your experience with Roy, in the reading of this book, will be very positive as well, because this book is something special.

Have you ever read a Michener novel? I haven't; but I've been told that they all start at "the atom." The book you're holding isn't a James Michener novel, but it does start at the atom—the atom of unit testing.

Don't be misled as you thumb through the early pages. This is *not* a mere introduction to unit testing. It starts that way, and if you're experienced you can skim those first chapters. As the book progresses, the chapters start to build on each other into a rather startling accumulation of depth. Indeed, as I read the last chapter (not knowing it was the last chapter), I thought to myself that the next chapter would be dealing with world peace—because, I mean, where else can you go after solving the problem of introducing unit testing into obstinate organizations with old legacy systems?

This book is technical—deeply technical. There's a lot of code. That's a good thing. But Roy doesn't restrict himself to the technical. From time to time he pulls out his guitar and breaks into song as he tells anecdotes from his professional past or waxes philosophical about the meaning of design or the definition of integration. He seems to relish regaling us with stories about some of the things he did really badly in the deep, dark past of 2006.

Oh, and don't be too concerned that the code is all in C#. I mean, who can tell the difference between C# and Java anyway? Right? And besides, it just doesn't matter. He may use C# as a vehicle to communicate his intent, but the lessons in this book also apply to Java, C, Ruby, Python, PHP, or any other programming language (except, perhaps COBOL).

If you're a newcomer to unit testing and test-driven development, or if you're an old hand at it, you'll find this book has something for you. So get ready for a treat as Roy sings you the song, "The Art of Unit Testing."

And Roy, please tune that guitar!

—ROBERT C. MARTIN (Uncle Bob)
cleancoder.com

foreword to the first edition

When Roy Osherove told me that he was working on a book about unit testing, I was very happy to hear it. The testing meme has been rising in the industry for years, but there has been a relative dearth of material available about unit testing. When I look at my bookshelf, I see books that are about test-driven development specifically and books about testing in general, but until now there has been no comprehensive reference for unit testing—no book that introduces the topic and guides the reader from first steps to widely accepted best practices. The fact that this is true is stunning. Unit testing isn't a new practice. How did we get to this point?

It's almost a cliché to say that we work in a very young industry, but it's true. Mathematicians laid the foundations of our work less than 100 years ago, but we've only had hardware fast enough to exploit their insights for the last 60 years. There was an initial gap between theory and practice in our industry, and we're only now discovering how it has impacted our field.

In the early days, machine cycles were expensive. We ran programs in batches. Programmers had a scheduled time slot, and they had to punch their programs into decks of cards and walk them to the machine room. If your program wasn't right, you lost your time, so you desk-checked your program with pencil and paper, mentally working out all of the scenarios, all of the edge cases. I doubt the notion of automated unit testing was even imaginable. Why use the machine for testing when you could use it to solve the problems it was meant to solve? Scarcity kept us in the dark.

Later, machines became faster and we became intoxicated with interactive computing. We could just type in code and change it on a whim. The idea of desk-checking code faded away, and we lost some of the discipline of the early years. We knew programming was hard, but that just meant that we had to spend more time at the computer, changing lines and symbols until we found the magical incantation that worked.

We went from scarcity to surplus and missed the middle ground, but now we're regaining it. Automated unit testing marries the discipline of desk-checking with a newfound appreciation for the computer as a development resource. We can write automated tests in the language we develop in to check our work—not just once, but as often as we're able to run them. I don't think there is any other practice that's quite as powerful in software development.

As I write this, in 2009, I'm happy to see Roy's book come into print. It's a practical guide that will help you get started and also serve as a great reference as you go about your testing tasks. *The Art of Unit Testing* isn't a book about idealized scenarios. It teaches you how to test code as it exists in the field, how to take advantage of widely used frameworks, and, most importantly, how to write code that's far easier to test.

The Art of Unit Testing is an important title that should have been written years ago, but we weren't ready then. We are ready now. Enjoy.

—MICHAEL FEATHERS
Object Mentor

preface

One of the biggest failed projects I worked on had unit tests. Or so I thought. I was leading a group of programmers creating a billing application, and we were doing it in a fully test-driven manner—writing the test, then writing the code, seeing the test fail, making the test pass, refactoring, and starting all over again.

The first few months of the project were great. Things were going well, and we had tests that proved that our code worked. But as time went by, requirements changed. We were forced to change our code to fit those new requirements, and when we did, tests broke and had to be fixed. The code still worked, but the tests we wrote were so brittle that any little change in our code broke them, even though the code was working fine. It became a daunting task to change code in a class or method because we also had to fix all the related unit tests.

Worse yet, some tests became unusable because the people who wrote them left the project, and no one knew how to maintain the tests or what they were testing. The names we gave our unit testing methods weren't clear enough, and we had tests relying on other tests. We ended up throwing out most of the tests less than six months into the project.

The project was a miserable failure because we let the tests we wrote do more harm than good. They took more time to maintain and understand than they saved us in the long run, so we stopped using them. I moved on to other projects, where we did a better job writing our unit tests, and we had some great successes using them, saving huge amounts of debugging and integration time. Since that first failed project, I've been compiling best practices for unit tests and using them on subsequent projects. I find a few more best practices with every project I work on.

Understanding how to write unit tests—and how to make them maintainable, readable, and trustworthy—is what this book is about, no matter what language or integrated development environment you work with. This book covers the basics of writing a unit test, moves on to the basics of interaction testing, and introduces best practices for writing, managing, and maintaining unit tests in the real world.

—ROY OSHEROVE

When Manning asked me to help complete a book on unit testing that was nearly finished, my initial thought was to decline. After all, I already had my own book on unit testing, so why should I work on someone else's project? But I changed my mind when I realized that the book in question was none other than Roy's *The Art of Unit Testing*. The first edition of *The Art of Unit Testing* was one of the first books I read on the topic, and it helped shape my views on unit testing. I feel honored to contribute to the third edition of this momentous work.

I personally see this book as an excellent introduction to the subject of unit testing. Once you have completed it and are ready to delve deeper, pick up my book, *Unit Testing Principles, Practices, and Patterns* (Manning, 2020).

—VLADIMIR KHORIKOV

acknowledgments

We would like to thank the many reviewers of the manuscript, whose feedback helped us to improve the book. Thanks go to Aboudou Samadou Sare, Adhir Ramjiawan, Adriaan Beiertz, Alain Lompo, Barnaby Norman, Charles Lam, Conor Redmond, Daut Morina, Esref Durna, Foster Haines, Harinath Mallepally, Jared Duncan, Jason Hales, Jaume López, Jeremy Chen, Joel Holmes, John Larsen, Jonathan Reeves, Jorge E. Bo, Kent Spillner, Kim Gabrielsen, Marcel van den Brink, Mark Graham, Matt Van Winkle, Matteo Battista, Matteo Gildone, Mike Holcomb, Oliver Korten, Onofrei George, Paul Roebuck, Pablo Herrera J., Patrice Maldague, Rahul Modpur, Ranjit Sahai, Rich Yonts, Richard Meinsen, Rodrigo Encinas, Ronald Borman, Sachin Singhi, Samantha Berk, Sander Zegveld, Satej Kumar Sahu, Shayn Cornwell, Tanya Wilke, Tom Madden, Udit Bhardwaj, and Vadim Turkov.

Many hands go into the making of a successful book. We would like to thank Manning acquisitions editor Michael Stephens, development editor Connor O'Brien, technical development editor Mike Shepard, technical proofreader Jean-François Morin, and review editors Adriana Sabo and Dunja Nikitović. We also thank everyone else at Manning who worked on the third edition in production and behind the scenes.

A final word of thanks goes to the early readers of the book in Manning's Early Access Program for their comments in the online forum. You helped shape the book.

about this book

One of the smartest things I ever heard anyone say about learning (and I forget who it was) is that to truly learn something, teach it. Writing the first edition of this book and publishing it in 2009 was nothing short of a true learning experience for me. I initially wrote the book because I got tired of answering the same questions over and over again. But there were other reasons, too. I wanted to try something new; I wanted to try an experiment; I wondered what I could learn from writing a book—any book. Unit testing was what I was good at, I thought. The curse is that the more experience you have, the more stupid you feel.

There are parts of the first edition that today I do not agree with—for example, that a *unit* refers to a method. That's not true at all. A unit is a unit of work, as I discuss in chapter 1 of this third edition. It can be as small as a method, or as big as several classes (possibly assemblies), and there are other things as well that have changed, as you will learn next.

What's new in the third edition

In this third edition, we switched from .NET to JavaScript and TypeScript. All the related tools and frameworks got updated, too, of course. For example, instead of NUnit test runner and NSubstitute, we used Jest, both as a unit testing framework and as a mocking library.

We added more techniques to the chapter about implementing unit testing at the organizational level.

There are plenty of design changes in the code we show in the book. They are mostly related to the use of dynamically typed languages such as JavaScript, but we talk about statically typed techniques as well with the help of TypeScript.

The discussion about test trustworthiness, maintainability, and readability has been expanded into three separate chapters. We also added a new chapter about testing strategies: how to decide between different test types and what techniques to use.

Who should read this book

The book is for anyone who writes code and is interested in learning best practices for unit testing. All the examples are written in JavaScript and TypeScript, so JavaScript developers will find the examples particularly useful. But the lessons we teach apply equally to most, if not all, object-oriented and statically typed languages (C#, VB.NET, Java, and C++, to name a few). If you're an architect, developer, team lead, QA engineer (who writes code), or novice programmer, this book should suit you well.

How this book is organized: A road map

If you've never written a unit test, it's best to read this book from start to finish so you get the full picture. If you have experience, you should feel comfortable jumping into the chapters as you see fit. The book is divided into four parts.

Part 1 takes you from 0 to 60 in writing unit tests. Chapters 1 and 2 cover the basics, such as how to use a testing framework (Jest), and they introduce automated test concepts, such as test libraries, assertion libraries, and test runners. They also introduce the ideas of asserts, ignoring tests, unit-of-work testing, the three types of end results of a unit test, and the three types of tests you need for them: value tests, state-based tests, and interaction tests.

Part 2 discusses advanced techniques for breaking dependencies: mock objects, stubs, isolation frameworks, and patterns for refactoring your code to use them. Chapter 3 introduces the idea of stubs and shows how to manually create and use them. Chapter 4 introduces interaction testing with mock objects. Chapter 5 merges these two concepts and shows how isolation frameworks combine these two ideas and allow them to be automated. Chapter 6 dives deeper into understanding how to test asynchronous code.

Part 3 is about ways to organize test code, patterns for running and refactoring its structure, and best practices when writing tests. Chapter 7 discusses techniques for writing tests that you can trust. Chapter 8 discusses best practices in unit testing for creating maintainable tests.

Part 4 is all about how to implement change in an organization and how to work on existing code. Chapter 9 is about test readability. Chapter 10 shows how to develop a testing strategy. Chapter 11 discusses problems and solutions you'd encounter when trying to introduce unit testing into an organization, and it identifies and answers some questions you might be asked in the course of such an effort. Chapter 12 talks about introducing unit testing into legacy code. It identifies a couple of ways to determine where to begin testing and discusses some tools for testing untestable code.

The appendix has a list of monkey-patching techniques you might find useful in your testing efforts.

Code conventions and downloads

All source code in listings or in the text is in a `fixed-width font` like this to distinguish it from ordinary text. In listings, **bold code** indicates code that has changed from the previous example or that will change in the next example. In many listings, the code is annotated to point out the key concepts.

You can download the source code for this book from GitHub at https://github .com/royosherove/aout3-samples, as well as from the publisher's website at https:// www.manning.com/books/the-art-of-unit-testing-third-edition. You can get executable snippets of code from the liveBook (online) version of this book at https://livebook .manning.com/book/the-art-of-unit-testing-third-edition.

Software requirements

To use the code in this book, you'll need VS Code (which is free). You'll also need Jest (an open source and free framework) and other tools that will be referenced where they're relevant. All the tools mentioned are either free, open source, or have trial versions you can use freely as you read this book.

liveBook discussion forum

Purchase of *The Art of Unit Testing, Third Edition*, includes free access to liveBook, Manning's online reading platform. Using liveBook's exclusive discussion features, you can attach comments to the book globally or to specific sections or paragraphs. It's a snap to make notes for yourself, ask and answer technical questions, and receive help from the author and other users. To access the forum, go to https://livebook .manning.com/book/the-art-of-unit-testing-third-edition/discussion. You can also learn more about Manning's forums and the rules of conduct at https://livebook.manning .com/discussion.

Manning's commitment to our readers is to provide a venue where a meaningful dialogue between individual readers and between readers and authors can take place. It is not a commitment to any specific amount of participation on the part of the authors, whose contribution to the forum remains voluntary (and unpaid). We suggest you try asking them some challenging questions, lest their interest stray! The forum and the archives of previous discussions will be accessible from the publisher's website as long as the book is in print.

Other projects by Roy Osherove

Roy is also the author of *Elastic Leadership: Growing Self-organizing Teams,* available at www.manning.com/books/elastic-leadership, and *Notes to a Software Team Leader: Growing Self-Organizing Teams* (Team Agile Publishing, 2014).

Other resources:

- A blog for team leaders related to this book is available at http://5whys.com.
- An online video TDD Master Class by Roy is available at https://courses.osherove.com/courses.
- Many free videos about unit testing are available at http://ArtOfUnitTesting.com and http://Osherove.com/Videos.
- Roy is continuously training and consulting around the world. You can contact him at http://contact.osherove.com to book training at your own company.

And you can follow him on X at @RoyOsherove.

Other projects by Vladimir Khorikov

Vladimir is also the author of *Unit Testing Principles, Practices, and Patterns,* which you can find at https://www.manning.com/books/unit-testing.

Other resources:

- A blog for developers striving to learn about unit testing and domain-driven design: https://enterprisecraftsmanship.com/.
- Video courses on Pluralsight are available at https://bit.ly/ps-all.

And you can follow him on X at @vkhorikov.

about the authors

ROY OSHEROVE is one of the original ALT.NET organizers and previously worked at Typemock as a chief architect. He consults and trains teams worldwide on the gentle art of unit testing and test-driven development, and he teaches team leaders how to lead better at 5whys.com. Roy tweets at @RoyOsherove and has many videos about unit testing at ArtOfUnitTesting.com. He can also be booked for talks and training at Osherove.com.

VLADIMIR KHORIKOV is a Microsoft MVP, blogger, and Pluralsight author. He has been professionally involved in software development for more than 10 years, including mentoring teams on the ins and outs of unit testing. Vladimir is the author of *Unit Testing, Principles, Practices, and Patterns* from Manning, and he has written several popular blog post series and an online training course on the topic of unit testing. The biggest advantage of his teaching style, and the one students often praise, is his tendency to have a strong theoretic background, which he then applies to practical examples. His blog is at EnterpriseCraftsmanship.com.

about the cover illustration

The figure on the cover of *The Art of Unit Testing, Third Edition,* is a "Japonais en costume de cérémonie," or a "Japanese man in ceremonial dress." The illustration is taken from James Prichard's *Natural History of Man,* a book of hand-colored lithographs published in England in 1847. It was found by our cover designer in an antique shop in San Francisco.

In those days, it was easy to identify where people lived and what their trade or station in life was just by their dress. Manning celebrates the inventiveness and initiative of the computer business with book covers based on the rich diversity of regional culture centuries ago, brought back to life by pictures from collections such as this one.

Part 1

Getting started

This part of the book covers the basics of unit testing.

In chapter 1, I'll define what a "unit" is and what "good" unit testing means, and I'll compare *unit testing* with *integration testing*. Then we'll look at test-driven development and its role in relation to unit testing.

You'll take a stab at writing your first unit test using Jest (a common JavaScript test framework) in chapter 2. You'll get to know Jest's basic API, how to assert things, and how to execute tests continuously.

The basics of unit testing 1

This chapter covers
- Identifying entry points and exit points
- The definitions of *unit test* and *unit of work*
- The difference between unit testing and integration testing
- A simple example of unit testing
- Understanding test-driven development

Manual tests suck. You write your code, you run it in the debugger, you hit all the right keys in your app to get things just right, and then you repeat all this the next time you write new code. And you have to remember to check all the other code that might have been affected by the new code. More manual work. Great.

Doing tests and regression testing completely manually, repeating the same actions again and again like a monkey, is error prone and time consuming, and people seem to hate doing that as much as anything can be hated in software development. These problems are alleviated by tooling and our decision to use it for good, by writing automated tests that save us precious time and debugging pain. Integration and unit testing frameworks help developers write tests more quickly with a set of known APIs, execute those tests automatically, and review the results of

3

those tests easily. And they never forget! I'm assuming you're reading this book because either you feel the same way, or because someone forced you to read it, and that someone feels the same way. Or maybe that someone was forced to force you into reading this book. Doesn't matter. If you believe repetitive manual testing is awesome, this book will be very difficult to read. The assumption is that you *want* to learn how to write good unit tests.

This book also assumes that you know how to write code using JavaScript or Type-Script, using at least ECMAScript 6 (ES6) features, and that you are comfortable with node package manager (npm). Another assumption is that you are familiar with Git source control. If you've seen github.com before and you know how to clone a repository from there, you are good to go.

Although all the book's code listings are in JavaScript and TypeScript, you don't have to be a JavaScript programmer to read this book. The previous editions of this book were in C#, and I've found that about 80% of the patterns there have transferred over quite easily. You should be able to read this book even if you come from Java, .NET, Python, Ruby, or other languages. The patterns are just patterns. The language is used to demonstrate those patterns, but they are not language-specific.

JavaScript vs. TypeScript in this book

This book contains both vanilla JavaScript and TypeScript examples throughout. I take full responsibility for creating such a Tower of Babel (no pun intended), but I promise, there's a good reason: this book is dealing with three programming paradigms in JavaScript: *procedural, functional,* and *object-oriented* design.

I use regular JavaScript for the samples dealing with procedural and functional designs. I use TypeScript for the object-oriented examples, because it provides the structure needed to express these ideas.

In previous editions of this book, when I was working in C#, this wasn't an issue. When moving to JavaScript, which supports these multiple paradigms, using Type-Script makes sense.

Why not just use TypeScript for all the paradigms, you ask? Both to show that Type-Script is not needed to write unit tests and that the concepts of unit testing do not depend on one language or another, or on any type of compiler or linter, to work.

This means that if you're into functional programming, some of the examples in this book will make sense, and others will seem like they are overcomplicated or needlessly verbose. Feel free to focus only on the functional examples.

If you're into object-oriented programming or are coming from a C#/Java background, you'll find that some of the non-object-oriented examples are simplistic and don't represent your day-to-day work in your own projects. Fear not, there will be plenty of sections relating to the object-oriented style.

1.1   The first step

There's always a first step: the first time you wrote a program, the first time you failed a project, and the first time you succeeded in what you were trying to accomplish. You never forget your first time, and I hope you won't forget your first tests.

You may have come across tests in some form. Some of your favorite open source projects come with bundled "test" folders—you have them in your own projects at work. You might have already written a few tests yourself, and you may even remember them as being bad, awkward, slow, or unmaintainable. Even worse, you might have felt they were useless and a waste of time. (Many people sadly do.) Or you may have had a great first experience with unit tests, and you're reading this book to see what more you might be missing.

This chapter will analyze the "classic" definition of a unit test and compare it to the concept of integration testing. This distinction is confusing to many, but it's very important to learn, because, as you'll learn later in the book, separating unit tests from other types of tests can be crucial to having high confidence in your tests when they fail or pass.

We'll also discuss the pros and cons of unit testing versus integration testing, and we'll develop a better definition of what might be a "good" unit test. We'll finish with a look at test-driven development (TDD), because it's often associated with unit testing but is a separate skill that I highly recommend giving a chance (it's not the main topic of this book, though). Throughout this chapter, I'll also touch on concepts that are explained more thoroughly elsewhere in the book.

First, let's define what a unit test should be.

1.2   Defining unit testing, step by step

Unit testing isn't a new concept in software development. It's been floating around since the early days of the Smalltalk programming language in the 1970s, and it proves itself time and time again as one of the best ways a developer can improve code quality while gaining a deeper understanding of the functional requirements of a module, class, or function. Kent Beck introduced the concept of unit testing in Smalltalk, and it has carried on into many other programming languages, making unit testing an extremely useful practice.

To see what we *don't* want to use as our definition of unit testing, let's look to Wikipedia as a starting point. I'll use its definition with reservations, because, in my opinion, there are many important parts missing, but it is largely accepted by many for lack of other good definitions. Our definition will slowly evolve throughout this chapter, with the final definition appearing in section 1.9.

> *Unit tests are typically automated tests written and run by software developers to ensure that a section of an application (known as the "unit") meets its design and behaves as intended. In procedural programming, a unit could be an entire module, but it is more commonly an individual function or procedure. In object-oriented programming, a unit*

is often an entire interface, such as a class, or an individual method (https://en
.wikipedia.org/wiki/Unit_testing).

The thing you'll write tests for is the *subject, system, or suite under test* (SUT).

> **DEFINITION**   SUT stands for *subject, system, or suite under test*, and some people
> like to use CUT (*component, class, or code under test*). When you test something,
> you refer to the thing you're testing as the SUT.

Let's talk about the word "unit" in unit testing. To me, *unit* stands for a "unit of work"
or a "use case" inside the system. A unit of work has a beginning and an end, which I
call an *entry point* and an *exit point*. A simple example of a unit of work is a function
that calculates something and returns a value. However, a function could also use
other functions, other modules, and other components in the calculation process,
which means the unit of work (from entry point to exit point), could span more than
just a function.

> **Unit of work**
>
> A *unit of work* is all the actions that take place between the invocation of an *entry
> point* up until a noticeable end result through one or more *exit points*. The *entry point*
> is the thing we trigger. Given a publicly visible function, for example
>
> - The function's body is all or part of the unit of work.
> - The function's declaration and signature are the entry point into the body.
> - The resulting outputs or behaviors of the function are its exit points.

1.3   *Entry points and exit points*

A unit of work always has an entry point and one or
more exit points. Figure 1.1 shows a simple diagram
of a unit of work.

A unit of work can be a single function, multiple
functions, or even multiple modules or components.
But it always has an entry point that we can trigger
from the outside (via tests or other production code),
and it always ends up doing something useful. If it
doesn't do anything useful, we might as well remove it
from our codebase.

What's *useful?* Something publicly noticeable that
happens in the code: a return value, a state change,
or calling an external party, as shown in figure 1.2.
Those noticeable behaviors are what I call *exit points*.

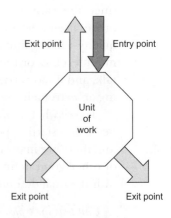

**Figure 1.1   A unit of work has
entry points and exit points.**

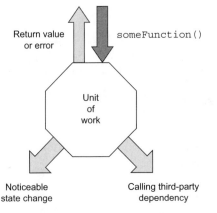

Figure 1.2 Types of exit points

Why "exit point"?

Why use the term "exit point" and not something like "behavior"? My thinking is that behaviors can be purely internal, whereas we're looking for externally visible behaviors from the caller. That difference might be difficult to distinguish at a glance. Also, "exit point" nicely suggests we are leaving the context of a unit of work and going back to the test context, though behaviors might be a bit more fluid than that. There's an extensive discussion about types of behavior, including observable behavior, in *Unit Testing Principles, Practices, and Patterns* by Vladimir Khorikov (Manning, 2020). Refer to that book to learn more about this topic.

The following listing shows a quick code example of a simple unit of work.

Listing 1.1 A simple function that we'd like to test

```
const sum = (numbers) => {
  const [a, b] = numbers.split(',');
  const result = parseInt(a) + parseInt(b);
  return result;
};
```

About the JavaScript version used in this book

I've chosen to use Node.js 12.8 with plain ES6 JavaScript along with JSDoc-style comments. The module system I'll use is CommonJS, to keep things simple. Perhaps in a future edition I'll start using ES modules (.mjs files), but for now, and for the rest of this book, CommonJS will do. It doesn't really matter for the patterns in this book anyway.

You should be able to easily extrapolate the techniques used here for whatever JavaScript stack you're currently working with, whether you're using TypeScript, Plain JS, ES modules, backend or frontend, Angular, or React. It shouldn't matter.

Getting the code for this chapter

You can download all the code samples shown in this book from GitHub. You can find the repository at https://github.com/royosherove/aout3-samples. Make sure you have Node 12.8 or higher installed, and run `npm install` followed by `npm run ch[chapter number]`. For this chapter, you would run `npm run ch1`. This will run all the tests for this chapter so you can see their outputs.

This unit of work is completely encompassed in a single function. The function is the entry point, and because its end result returns a value, it also acts as the exit point. We get the end result in the same place we trigger the unit of work, so the entry point is also the exit point.

If we drew this function as a unit of work, it would look something like figure 1.3. I used `sum(numbers)` as the entry point, not `numbers`, because the entry point is the function signature. The parameters are the context or input given through the entry point.

The following listing shows a variation on this idea.

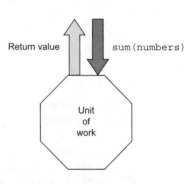

Figure 1.3   A function that has the same entry point as exit point

Listing 1.2   A unit of work with entry points and exit points

```
let total = 0;

const totalSoFar = () => {
  return total;
};

const sum = (numbers) => {
  const [a, b] = numbers.split(',');
  const result = parseInt(a) + parseInt(b);
  total += result;              ⟵──┐ New functionality:
  return result;                    │ calculating a
};                                   │ running total
```

This new version of `sum` has *two* exit points. It does two things:

- It returns a value.
- It introduces new functionality: a running total of all the sums. It sets the state of the module in a way that is noticeable (via `totalSoFar`) from the caller of the entry point.

Figure 1.4 shows how I would draw this unit of work. You can think of these two exit points as two different paths, or requirements, from the same unit of work, because they indeed *are* two different useful things the code is expected to do. This also means I'd be very likely to write two different unit tests here: one for each exit point. Very soon we'll do exactly that.

What about `totalSoFar`? Is this also an entry point? Yes, it could be, *in a separate test*. I could write a test that proves that calling `totalSoFar` without triggering prior to that call returns `0`. That would make it its own little unit of work, which would be perfectly fine. Often one unit of work (such as `sum`) can be composed of smaller units.

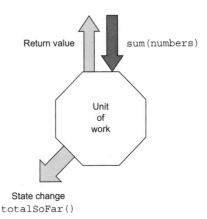

Return value   sum(numbers)

Unit
of
work

State change
totalSoFar()

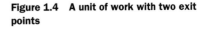

Figure 1.4 A unit of work with two exit points

As you can see, the scope of our tests can change and mutate, but we can still define them with entry points and exit points. Entry points are always where the test triggers the unit of work. You can have multiple entry points into a unit of work, each used by a different set of tests.

A note on design

There are two main types of actions: "query" actions and "command" actions. Query actions don't change stuff; they just return values. Command actions change stuff but don't return values.

We often combine the two, but there are many cases where separating them might be a better design choice. This book isn't primarily about design, but I urge you to read more about the concept of *command query separation* over on Martin Fowler's website: https://martinfowler.com/bliki/CommandQuerySeparation.html.

Exit points signifying requirements and new tests, and vice versa

Exit points are end results of a unit of work. For unit tests, I usually write at least one test, with its own readable name, for each exit point. I may then add more tests with variations on the inputs, all using the same entry point, to gain more confidence.

Integration tests, which we'll discuss later in this chapter and in the book, usually include multiple end results, since it can be impossible to separate code paths at those levels. That's also one of the reasons integration tests are harder to debug, get up and running, and maintain: they do much more than unit tests, as you'll soon see.

A third version of our example function is shown in the following listing.

> **Listing 1.3　Adding a logger call to the function**

```
let total = 0;

const totalSoFar = () => {
  return total;
};

const logger = makeLogger();

const sum = (numbers) => {
  const [a, b] = numbers.split(',');
  logger.info(
    'this is a very important log output',
    { firstNumWas: a, secondNumWas: b });

  const result = parseInt(a) + parseInt(b);
  total += result;
  return result;
};
```

A new exit point

You can see that there's a new exit point (or requirement, or end result) in the function. It logs something to an external entity—perhaps to a file, or the console, or a database. We don't know, and we don't care. This is the third type of exit point: *calling a third party.* I also like to refer to it as "calling a *dependency.*"

> **DEFINITION**　A *dependency* is something we don't have full control over during a unit test. Or it can be something that trying to control in a test would make our lives miserable. Some examples would include loggers that write to files, things that talk to the network, code that's controlled by other teams, components that take a long time (calculations, threads, database access), and more. The rule of thumb is that if we can fully and easily control what it's doing, and it runs in memory, and it's fast, then it's not a dependency. There are always exceptions to the rule, but this should get you through 80% of the cases, at least.

Figure 1.5 shows how I'd draw this unit of work with all three exit points. At this point we're still discussing a function-sized unit of work. The entry point is the function call, but now we have three possible paths, or exit points, that do something useful and that the caller can verify publicly.

　Here's where it gets interesting: it's a good idea to have a *separate test for each exit point.* This will make the tests more readable and simpler to debug or change without affecting other outcomes.

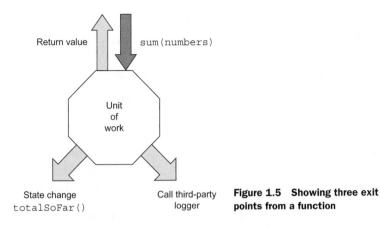

Figure 1.5 **Showing three exit points from a function**

Return value

`sum(numbers)`

Unit of work

State change `totalSoFar()`

Call third-party logger

1.4 Exit point types

We've seen that we have three different types of end results:

- The invoked function returns a useful value (not undefined). If this was in a statically typed language such as Java or C#, we'd say it is a public, non-void function.
- There's a *noticeable* change to the state or behavior of the system before and after invocation that can be determined without interrogating private state.
- There's a callout to a third-party system over which the test has no control. That third-party system doesn't return any value, or that value is ignored. (Example: the code calls a third-party logging system that was not written by you, and you don't control its source code.)

> **XUnit Test Patterns' definition of entry and exit points**
>
> Gerard Meszaros' book *XUnit Test Patterns* (Addison-Wesley Professional, 2007) discusses the notion of *direct inputs and outputs,* and *indirect inputs and outputs. Direct inputs* are what I like to call entry points. Meszaros refers to it as "using the front door" of a component. *Indirect output*s in that book are the other two types of exit points I mentioned (state change and calling a third party).
>
> Both versions of these ideas have evolved in parallel, but the idea of a "unit of work" only appears in this book. A unit of work, coupled with entry and exit points, makes much more sense to me than direct and indirect inputs and outputs, but you can consider this a stylistic choice about how to teach the concept of test scopes. You can find more about *XUnit Test Patterns* at xunitpatterns.com.

Let's see how the idea of entry and exit points affects the definition of a unit test: A *unit test* is a piece of code that invokes a unit of work and checks one specific exit point as an end result of that unit of work. If the assumptions about the end result turn out to be wrong, the unit test has failed. A unit test's scope can span as little as a function or as much as multiple modules or components, depending on how many functions and modules are used between the entry point and the exit point.

1.5   *Different exit points, different techniques*

Why am I spending so much time talking about types of exit points? Because not only is it a great idea to separate the tests for each exit point, but different types of exit points might require different techniques to test successfully:

- Return-value-based exit points (direct outputs in Meszaros' *XUnit Test Patterns*) should be the easiest exit points to test. You trigger an entry point, you get something back, and you check the value you got back.
- State-based tests (indirect outputs) usually require a little more gymnastics. You call something, and then you do another call to check something else (or you call the previous thing again) to see if everything went according to plan.

In a third-party situation (indirect outputs), we have the most hoops to jump through. We haven't discussed this yet, but that's where we're forced to use things like *mock objects* to replace the external system with something we can control and interrogate in our tests. I'll cover this idea deeply later in the book.

Which exit points make the most problems?

As a rule of thumb, I try to mostly use either return-value-based or state-based tests. I try to avoid mock-object-based tests if I can, and usually I can. As a result, I usually have no more than 5% of my tests using mock objects for verification. Those types of tests complicate things and make maintainability more difficult. Sometimes there's no escape, though, and we'll discuss them as we proceed in the next chapters.

1.6   *A test from scratch*

Let's go back to the first, simplest version of the code (listing 1.1) and try to test it, shall we? If we were to try to write a test for this, what would it look like?

Let's take the visual approach first with figure 1.6. Our entry point is sum with an input of a string called numbers. sum is also our exit point, since we will get a return value back from it and check its value.

It's possible to write an automated unit test without using a test framework. In fact, because developers have gotten more into the habit of automating their testing, I've seen plenty of them doing this before discovering test frameworks. In this section, we'll write such a test without a framework, so that you can contrast this approach with using a framework in chapter 2.

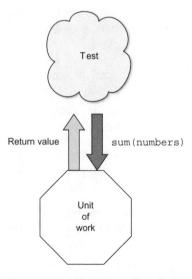

Figure 1.6   A visual view of our test

So, let's assume test frameworks don't exist (or that we don't know they do). We have decided to write our own little automated test from scratch. The following listing shows a very naive example of testing our own code with plain JavaScript.

Listing 1.4 A very naive test against `sum()`

```
const parserTest = () => {
  try {
    const result = sum('1,2');
    if (result === 3) {
      console.log('parserTest example 1 PASSED');
    } else {
      throw new Error(`parserTest: expected 3 but was ${result}`);
    }
  } catch (e) {
    console.error(e.stack);
  }
};
```

No, this code is not lovely. But it's good enough to explain how tests work. To run this code, we can do the following:

1 Open the command line and type an empty string.
2 Add an entry under package.json's `"scripts"` entry under `"test"` to execute `"node mytest.js"` and then execute `npm test` on the command line.

The following listing shows this.

Listing 1.5 The beginning of our package.json file

```
{
  "name": "aout3-samples",
  "version": "1.0.0",
  "description": "Code Samples for Art of Unit Testing 3rd Edition",
  "main": "index.js",
  "scripts": {
    "test": "node ./ch1-basics/custom-test-phase1.js",
  }
}
```

The test method invokes the *production module* (the SUT) and then checks the returned value. If it's not what's expected, the test method writes to the console an error and a stack trace. The test method also catches any exceptions that occur and writes them to the console, so that they don't interfere with the running of subsequent methods. When we use a test framework, that's usually handled for us automatically.

Obviously, this is an ad hoc way of writing such a test. If you were to write multiple tests like this, you might want to have a generic `test` or `check` method that all tests could use, and which would format the errors consistently. You could also add special helper methods that would check on things like null objects, empty strings, and so on, so that you don't need to write the same long lines of code in many tests.

The following listing shows what this test would look like with a slightly more generic check and assertEquals functions.

```
const assertEquals = (expected, actual) => {
  if (actual !== expected) {
    throw new Error(`Expected ${expected} but was ${actual}`);
  }
};

const check = (name, implementation) => {
  try {
    implementation();
    console.log(`${name} passed`);
  } catch (e) {
    console.error(`${name} FAILED`, e.stack);
  }
};

check('sum with 2 numbers should sum them up', () => {
  const result = sum('1,2');
  assertEquals(3, result);
});

check('sum with multiple digit numbers should sum them up', () => {
  const result = sum('10,20');
  assertEquals(30, result);
});
```

We've now created two helper methods: assertEquals, which removes boilerplate code for writing to the console or throwing errors, and check, which takes a string for the name of the test and a callback to the implementation. It then takes care of catching any test errors, writing them to the console, and reporting on the status of the test.

Built-in asserts

It's important to note that we don't need to write our own asserts. We could have easily used Node.js's built-in assert functions, which were originally built for internal use in testing Node.js itself. We could do so by importing the functions with

```
const assert = require('assert');
```

However, I'm trying to demonstrate the underlying simplicity of the concept, so we'll avoid that. You can find more info about Node.js's assert module at https://nodejs .org/api/assert.html.

Notice how the tests are easier to read and faster to write with just a couple of helper methods. Unit testing frameworks such as Jest can provide even more generic helper methods like this, so tests are even easier to write. I'll talk about that in chapter 2. First, let's talk a bit about the main subject of this book: good unit tests.

1.7 Characteristics of a good unit test

No matter what programming language you're using, one of the most difficult aspects of defining a unit test is defining what's meant by a *good* one. Of course, good is relative, and it can change whenever we learn something new about coding. That may seem obvious, but it really isn't. I need to explain *why* we need to write better tests— understanding what a unit of work is isn't enough.

Based on my own experience, involving many companies and teams over the years, most people who try to unit test their code either give up at some point or don't actually perform unit tests. They waste a lot of time writing problematic tests, and they give up when they have to spend a lot of time maintaining them, or worse, they don't trust their results.

There's no point in writing a bad unit test, unless you're in the process of learning how to write a good one. There are more downsides than upsides to writing bad tests, such as wasting time debugging buggy tests, wasting time writing tests that bring no benefit, wasting time trying to understand unreadable tests, and wasting time writing tests only to delete them a few months later. There's also a huge issue with maintaining bad tests, and with how they affect the maintainability of production code. Bad tests can actually slow down your development speed, not only when writing test code, but also when writing production code. I'll touch on all these things later in the book.

By learning what a good unit test is, you can be sure you aren't starting off on a path that will be hard to fix later on, when the code becomes a nightmare. We'll also define other forms of tests (component, end to end, and more) later in the book.

1.7.1 What is a good unit test?

Every good automated test (not just unit tests) should have the following properties:

- It should be easy to understand the intent of the test author.
- It should be easy to read and write.
- It should be automated.
- It should be consistent in its results (it should always return the same result if you don't change anything between runs).
- It should be useful and provide actionable results.
- Anyone should be able to run it with the push of a button.
- When it fails, it should be easy to detect what was expected and determine how to pinpoint the problem.

A good unit test should also exhibit the following properties:

- It should run quickly.
- It should have *full control* of the code under test (more on that in chapter 3).
- It should be fully isolated (run independently of other tests).

- It should run in memory without requiring system files, networks, or databases.
- It should be as synchronous and linear as possible when that makes sense (no parallel threads if we can help it).

It's impossible for all tests to follow the properties of a good unit test, and that's fine. Such tests will simply transition to the realm of integration testing (the topic of section 1.8). Still, there are ways to refactor some of your tests to conform to these properties.

REPLACING THE DATABASE (OR ANOTHER DEPENDENCY) WITH A STUB

We'll discuss stubs in later chapters, but, in short, they are fake dependencies that emulate the real ones. Their purpose is to simplify the process of testing because they are easier to set up and maintain.

Beware of in-memory databases, though. They can help you isolate tests from each other (as long as you don't share database instances between tests) and thus adhere to the properties of good unit tests, but such databases lead to an awkward, in-between spot. In-memory databases aren't as easy to set up as stubs. At the same time, they don't provide as strong guarantees as real databases. Functionality-wise, an in-memory database may differ drastically from the production one, so tests that pass an in-memory database may fail the real one, and vice versa. You'll often have to rerun the same tests manually against the production database to gain additional confidence that your code works. Unless you use a small and standardized set of SQL features, I recommend sticking to either stubs (for unit tests) or real databases (for integration testing).

The same is true for solutions like jsdom. You can use it to replace the real DOM, but make sure it supports your particular use cases. Don't write tests that require you to manually recheck them.

EMULATING ASYNCHRONOUS PROCESSING WITH LINEAR, SYNCHRONOUS TESTS

With the advent of promises and `async/await`, asynchronous coding has become standard in JavaScript. Our tests can still verify asynchronous code synchronously, though. Usually that means triggering callbacks directly from the test or explicitly waiting for an asynchronous operation to finish executing.

1.7.2 A unit test checklist

Many people confuse the act of testing their software with the concept of a unit test. To start off, ask yourself the following questions about the tests you've written and executed up to now:

- Can I run and get results from a test I wrote two weeks or months or years ago?
- Can any member of my team run and get results from tests I wrote two months ago?
- Can I run all the tests I've written in no more than a few minutes?
- Can I run all the tests I've written at the push of a button?

- Can I write a basic test in no more than a few minutes?
- Do my tests pass when there are bugs in another team's code?
- Do my tests show the same results when run on different machines or environments?
- Do my tests stop working if there's no database, network, or deployment?
- If I delete, move, or change one test, do other tests remain unaffected?

If you answered "no" to any of these questions, there's a high probability that what you're implementing either isn't fully automated or it isn't a unit test. It's definitely *some* kind of test, and it might be as important as a unit test, but it has drawbacks compared to tests that would let you answer yes to all of those questions.

"What was I doing until now?" you might ask. You've been doing integration testing.

1.8 *Integration tests*

I consider *integration tests* to be any tests that don't live up to one or more of the conditions outlined previously for good unit tests. For example, if the test uses the real network, the real rest APIs, the real system time, the real filesystem, or a real database, it has stepped into the realm of integration testing.

If a test doesn't have control of the system time, for example, and it uses the current `new Date()` in the test code, then every time the test executes, it's essentially a different test because it uses a different time. It's no longer consistent. That's not a bad thing per se. I think integration tests are important counterparts to unit tests, but they should be separated from them to achieve a feeling of "safe green zone," which is discussed later in this book.

If a test uses the real database, it's no longer only running in memory—its actions are harder to erase than when using only in-memory fake data. The test will also run longer, and we won't easily be able to control how long data access takes. Unit tests should be *fast*. Integration tests are usually much slower. When you start having hundreds of tests, every half-second counts.

Integration tests increase the risk of another problem: testing too many things at once. For example, suppose your car breaks down. How do you learn what the problem is, let alone fix it? An engine consists of many subsystems working together, each relying on the others to help produce the final result: a moving car. If the car stops moving, the fault could be with any of the subsystems—or with more than one. It's the integration of those subsystems (or layers) that makes the car move. You could think of the car's movement as the ultimate integration test of these parts as the car goes down the road. If the test fails, all the parts fail together; if it succeeds, all the parts succeed.

The same thing happens in software. The way most developers test their functionality is through the final functionality of the app or REST API or UI. Clicking some button triggers a series of events—functions, modules, and components working together to produce the final result. If the test fails, all of these software components fail as a team, and it can be difficult to figure out what caused the failure of the overall operation (see figure 1.7).

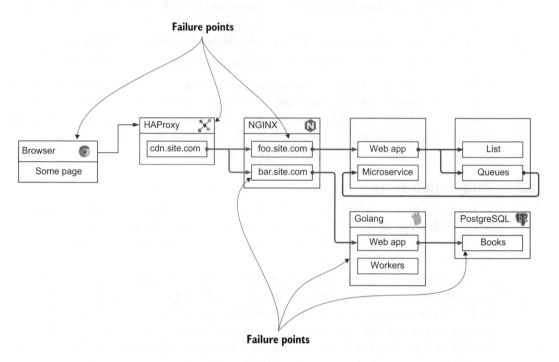

Figure 1.7   You can have many failure points in an integration test. All the units have to work together, and each could malfunction, making it harder to find the source of a bug.

As defined in *The Complete Guide to Software Testing* by Bill Hetzel (Wiley, 1988), integration testing is "an orderly progression of testing in which software and/or hardware elements are combined and tested until the entire system has been integrated." Here's my own variation on defining integration testing:

> *Integration testing is testing a unit of work without having full control over all of its real dependencies, such as other components by other teams, other services, the time, the network, databases, threads, random number generators, and more.*

To summarize, an integration test uses real dependencies; unit tests isolate the unit of work from its dependencies so that they're easily consistent in their results and can easily control and simulate any aspect of the unit's behavior.

Let's apply the questions from section 1.7.2 to integration tests and consider what you want to achieve with real-world unit tests:

- *Can I run and get results from a test I wrote two weeks or months or years ago?*
  If you can't, how would you know whether you broke a feature that you created earlier? Shared data and code changes regularly during the life of an application,

and if you can't (or won't) run tests for all the previously working features after changing your code, you just might break it without knowing—this is known as a *regression*. Regressions seem to occur a lot near the end of a sprint or release, when developers are under pressure to fix existing bugs. Sometimes they introduce new bugs inadvertently as they resolve old ones. Wouldn't it be great to know that you broke something within 60 seconds of breaking it? You'll see how that can be done later in this book.

DEFINITION A *regression* is broken functionality—code that used to work. You can also think of it as one or more units of work that once worked and now don't.

- *Can any member of my team run and get results from tests I wrote two months ago?*
  This goes with the previous point but takes it up a notch. You want to make sure that you don't break someone else's code when you change something. Many developers fear changing legacy code in older systems for fear of not knowing what other code depends on what they're changing. In essence, they risk changing the system into an unknown state of stability.

  Few things are scarier than not knowing whether the application still works, especially when you didn't write that code. If you have that safety net of unit tests and know you aren't breaking anything, you'll be much less afraid of taking on code you're less familiar with.

  Good tests can be accessed and run by anyone.

DEFINITION *Legacy code* is defined by Wikipedia as "old computer source code that is no longer supported on the standard hardware and environments" (https://en.wikipedia.org/wiki/Legacy_system), but many shops refer to any older version of the application currently under maintenance as legacy code. It often refers to code that's hard to work with, hard to test, and usually even hard to read. A client once defined legacy code in a down-to-earth way: "code that works." Many people like to define legacy code as "code that has no tests." *Working Effectively with Legacy Code* by Michael Feathers (Pearson, 2004) uses "code that has no tests" as an official definition of legacy code, and it's a definition to be considered while reading this book.

- *Can I run all the tests I've written in no more than a few minutes?*
  If you can't run your tests quickly (seconds are better than minutes), you'll run them less often (daily, or even weekly or monthly in some places). The problem is that when you change code, you want to get feedback as early as possible to see if you broke something. The more time required between running the tests, the more changes you make to the system, and the (many) more places you'll have to search for bugs when you find that you broke something.

  Good tests should run *quickly*.

- *Can I run all the tests I've written at the push of a button?*
  If you can't, it probably means that you have to configure the machine on which the tests will run so that they run correctly (setting up a Docker environment, or setting connection strings to the database, for example), or it may mean that your unit tests aren't fully automated. If you can't fully automate your unit tests, you'll probably avoid running them repeatedly, as will everyone else on your team.

  No one likes to get bogged down with configuring details to run tests, just to make sure that the system still works. Developers have more important things to do, like writing more features into the system. But they can't do that if they don't know the state of the system.

  Good tests should be easily executed in their original form, not manually.

- *Can I write a basic test in no more than a few minutes?*
  One of the easiest ways to spot an integration test is that it takes time to prepare correctly and to implement, not just to execute. It takes time to figure out how to write it because of all the internal, and sometimes external, dependencies. (A database may be considered an external dependency.) If you're not automating the test, dependencies are less of a problem, but you're losing all the benefits of an automated test. The harder it is to write a test, the less likely you are to write more tests or to focus on anything other than the "big stuff" that you're worried about. One of the strengths of unit tests is that they tend to test every little thing that might break, not only the big stuff. People are often surprised at how many bugs they can find in code they thought was simple and bug free.

  When you concentrate only on the big tests, the overall confidence in your code is still very much lacking. Many parts of the code's core logic aren't tested (even though you may be covering more components), and there may be many bugs that you haven't considered and might be "unofficially" worried about.

  Good tests against the system should be easy and quick to write, once you've figured out the patterns you want to use to test your specific set of objects, functions, and dependencies (the *domain model*).

- *Do my tests pass when there are bugs in another team's code? Do my tests show the same results when run on different machines or environments? Do my tests stop working if there's no database, network, or deployment?*
  These three points refer to the idea that our test code is isolated from various dependencies. The test results are consistent because we have control over what those indirect inputs into our system provide. We can have fake databases, fake networks, fake time, and fake machine culture. In later chapters, I'll refer to those points as *stubs* and *seams* in which we can inject those stubs.

- *If I delete, move, or change one test, do other tests remain unaffected?*
  Unit tests usually don't need to have any shared state, but integration tests often do, such as an external database or service. Shared state can create a dependency

between tests. For example, running tests in the wrong order can corrupt the state for future tests.

> **WARNING**   Even experienced unit testers can find that it may take 30 minutes or more to figure out how to write the very *first* unit test against a domain model they've never unit tested before. This is part of the work and is to be expected. The second and subsequent tests on that domain model should be very easy to accomplish once you've figured out the entry and exit points of the unit of work.

We can recognize three main criteria in the previous questions and answers:

- *Readability*—If we can't read it, then it's hard to maintain, hard to debug, and hard to know what's wrong.
- *Maintainability*—If maintaining the test or production code is painful because of the tests, our lives will become a living nightmare.
- *Trust*—If we don't trust the results of our tests when they fail, we'll start manually testing again, losing all the time benefit the tests are supposed to provide. If we don't trust the tests when they *pass*, we'll start debugging more, again losing any time benefit.

From what I've explained so far about what a unit test is not and what features need to be present for testing to be useful, I can now start to answer the primary question this chapter poses: what is a good unit test?

1.9   *Finalizing our definition*

Now that I've covered the important properties that a unit test should have, I'll define unit tests once and for all:

> *A unit test is an automated piece of code that invokes the unit of work through an entry point and then checks one of its exit points. A unit test is almost always written using a unit testing framework. It can be written easily and runs quickly. It's trustworthy, readable, and maintainable. It is consistent as long as the production code we control has not changed.*

This definition certainly looks like a tall order, particularly considering how many developers implement unit tests poorly. It makes us take a hard look at the way we, as developers, have implemented testing up until now, compared to how we'd like to implement it. (Trustworthy, readable, and maintainable tests are discussed in depth in chapters 7 through 9.)

In the first edition of this book, my definition of a unit test was slightly different. I used to define a unit test as "only running against control flow code," but I no longer think that's true. Code without logic is usually used as part of a unit of work. Even properties with no logic will get used by a unit of work, so they don't have to be specifically targeted by tests.

> **DEFINITION**   *Control flow code* is any piece of code that has some sort of logic in
> it, small as it may be. It has one or more of the following: an `if` statement, a
> loop, calculations, or any other type of decision-making code.

Getters and setters are good examples of code that usually doesn't contain any logic
and so don't require specific targeting by the tests. It's code that will probably get used
by the unit of work you're testing, but there's no need to test it directly. But watch out:
once you add any logic inside a getter or setter, you'll want to make sure that logic is
being tested.

In the next section, we'll stop talking about what is a good test and talk about *when*
you might want to write tests. I'll discuss test-driven development, because it is often
put in the same bucket as doing unit testing. I want to make sure we set the record
straight on that.

1.10 *Test-driven development*

Once you know how to write readable, maintainable, and trustworthy tests with a unit
testing framework, the next question is *when* to write the tests. Many people feel that
the best time to write unit tests for software is after they've created some functionality
and just before they merge their code into remote source control.

Also, to be a bit blunt, a lot of people don't believe writing tests is a good idea, but
have realized through trial and error that there are strict testing requirements in
source control reviews, so they *have* to write tests to appease the code review gods and
get their code merged into the main branch. (That kind of dynamic is a great source
of bad tests, and I'll address it in the third part of this book.)

A growing number of developers prefer writing unit tests incrementally, during the
coding session and before each piece of very small functionality is implemented. This
approach is called *test-first* or *test-driven* development (TDD).

> **NOTE**   There are many different views on exactly what test-driven develop-
> ment means. Some say it's test-first development, and some say it means you
> have a lot of tests. Some say it's a way of designing, and others feel it could be
> a way to drive your code's behavior with only some design. In this book, TDD
> means test-first development, with design taking an incremental role in the
> technique (besides this section, TDD won't be discussed in this book).

Figures 1.8 and 1.9 show the differences between traditional coding and TDD. TDD is
different from traditional development, as figure 1.9 shows. You begin by writing a test
that fails; then you move on to creating the production code, seeing the test pass, and
continuing on to either refactor your code or create another failing test.

This book focuses on the technique of writing good unit tests, rather than on
TDD, but I'm a big fan of TDD. I've written several major applications and frameworks using TDD, I've managed teams that utilize it, and I've taught hundreds of
courses and workshops on TDD and unit testing techniques. Throughout my career,
I've found TDD to be helpful in creating quality code, quality tests, and better designs

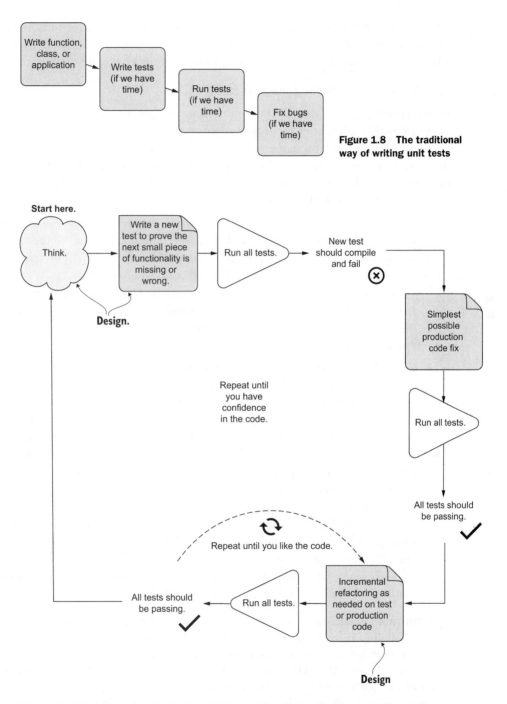

Figure 1.8   The traditional way of writing unit tests

Figure 1.9   Test-driven development—a bird's-eye view. Notice the circular nature of the process: write the test, write the code, refactor, write the next test. It shows the incremental nature of TDD: small steps lead to a quality end result with confidence.

for the code I was writing. I'm convinced that it can work to your benefit, but it's not without a price (time to learn, time to implement, and more). It's definitely worth the admission price, though, if you're willing to take on the challenge of learning it.

1.10.1 *TDD: Not a substitute for good unit tests*

It's important to realize that TDD doesn't ensure project success or tests that are robust or maintainable. It's quite easy to get caught up in the technique of TDD and not pay attention to the way unit tests are written: their naming, how maintainable or readable they are, and whether they test the right things or might themselves have bugs. That's why I'm writing this book—because writing good tests is a separate skill from TDD.

The technique of TDD is quite simple:

1 *Write a failing test to prove code or functionality is missing from the end product.* The test is written *as if* the production code were already working, so the test failing means there's a bug in the production code. How do I know? The test is written such that it would pass if the production code had no bugs.

   In some languages other than JavaScript, the test might not even compile at first, since the code doesn't exist yet. Once it does run, it should be failing, because the production code is still not working. This is where a lot of the "design" in test-driven-design thinking happens.

2 *Make the test pass by adding functionality to the production code that meets the expectations of your test.* The production code should be kept as simple as possible. Don't touch the test. You have to make it pass only by touching production code.

3 *Refactor your code.* When the test passes, you're free to move on to the next unit test or to refactor your code (both production code and tests) to make it more readable, to remove code duplication, and so on. This is another point where the "design" part happens. We refactor and can even redesign our components while still keeping the old functionality.

   Refactoring steps should be very small and incremental, and we run all the tests after each small step to make sure we didn't break anything with our changes. Refactoring can be done after writing several tests or after writing each test. It's an important practice, because it ensures your code gets easier to read and maintain, while still passing all of the previously written tests. There's a whole section (8.3) on refactoring later in the book.

> **DEFINITION** *Refactoring* means changing a piece of code *without* changing its functionality. If you've ever renamed a method, you've done refactoring. If you've ever split a large method into multiple smaller method calls, you've refactored your code. The code still does the same thing, but it becomes easier to maintain, read, debug, and change.

The preceding steps sound technical, but there's a lot of wisdom behind them. Done correctly, TDD can make your code quality soar, decrease the number of bugs, raise your confidence in the code, shorten the time it takes to find bugs, improve your code's design, and keep your manager happier. If TDD is done incorrectly, it can cause your project schedule to slip, waste your time, lower your motivation, and lower your code quality. It's a double-edged sword, and many people find this out the hard way.

Technically, one of the biggest benefits of TDD that nobody tells you about is that by seeing a test fail, and then seeing it pass without changing the test, you're basically testing the test itself. If you expect it to fail and it passes, you might have a bug in your test or you're testing the wrong thing. If the test failed, you fixed it, and now you expect it to pass, and it still fails, your test could have a bug, or maybe it's expecting the wrong thing to happen.

This book deals with readable, maintainable, and trustworthy tests, but if you add TDD on top, your confidence in your own tests will increase by seeing the failed, you fixed it, tests failing when they should and passing when they should. In test-after style, you'll usually only see them pass when they should, and fail when they shouldn't (since the code they test should already be working). TDD helps with that a lot, and it's also one of the reasons developers do far less debugging when practicing TDD than when they're simply unit testing after the fact. If they trust the tests, they don't feel a need to debug it "just in case." That's the kind of trust you can only gain by seeing both sides of the test—failing when it should and passing when it should.

1.10.2   *Three core skills needed for successful TDD*

To be successful in test-driven development, you need three different skill sets: knowing how to write good tests, writing them test-first, and designing the tests and the production code well. Figure 1.10 shows these more clearly:

- *Just because you write your tests first doesn't mean they're maintainable, readable, or trustworthy.* Good unit testing skills are what this book is all about.
- *Just because you write readable, maintainable tests doesn't mean you'll get the same benefits as when writing them test-first.* Test-first skills are what most of the TDD books out there teach, without teaching the skills of good testing. I would especially recommend Kent Beck's *Test-Driven Development: By Example* (Addison-Wesley Professional, 2002).

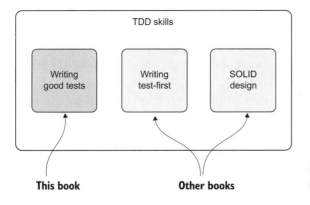

Figure 1.10   Three core skills of test-driven development

- *Just because you write your tests first, and they're readable and maintainable, doesn't mean you'll end up with a well-designed system.* Design skills are what make your code beautiful and maintainable. I recommend *Growing Object-Oriented Software, Guided by Tests* by Steve Freeman and Nat Pryce (Addison-Wesley Professional, 2009) and *Clean Code* by Robert C. Martin (Pearson, 2008) as good books on the subject.

A pragmatic approach to learning TDD is to learn each of these three aspects separately; that is, to focus on one skill at a time, ignoring the others in the meantime. The reason I recommend this approach is that I often see people trying to learn all three skill sets at the same time, having a really hard time in the process, and finally giving up because the wall is too high to climb. By taking a more incremental approach to learning this field, you relieve yourself of the constant fear that you're getting it wrong in a different area than you're currently focusing on.

In the next chapter, you'll start writing your first unit tests using Jest, one of the most commonly used test frameworks for JavaScript.

Summary

- A good unit test has these qualities:
  - It should run quickly.
  - It should have full control of the code under test.
  - It should be fully isolated (it should run independently of other tests).
  - It should run in memory without requiring filesystem files, networks, or databases.
  - It should be as synchronous and linear as possible (no parallel threads).
- Entry points are public functions that are the doorways into our units of work and trigger the underlying logic. Exit points are the places you can inspect with your test. They represent the effects of the units of work.
- An exit point can be a return value, a change of state, or a call to a third-party dependency. Each exit point usually requires a separate test, and each type of exit point requires a different testing technique.
- A unit of work is the sum of actions that take place between the invocation of an entry point up until a noticeable end result through one or more exit points. A unit of work can span a function, a module, or multiple modules.
- Integration testing is just unit testing with some or all of the dependencies being real and residing outside of the current execution process. Conversely, unit testing is like integration testing, but with all of the dependencies in memory (both real and fake), and we have control over their behavior in the test.
- The most important attributes of any test are readability, maintainability, and trust. *Readability* tells us how easy it is to read and understand the test. *Maintainability* is the measure of how painful it is to maintain the test code. Without *trust,*

it's harder to introduce important changes (such as refactoring) in a codebase, which leads to code deterioration.

- Test-driven development (TDD) is a technique that advocates for writing tests before the production code. This approach is also referred to as a test-first approach (as opposed to code-first).

- The main benefit of TDD is verifying the correctness of your tests. Seeing your tests fail before writing production code ensures that these same tests would fail if the functionality they cover stops working properly.

A first unit test 2

This chapter covers

- Writing your first test with Jest
- Test structure and naming conventions
- Working with the assertion library
- Refactoring tests and reducing repetitive code

When I first started writing unit tests with a real unit testing framework, there was little documentation, and the frameworks I worked with didn't have proper examples. (I was mostly coding in VB 5 and 6 at the time.) It was a challenge learning to work with them, and I started out writing rather poor tests. Fortunately, times have changed. In JavaScript, and in practically any language out there, there's a wide range of choices and plenty of documentation and support from the community for trying out these bundles of helpfulness.

In the previous chapter, we wrote a very simple home-grown test framework. In this chapter, we'll take a look at Jest, which will be our framework of choice for this book.

2.1 Introducing Jest

Jest is an open source test framework created by Facebook. It's easy to use, easy to remember, and has lots of great features. Jest was originally created for testing front-end React components in JavaScript. These days it's widely used in many parts of the industry for both backend and frontend project testing. It supports two major flavors of test syntax (one that uses the word `test` and another that's based on the Jasmin syntax, a framework that has inspired many of Jest's features). We'll try both of them to see which one we like better.

Aside from Jest, there are many other testing frameworks in JavaScript, pretty much all open source as well. There are some differences between them in style and APIs, but for the purposes of this book, that shouldn't matter too much.

2.1.1 Preparing our environment

Make sure you have Node.js installed locally. You can follow the instructions at https://nodejs.org/en/download/ to get it up and running on your machine. The site will provide you with the option of either a long-term support (LTS) release or a current release. The LTS release is geared toward enterprises, whereas the current release has more frequent updates. Either will work for the purposes of this book.

Make sure that the node package manager (npm) is installed on your machine. It is included with Node.js, so run the command `npm -v` on the command line, and if you see a version of 6.10.2 or higher, you should be good to go. If not, make sure Node.js is installed.

2.1.2 Preparing our working folder

To get started with Jest, let's create a new empty folder named "ch2" and initialize it with a package manager of your choice. I'll use npm, since I have to choose one. Yarn is an alternative package manager. It shouldn't matter, for the purposes of this book, which one you use.

Jest expects either a jest.config.js or a package.json file. We're going with the latter, and `npm init` will generate one for us:

```
mkdir ch2
cd ch2
npm init --yes
//or
yarn init -yes
git init
```

I'm also initializing Git in this folder. This would be recommended anyway, to track changes, but for Jest this file is used under the covers to track changes to files and run specific tests. It makes Jest's life easier.

By default, Jest will look for its configuration either in the package.json file that is created by this command or in a special jest.config.js file. For now, we won't need anything but the default package.json file. If you'd like to learn more about the Jest configuration options, refer to https://jestjs.io/docs/en/configuration.

2.1.3   *Installing Jest*

Next, we'll install Jest. To install Jest as a dev dependency (which means it does not get distributed to production) we can use this command:

```
npm install --save-dev jest
//or
yarn add jest -dev
```

This will create a new jest.js file under our [root folder]/node_modules/bin. We can then execute Jest using the `npx jest` command.

We can also install Jest *globally* on the local machine (I recommend doing this on top of the `save-dev` installation) by executing this command:

```
npm install -g jest
```

This will give us the freedom to execute the `jest` command directly from the command line in any folder that has tests, without going through npm to execute it.

In real projects, it is common to use `npm` commands to run tests instead of using the global `jest`. I'll show how this is done in the next few pages.

2.1.4   *Creating a test file*

Jest has a couple of default ways to find test files:

- If there's a __tests__ folder, it loads all the files in it as test files, regardless of their naming conventions.
- It tries to find any file that ends with *.spec.js or *.test.js, in any folder under the root folder of your project, recursively.

We'll use the first variation, but we'll also name our files with either *test.js or *.spec.js to make things a bit more consistent in case we want to move them around later (and stop using the __tests_ folder altogether).

You can also configure Jest to your heart's content, specifying how to find which files where, with a jest.config.js file or through package.json. You can look up the Jest docs at https://jestjs.io/docs/en/configuration to find all the gory details.

The next step is to create a special folder under our ch2 folder called __tests__. Under this folder, create a file that ends with either test.js or spec.js—my-component.test.js, for example. Which suffix you choose is up to you—it's about your own style. I'll use them interchangeably in this book because I think of "test" as the simplest version of "spec," so I use it when showing very simple things.

We don't need `require()` at the top of the file to start using Jest. It automatically imports global functions for us to use. The main functions you should be interested in include `test`, `describe`, `it`, and `expect`. Listing 2.1 shows what a simple test might look like.

Test file locations

There are two main patterns I see for placing test files: Some people prefer to place the test files directly next to the files or modules being tested. Others prefer to place all the files under a test directory. Which approach you choose doesn't really matter; just be consistent in your choice throughout a project, so it's easy to know where to find the tests for a specific item.

I find that placing tests in a test folder allows me to also put helper files under the test folder close to the tests. As for easily navigating between tests and the code under test, there are plugins for most IDEs today that allow you to navigate between code and its tests with a keyboard shortcut.

Listing 2.1   Hello Jest

```
test('hello jest', () => {
    expect('hello').toEqual('goodbye');
});
```

We haven't used `describe` and `it` yet, but we'll get to them soon.

2.1.5   *Executing Jest*

To run this test, we need to be able to execute Jest. For Jest to be recognized from the command line, we need to do either of the following:

- Install Jest globally on the machine by running `npm install jest -g`.
- Use `npx` to execute Jest from the node_modules directory by typing `jest` in the root of the ch2 folder.

If all the stars lined up correctly, you should see the results of the Jest test run and a failure. Your first failure. Yay! Figure 2.1 shows the output on my terminal when I run the command. It's pretty cool to see such lovely, colorful (if you're reading the e-book), useful output from a test tool. It looks even cooler if your terminal is in dark mode.

Let's take a closer look at the details. Figure 2.2 shows the same output, but with numbers to follow along. Let's see how many pieces of information are presented here:

1. A quick list of all the failing tests (with names) with nice red Xs next to them
2. A detailed report on the expectation that failed (aka our assertion)
3. The exact difference between the actual value and expected value
4. The type of comparison that was executed
5. The code for the test
6. The exact line (visually) where the test failed
7. A report of how many tests ran, failed, and passed
8. The time it took
9. The number of snapshots (not relevant to our discussion)

```
[aout3-samples/ch2 [ jest
 FAIL  __tests__/hellojest.test.js
  ✕ hello jest (14ms)

  ● hello jest

    expect(received).toEqual(expected) // deep equality

    Expected: "goodbye"
    Received: "hello"

      1 | test('hello jest', () => {
    > 2 |     expect('hello').toEqual('goodbye');
        |                     ^
      3 | });
      4 |

      at Object.toEqual (__tests__/hellojest.test.js:2:21)

Test Suites: 1 failed, 1 total
Tests:       1 failed, 1 total
Snapshots:   0 total
Time:        1.145s
Ran all test suites.
aout3-samples/ch2 [ ▇
```

Figure 2.1   Terminal output from Jest

```
 FAIL  __tests__/hellojest.test.js
  ✕ hello jest (6ms) ❶

  ● hello jest

 ❷ expect(received).toEqual(expected) // deep equality ❹

    Expected: "goodbye"
    Received: "hello" ❸

      1 | test('hello jest', () => {        ❺
 ❻  > 2 |     expect('hello').toEqual('goodbye');
        |                     ^
      3 | });
      4 |

      at Object.toEqual (__tests__/hellojest.test.js:2:21)
 ❼
Test Suites: 1 failed, 1 total
Tests:       1 failed, 1 total
Snapshots:   0 total
Time:        0.743s, estimated 1s ❽  ❾
Ran all_test suites matching /__tests__\/hellojest.test.js/i.
```

Figure 2.2   Annotated terminal output from Jest

Imagine trying to write all this reporting functionality yourself. It's possible, but who's got the time and the inclination? Plus, you'd have to take care of any bugs in the reporting mechanism.

If we change `goodbye` to `hello` in the test, we can see what happens when the test passes (figure 2.3). Nice and green, as all things should be (again, in the digital version—otherwise it's nice and grey).

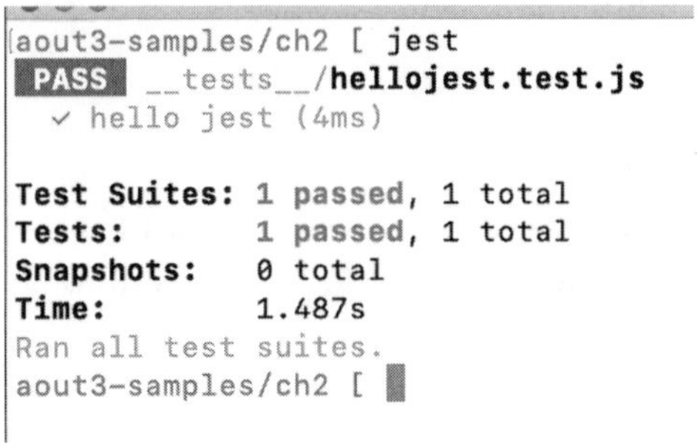

```
[aout3-samples/ch2 [ jest
 PASS  __tests__/hellojest.test.js
  ✓ hello jest (4ms)

Test Suites: 1 passed, 1 total
Tests:       1 passed, 1 total
Snapshots:   0 total
Time:        1.487s
Ran all test suites.
aout3-samples/ch2 [ ▮
```

Figure 2.3 Jest terminal output for a passing test

You might note that it takes 1.5 seconds to run this single Hello World test. If we used the command `jest --watch` instead, we could have Jest monitor filesystem activity in our folder and automatically run tests for files that have changed without re-initializing itself every time. This can save a considerable amount of time, and it really helps with the whole notion of *continuous testing*. Set a terminal in the other window of your workstation with `jest --watch` on it, and you can keep coding and getting fast feedback on issues you might be creating. That's a good way to get into the flow of things.

Jest also supports async-style testing and callbacks. I'll touch on these when we get to those topics later in the book, but if you'd like to learn more about this style now, head over to the Jest documentation on the subject: https://jestjs.io/docs/en/asynchronous.

2.2 The library, the assert, the runner, and the reporter

Jest has acted in several capacities for us:

- It acted as a *test library* to use when writing the test.
- It acted as an *assertion library* for asserting inside the test (`expect`).
- It acted as the *test runner*.
- It acted as the *test reporter* for the test run.

Jest also provides *isolation* facilities to create mocks, stubs, and spies, though we haven't seen that yet. We'll touch on these ideas in later chapters.

Other than isolation facilities, it's very common in other languages for a test framework to fill all the roles I just mentioned—library, assertions, test runner, and test reporter—but the JavaScript world seems a bit more fragmented. Many other test frameworks provide only some of these facilities. Perhaps this is because the mantra of "do one thing, and do it well" has been taken to heart, or perhaps it's for other reasons. In any case, Jest stands out as one of a handful of all-in-one frameworks. It is a testament to the strength of the open source culture in JavaScript that for each one of these categories, there are multiple tools that you can mix and match to create your own super toolset.

One of the reasons I chose Jest for this book is so we don't have to bother too much with the tooling or deal with missing features—we can just focus on the patterns. That way we won't have to use multiple frameworks in a book that is mostly concerned with patterns and antipatterns.

2.3   *What unit testing frameworks offer*

Let's zoom out for a second and see where we are. What do frameworks like Jest offer us over creating our own framework, like we started to do in the previous chapter, or over manually testing things?

- *Structure*—Instead of reinventing the wheel every time you want to test a feature, when you use a test framework you always start out the same way—by writing a test with a well-defined structure that everyone can easily recognize, read, and understand.
- *Repeatability*—When using a test framework, it's easy to repeat the act of writing a new test. It's also easy to repeat the execution of the test, using a test runner, and it's easy to do this quickly and many times a day. It's also easy to understand failures and their causes. Someone has already done all the hard work for us, instead of us having to code all that stuff into our hand-rolled framework.
- *Confidence and time savings*—When we roll our own test framework, the framework is more likely to have bugs in it, since it is less battle-tested than an existing mature and widely used framework. On the other hand, manually testing things is usually very time consuming. When we're short on time, we'll likely focus on testing the things that feel the most critical and skip over things that might feel less important. We could be skipping small but significant bugs. By making it easy to write new tests, it's more likely that we'll also write tests for the stuff that feels less significant because we won't be spending too much time writing tests for the big stuff.
- *Shared understanding*—The framework's reporting can be helpful for managing tasks at the team level (when a test is passing, it means the task is done). Some people find this useful.

In short, frameworks for writing, running, and reviewing unit tests and their results can make a huge difference in the daily lives of developers who are willing to invest the time in learning how to use them properly. Figure 2.4 shows the areas in software development in which a unit testing framework and its helper tools have influence, and table 2.1 lists the types of actions we usually execute with a test framework.

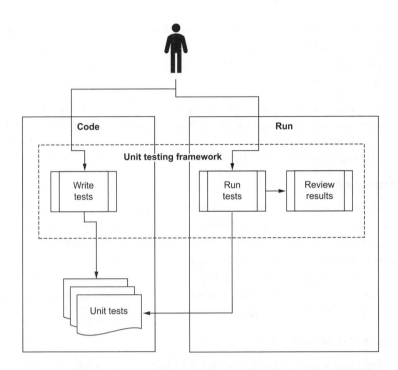

Figure 2.4   Unit tests are written as code, using libraries from the unit testing framework. The tests are run from a test runner inside the IDE or through the command line, and the results are reviewed through a test reporter (either as output text or in the IDE) by the developer or an automated build process.

Table 2.1   How testing frameworks help developers write and execute tests and review results

Unit testing practice	How the framework helps
Write tests easily and in a structured manner.	A framework supplies the developer with helper functions, assertion functions, and structure-related functions.
Execute one or all of the unit tests.	A framework provides a test runner, usually at the command line, that ■ Identifies tests in your code ■ Runs tests automatically ■ Indicates test status while running
Review the results of the test runs.	A test runner will usually provide information such as ■ How many tests ran ■ How many tests didn't run ■ How many tests failed ■ Which tests failed ■ The reason tests failed ■ The code location that failed ■ Possibly provide a full stack trace for any exceptions that caused the test to fail, and let you go to the various method calls inside the call stack

At the time of writing, there are around 900 unit testing frameworks out there, with more than a couple for most programming languages in public use (and a few dead ones). You can find a good list on Wikipedia: https://en.wikipedia.org/wiki/List_of_unit_testing_frameworks.

> **NOTE**   Using a unit testing framework doesn't ensure that the tests you write are *readable*, *maintainable*, or *trustworthy*, or that they cover all the logic you'd like to test. We'll look at how to ensure your unit tests have these properties in chapters 7 through 9 and in various other places throughout this book.

2.3.1   *The xUnit frameworks*

When I started writing tests (in the Visual Basic days), the standard by which most unit test frameworks were measured was collectively called xUnit. The grandfather of the xUnit frameworks idea was SUnit, the unit testing framework for Smalltalk.

These unit testing frameworks' names usually start with the first letters of the language for which they were built; you might have CppUnit for C++, JUnit for Java, NUnit and xUnit for .NET, and HUnit for the Haskell programming language. Not all of them follow these naming guidelines, but most do.

2.3.2   *xUnit, TAP, and Jest structures*

It's not just the names that were reasonably consistent. If you were using an xUnit framework, you could also expect a specific structure in which the tests were built. When these frameworks would run, they would output their results in the same structure, which was usually an XML file with a specific schema.

This type of xUnit XML report is still prevalent today, and it's widely used in most build tools, such as Jenkins, which support this format with native plugins and use it to report the results of test runs. Most unit test frameworks in static languages still use the xUnit model for structure, which means that once you've learned to use one of them, you should be able to easily use any of them (assuming you know the particular programming language).

The other interesting standard for the reporting structure of test results and more is called *TAP*, the Test Anything Protocol. TAP started life as part of the test harness for Perl, but now it has implementations in C, C++, Python, PHP, Perl, Java, JavaScript, and other languages. TAP is much more than just a reporting specification. In the JavaScript world, the TAP framework is the best-known test framework that natively supports the TAP protocol.

Jest is not strictly an xUnit or TAP framework. Its output is not xUnit- or TAP-compliant by default. However, because xUnit-style reporting still rules the build sphere, we'll usually want to adapt to that protocol for our reporting on a build server. To get Jest test results that are easily recognized by most build tools, you can install npm modules such as `jest-xunit` (if you want TAP-specific output, use `jest-tap-reporter`) and then use a special jest.config.js file in your project to configure Jest to alter its reporting format.

Now let's move on and write something that feels a bit more like a real test with Jest, shall we?

2.4 Introducing the Password Verifier project

The project that we'll mostly use for testing examples in this book will start out simple, containing only one function. As the book moves along, we'll extend that project with new features, modules, and classes to demonstrate different aspects of unit testing. We'll call it the Password Verifier project.

The first scenario is pretty simple. We'll be building a password verification library, and it will just be a function at first. The function, `verifyPassword(rules)`, allows us to put in custom verification functions dubbed `rules`, and it outputs the list of errors, according to the rules that have been input. Each rule function will output two fields:

```
{
    passed: (boolean),
    reason: (string)
}
```

In this book, I'll teach you to write tests that check `verifyPassword`'s functionality in multiple ways as we add more features to it.

The following listing shows version 0 of this function, with a very naive implementation.

Listing 2.2 Password Verifier version 0

```
const verifyPassword = (input, rules) => {
  const errors = [];
  rules.forEach(rule => {
    const result = rule(input);
    if (!result.passed) {
      errors.push(`error ${result.reason}`);
    }
  });
  return errors;
};
```

Granted, this is not the most functional-style code, and we might refactor it a bit later, but I wanted to keep things very simple here so we can focus on the tests.

The function doesn't really do much. It iterates over all the rules given and runs each one with the supplied input. If the rule's result is not *passed*, then an error is added to the final errors array that is returned as the final result.

2.5 The first Jest test for verifyPassword

Assuming you have Jest installed, you can go ahead and create a new file named password-verifier0.spec.js under the __tests__ folder.

Using the __tests__ folder is only one convention for organizing your tests, and it's part of Jest's default configuration. There are many who prefer to place the test files alongside the code being tested. There are pros and cons to each approach, and we'll get into that in later parts of the book. For now, we'll go with the defaults.

Here's a first version of a test against our new function.

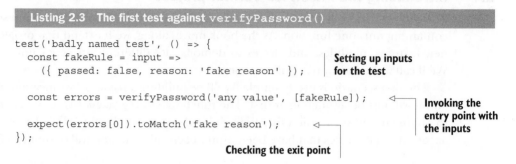

Listing 2.3   The first test against `verifyPassword()`

```
test('badly named test', () => {
  const fakeRule = input =>
    ({ passed: false, reason: 'fake reason' });        Setting up inputs
                                                       for the test

  const errors = verifyPassword('any value', [fakeRule]);    ◁───  Invoking the
                                                                   entry point with
  expect(errors[0]).toMatch('fake reason');     ◁───               the inputs
});
                                       Checking the exit point
```

2.5.1   *The Arrange-Act-Assert pattern*

The structure of the test in listing 2.3 is colloquially called the *Arrange-Act-Assert* (AAA) pattern. It's quite nice! I find it very easy to reason about the parts of a test by saying things like "that 'arrange' part is too complicated" or "where is the 'act' part?"

In the arrange part, we're creating a fake rule that always returns false, so that we can prove it's actually used by asserting *on its reason* at the end of the test. We then send it to `verifyPassword` along with a simple input. We check in the assert section that the first error we get matches the fake reason we gave in the arrange part. `.toMatch(/string/)` uses a regular expression to find a part of the string. It's the same as using `.toContain('fake reason')`.

It's tedious to run Jest manually after we write a test or fix something, so let's configure npm to run Jest automatically. Go to package.json in the root folder of ch2 and add the following items under the `scripts` item:

```
"scripts": {
  "test": "jest",
  "testw": "jest --watch" //if not using git, change to --watchAll
},
```

If you don't have Git initialized in this folder, you can use the command `--watchAll` instead of `--watch`.

If everything went well, you can now type npm `test` in the command line from the ch2 folder, and Jest will run the tests once. If you type npm `run testw`, Jest will run and wait for changes in an endless loop, until you kill the process with Ctrl-C. (You need to use the word `run` because `testw` is not one of the special keywords that npm recognizes automatically.)

If you run the test, you can see that it passes, since the function works as expected.

2.5.2 Testing the test

Let's put a bug in the production code and see if the test fails when it should.

> **Listing 2.4 Adding a bug**

```
const verifyPassword = (input, rules) => {
  const errors = [];
  rules.forEach(rule => {
    const result = rule(input);
    if (!result.passed) {
      // errors.push(`error ${result.reason}`);     ◁─── We've accidentally
    }                                                     commented out
  });                                                     this line.
  return errors;
};
```

You should now see your test failing with a nice message. Let's uncomment the line and see the test pass again. This is a great way to gain some confidence in your tests, if you're not doing test-driven development and are writing the tests after the code.

2.5.3 USE naming

Our test has a really bad name. It doesn't explain anything about what we're trying to accomplish here. I like to put three pieces of information in test names, so that the reader of the test will be able to answer most of their mental questions just by looking at the test name. These three parts include

- The unit of work under test (the `verifyPassword` function, in this case)
- The scenario or inputs to the unit (the failed rule)
- The expected behavior or exit point (returns an error with a reason)

During the review process, Tyler Lemke, a reviewer of the book, came up with a nice acronym for this, USE: unit under test, scenario, expectation. I like it, and it's easy to remember. Thanks Tyler!

The following listing shows our next revision of the test with a USE name.

> **Listing 2.5 Naming a test with USE**

```
test('verifyPassword, given a failing rule, returns errors', () => {
  const fakeRule = input => ({ passed: false, reason: 'fake reason' });

  const errors = verifyPassword('any value', [fakeRule]);
  expect(errors[0]).toContain('fake reason');
});
```

This is a bit better. When a test fails, especially during a build process, you don't see comments or the full test code. You usually only see the name of the test. The name should be so clear that you might not even have to look at the test code to understand where the production code problem might be.

2.5.4   *String comparisons and maintainability*

We also made another small change in the following line:

```
expect(errors[0]).toContain('fake reason');
```

Instead of checking that one string is equal to another, as is very common in tests, we are checking that a string is contained in the output. This makes our test less brittle for future changes to the output. We can use `.toContain` or `.toMatch(/fake reason/)`, which uses a regular expression to match a part of the string, to achieve this.

Strings are a form of user interface. They are visible to humans, and they might change—especially the edges of strings. We might add whitespace, tabs, asterisks, or other embellishments to a string. We care that the *core* of the information contained in the string exists. We don't want to change our test every time someone adds a new line to the end of a string. This is part of the thinking we want to encourage in our tests: test maintainability over time, and resistance to test brittleness, are of high priority.

We'd ideally like the test to fail only when something is actually wrong in the production code. We'd like to reduce the number of false positives to a minimum. Using `toContain()` or `toMatch()` is a great way to move toward that goal.

I'll talk about more ways to improve test maintainability throughout the book, and especially in part 2 of the book.

2.5.5   *Using describe()*

We can use Jest's `describe()` function to create a bit more structure around our test and to start separating the three USE pieces of information from each other. This step and the ones after it are completely up you—you can decide how you want to style your test and its readability structure. I'm showing you these steps because many people either don't use `describe()` in an effective way, or they ignore it altogether. It can be quite useful.

The `describe()` functions wrap our tests with context: both logical context for the reader, and functional context for the test itself. The next listing shows how we can start using them.

Listing 2.6   Adding a `describe()` block

```
describe('verifyPassword', () => {
  test('given a failing rule, returns errors', () => {
    const fakeRule = input =>
      ({ passed: false, reason: 'fake reason' });

    const errors = verifyPassword('any value', [fakeRule]);

    expect(errors[0]).toContain('fake reason');
  });
});
```

I've made four changes here:

- I've added a `describe()` block that describes the unit of work under test. To me this looks clearer. It also feels like I can now add more nested tests under that block. This `describe()` block also helps the command-line reporter create nicer reports.
- I've nested the `test` under the new block and removed the name of the unit of work from the test.
- I've added the `input` into the fake rule's `reason` string.
- I've added an empty line between the arrange, act, and assert parts to make the test more readable, especially to someone new to the team.

2.5.6 *Structure implying context*

The nice thing about `describe()` is that it can be nested under itself. So we can use it to create another level that explains the scenario, and under that we'll nest our test.

Listing 2.7 Nested `describes` for extra context

```
describe('verifyPassword', () => {
  describe('with a failing rule', () => {
    test('returns errors', () => {
      const fakeRule = input => ({ passed: false,
                                   reason: 'fake reason' });

      const errors = verifyPassword('any value', [fakeRule]);

      expect(errors[0]).toContain('fake reason');
    });
  });
});
```

Some people will hate it, but I think there's a certain elegance to it. This nesting allows us to separate the three pieces of critical information to their own level. In fact, we can also extract the false rule outside of the test right under the relevant `describe()`, if we wish to.

Listing 2.8 Nested `describes` with an extracted input

```
describe('verifyPassword', () => {
  describe('with a failing rule', () => {
    const fakeRule = input => ({ passed: false,
                                 reason: 'fake reason' });

    test('returns errors', () => {
      const errors = verifyPassword('any value', [fakeRule]);

      expect(errors[0]).toContain('fake reason');
    });
  });
});
```

For the next example, I'll move this rule back into the test (I like it when things are close together—more on that later).

This nesting structure also implies very nicely that under a specific scenario you could have more than one expected behavior. You could check multiple exit points under a scenario, with each one as a separate test, and it will still make sense from the reader's point of view.

2.5.7   *The it() function*

There's one missing piece to the puzzle I've been building so far. Jest also exposes an `it()` function. This function is, for all intents and purposes, an *alias* to the `test()` function, but it fits in more nicely in terms of syntax with the describe-driven approach outlined so far.

The following listing shows what the test looks like when I replace `test()` with `it()`.

Listing 2.9   Replacing `test()` with `it()`

```
describe('verifyPassword', () => {
  describe('with a failing rule', () => {
    it('returns errors', () => {
      const fakeRule = input => ({ passed: false,
                                   reason: 'fake reason' });

      const errors = verifyPassword('any value', [fakeRule]);

      expect(errors[0]).toContain('fake reason');
    });
  });
});
```

In this test, it's very easy to understand what `it` refers to. This is a natural extension of the previous `describe()` blocks. Again, it's up to you whether you want to use this style. I'm showing one variation of how I like to think about it.

2.5.8   *Two Jest flavors*

As you've seen, Jest supports two main ways to write tests: a terse `test` syntax, and a more `describe`-driven (i.e., hierarchical) syntax.

The `describe`-driven Jest syntax can be largely attributed to Jasmine, one of the oldest JavaScript test frameworks. The style itself can be traced back to Ruby-land and the well-known RSpec Ruby test framework. This nested style is usually called *BDD style*, referring to *behavior-driven development*.

You can mix and match these styles as you like (I do). You can use the `test` syntax when it's easy to understand your test target and all of its context, without going to too much trouble. The `describe` syntax can help when you're expecting multiple results from the same entry point under the same scenario. I'm showing them both here because I sometimes use the terse `test` flavor and sometimes use the `describe`-driven flavor, depending on the complexity and expressiveness requirements.

BDD's dark present

BDD has quite an interesting background that might be worth talking about. BDD isn't related to TDD. Dan North, the person most associated with inventing the term, refers to BDD as using stories and examples to describe how an application should behave. Mainly this is targeted at working with non-technical stakeholders—product owners, customers, etc. RSpec (inspired by RBehave) brought the story-driven approach to the masses, and in the process, many other frameworks came along, including the famous Cucumber.

There is also a dark side to this story: many frameworks have been developed and used solely by developers without working with non-technical stakeholders, in complete opposition to the main ideas of BDD.

Today, to me, the term *BDD frameworks* mainly means "test frameworks with some syntactic sugar," since they are almost never used to create real conversations between stakeholders and are almost always used as just another shiny or prescribed tool for performing developer-based automated tests. I've even seen the mighty Cucumber fall into this pattern.

2.5.9 *Refactoring the production code*

Since there are many ways to build the same thing in JavaScript, I thought I'd show a couple of variations on our design and what happens if we change it. Suppose we'd like to make the password verifier an object with state.

One reason to change the design into a stateful one might be that I intend for different parts of the application to use this object. One part will configure and add rules to it, and a different part will use it to do the verification. Another reason is that we need to know how to handle a stateful design and look at which directions it pulls our tests in, and what we can do about that.

Let's look at the production code first.

> **Listing 2.10   Refactoring a function to a stateful class**

```
class PasswordVerifier1 {
  constructor () {
    this.rules = [];
  }

  addRule (rule) {
    this.rules.push(rule);
  }

  verify (input) {
    const errors = [];
    this.rules.forEach(rule => {
      const result = rule(input);
      if (result.passed === false) {
        errors.push(result.reason);
      }
```

```
    });
    return errors;
  }
}
```

I've highlighted the main changes from listing 2.9. There's nothing really special going on here, though this may feel more comfortable if you're coming from an object-oriented background. It's important to note that this is just one way to design this functionality. I'm using the class-based approach so that I can show how this design affects the test.

In this new design, where are the entry and exit points for the current scenario? Think about it for a second. The scope of the unit of work has increased. To test a scenario with a failing rule, we would have to invoke two functions that affect the state of the unit under test: addRule and `verify`.

Now let's see what the test might look like (changes are highlighted as usual).

Listing 2.11   Testing the stateful unit of work

```
describe('PasswordVerifier', () => {
  describe('with a failing rule', () => {
    it('has an error message based on the rule.reason', () => {
      const verifier = new PasswordVerifier1();
      const fakeRule = input => ({ passed: false,
                                    reason: 'fake reason'});

      verifier.addRule(fakeRule);
      const errors = verifier.verify('any value');

      expect(errors[0]).toContain('fake reason');
    });
  });
});
```

So far, so good; nothing fancy is happening here. Note that the surface of the unit of work has increased. It now spans two related functions that must work together (addRule and `verify`). There is a *coupling* that occurs due to the stateful nature of the design. We need to use two functions to test productively without exposing any internal state from the object.

The test itself looks innocent enough. But what happens when we want to write several tests for the same scenario? That would happen if we have multiple exit points, or if we want to test multiple results from the same exit point. For example, let's say we want to verify that we have only a single error. We could simply add a line to the test like this:

```
verifier.addRule(fakeRule);
const errors = verifier.verify('any value');        A new
expect(errors.length).toBe(1);            ⟵────     assertion
expect(errors[0]).toContain('fake reason');
```

What happens if the new assertion fails? The second assertion would never execute, because the test runner would receive an error and move on to the next test case.

We'd still want to know if the second assertion would have passed, right? So maybe we'd start commenting out the first one and rerunning the test. That's not a healthy way to run your tests. In Gerard Meszaros' book *xUnit Test Patterns*, this human behavior of commenting things out to test other things is called *assertion roulette*. It can create lots of confusion and false positives in your test runs (thinking that something is failing or passing when it isn't).

I'd rather separate this extra check into its own test case with a good name, as follows.

Listing 2.12   Checking an extra end result from the same exit point

```
describe('PasswordVerifier', () => {
  describe('with a failing rule', () => {
    it('has an error message based on the rule.reason', () => {
      const verifier = new PasswordVerifier1();
      const fakeRule = input => ({ passed: false,
                                   reason: 'fake reason'});

      verifier.addRule(fakeRule);
      const errors = verifier.verify('any value');

      expect(errors[0]).toContain('fake reason');
    });
    it('has exactly one error', () => {
      const verifier = new PasswordVerifier1();
      const fakeRule = input => ({ passed: false,
                                   reason: 'fake reason'});

      verifier.addRule(fakeRule);
      const errors = verifier.verify('any value');

      expect(errors.length).toBe(1);
    });
  });
});
```

This is starting to look *bad*. Yes, we have solved the assertion roulette issue. Each `it()` can fail separately and not interfere with the results from the other test case. But what did it cost? Everything. Look at all the duplication we have now. At this point, those of you with some unit testing background will start shouting at the book: "Use a `setup/beforeEach` method!"

Fine!

2.6   *Trying the beforeEach() route*

I haven't introduced `beforeEach()` yet. This function and its sibling, `afterEach()`, are used to set up and tear down a specific state required by the test cases. There's also `beforeAll()` and `afterAll()`, which I try to avoid using at all costs for unit testing scenarios. We'll talk more about the siblings later in the book.

`beforeEach()` can help us remove duplication in our tests because it runs once before each test in the `describe` block in which we nest it. We can also nest it multiple times, as the following listing demonstrates.

Listing 2.13   Using `beforeEach()` on two levels

```
describe('PasswordVerifier', () => {                    Setting up a new
  let verifier;                                         verifier that will be
  beforeEach(() => verifier = new PasswordVerifier1()); used in each test
  describe('with a failing rule', () => {
    let fakeRule, errors;
    beforeEach(() => {
      fakeRule = input => ({passed: false, reason: 'fake reason'});
      verifier.addRule(fakeRule);
    });
    it('has an error message based on the rule.reason', () => {
      const errors = verifier.verify('any value');
                                                        Setting up a fake
      expect(errors[0]).toContain('fake reason');       rule that will be
    });                                                 used within this
    it('has exactly one error', () => {                 describe() method
      const errors = verifier.verify('any value');

      expect(errors.length).toBe(1);
    });
  });
});
```

Look at all that extracted code.

In the first `beforeEach()`, we're setting up a new `PasswordVerifier1` that will be created for each test case. In the `beforeEach()` after that, we're setting up a fake rule and adding it to the new verifier for every test case under that specific scenario. If we had other scenarios, the second `beforeEach()` in line 6 wouldn't run for them, but the first one would.

The tests seem shorter now, which ideally is what you want in a test, to make it more readable and maintainable. We removed the creation line from each test and reused the same higher-level variable `verifier`.

There are a couple of caveats:

- We forgot to reset the `errors` array in `beforeEach()` on line 6. That could bite us later on.
- Jest runs unit tests in parallel by default. This means that moving the verifier to line 2 may cause an issue with parallel tests, where the verifier could be overwritten by a different test on a parallel run, which would screw up the state of our running test. Jest is quite different from unit test frameworks in most other languages I know, which make a point of running tests in a single thread, not in parallel (at least by default), to avoid such issues. With Jest, we have to remember that parallel tests are a reality, so stateful tests with a shared upper state, like

we have at line 2, can potentially be problematic and cause flaky tests that fail for unknown reasons.

We'll correct both of these issues soon.

2.6.1 beforeEach() and scroll fatigue

We lost a couple of things in the process of refactoring to `beforeEach()`:

- If I'm trying to read only the `it()` parts, I can't tell where the `verifier` is created and declared. I'd have to scroll up to understand.
- The same goes for understanding what rule was added. I'd have to look one level above the `it()` to see what rule was added, or look up the `describe()` block description.

Right now, this doesn't seem so bad. But we'll see later that this structure starts to get a bit hairy as the scenario list increases in size. Larger files can bring about what I like to call *scroll fatigue*, requiring the test reader to scroll up and down the test file to understand the context and state of the tests. This makes maintaining and reading the tests a chore instead of a simple act of reading.

This nesting is great for reporting, but it sucks for humans who have to keep looking up where something came from. If you've ever tried to debug CSS styles in the browser's inspector window, you'll know the feeling. You'll see that a specific cell is bold for some reason. Then you scroll up to see which style made that `<div>` inside nested cells in a special `table` under the third node bold.

Let's see what happens when we take it one step further in the following listing. Since we're in the process of removing duplication, we can also call `verify` in `beforeEach()` and remove an extra line from each `it()`. This is basically putting the arrange and act parts from the AAA pattern into the `beforeEach()` function.

Listing 2.14 Pushing the arrange and act parts into `beforeEach()`

```
describe('PasswordVerifier', () => {
  let verifier;
  beforeEach(() => verifier = new PasswordVerifier1());
  describe('with a failing rule', () => {
    let fakeRule, errors;
    beforeEach(() => {
      fakeRule = input => ({passed: false, reason: 'fake reason'});
      verifier.addRule(fakeRule);
      errors = verifier.verify('any value');
    });
    it('has an error message based on the rule.reason', () => {
      expect(errors[0]).toContain('fake reason');
    });
    it('has exactly one error', () => {
      expect(errors.length).toBe(1);
    });
  });
});
```

The code duplication has been reduced to a minimum, but now we also need to look up where and how we got the `errors` array if we want to understand each `it()`.

Let's double down and add a few more basic scenarios, and see if this approach is scalable as the problem space increases.

Listing 2.15   Adding extra scenarios

```
describe('v6 PasswordVerifier', () => {
  let verifier;
  beforeEach(() => verifier = new PasswordVerifier1());
  describe('with a failing rule', () => {
    let fakeRule, errors;
    beforeEach(() => {
      fakeRule = input => ({passed: false, reason: 'fake reason'});
      verifier.addRule(fakeRule);
      errors = verifier.verify('any value');
    });
    it('has an error message based on the rule.reason', () => {
      expect(errors[0]).toContain('fake reason');
    });
    it('has exactly one error', () => {
      expect(errors.length).toBe(1);
    });
  });
  describe('with a passing rule', () => {
    let fakeRule, errors;
    beforeEach(() => {
      fakeRule = input => ({passed: true, reason: ''});
      verifier.addRule(fakeRule);
      errors = verifier.verify('any value');
    });
    it('has no errors', () => {
      expect(errors.length).toBe(0);
    });
  });
  describe('with a failing and a passing rule', () => {
    let fakeRulePass,fakeRuleFail, errors;
    beforeEach(() => {
      fakeRulePass = input => ({passed: true, reason: 'fake success'});
      fakeRuleFail = input => ({passed: false, reason: 'fake reason'});
      verifier.addRule(fakeRulePass);
      verifier.addRule(fakeRuleFail);
      errors = verifier.verify('any value');
    });
    it('has one error', () => {
      expect(errors.length).toBe(1);
    });
    it('error text belongs to failed rule', () => {
      expect(errors[0]).toContain('fake reason');
    });
  });
});
```

Do we like this? I don't. Now we're seeing a couple of extra problems:

- I can already start to see lots of repetition in the beforeEach() parts.
- The potential for scroll fatigue has increased dramatically, with more options of which beforeEach() affects which it() state.

In real projects, beforeEach() functions tend to be the garbage bin of the test file. People throw all kinds of test-initialized stuff in there: things that only some tests need, things that affect all the other tests, and things that nobody uses anymore. It's human nature to put things in the easiest place possible, especially if everyone else before you has done so as well.

I'm not crazy about the beforeEach() approach. Let's see if we can mitigate some of these issues while still keeping duplication to a minimum.

2.7   *Trying the factory method route*

Factory methods are simple helper functions that help us build objects or special states and reuse the same logic in multiple places. Perhaps we can reduce some of the duplication and clunky-feeling code by using a couple of factory methods for the failing and passing rules in listing 2.16.

Listing 2.16   Adding a couple of factory methods to the mix

```
describe('PasswordVerifier', () => {
  let verifier;
  beforeEach(() => verifier = new PasswordVerifier1());
  describe('with a failing rule', () => {
    let errors;
    beforeEach(() => {
      verifier.addRule(makeFailingRule('fake reason'));
      errors = verifier.verify('any value');
    });
    it('has an error message based on the rule.reason', () => {
      expect(errors[0]).toContain('fake reason');
    });
    it('has exactly one error', () => {
      expect(errors.length).toBe(1);
    });
  });
  describe('with a passing rule', () => {
    let errors;
    beforeEach(() => {
      verifier.addRule(makePassingRule());
      errors = verifier.verify('any value');
    });
    it('has no errors', () => {
      expect(errors.length).toBe(0);
    });
  });
  describe('with a failing and a passing rule', () => {
    let errors;
```

```
      beforeEach(() => {
        verifier.addRule(makePassingRule());
        verifier.addRule(makeFailingRule('fake reason'));
        errors = verifier.verify('any value');
      });
      it('has one error', () => {
        expect(errors.length).toBe(1);
      });
      it('error text belongs to failed rule', () => {
        expect(errors[0]).toContain('fake reason');
      });
    });
. . .
  const makeFailingRule = (reason) => {
    return (input) => {
      return { passed: false, reason: reason };
    };
  };
  const makePassingRule = () => (input) => {
    return { passed: true, reason: '' };
  };
})
```

The `makeFailingRule()` and `makePassingRule()` factory methods have made our `beforeEach()` functions a little more clear.

2.7.1 *Replacing beforeEach() completely with factory methods*

What if we don't use `beforeEach()` to initialize various things at all? What if we switched to using small factory methods instead? Let's see what that looks like.

> **Listing 2.17 Replacing `beforeEach()` with factory methods**

```
const makeVerifier = () => new PasswordVerifier1();
const passingRule = (input) => ({passed: true, reason: ''});

const makeVerifierWithPassingRule = () => {
  const verifier = makeVerifier();
  verifier.addRule(passingRule);
  return verifier;
};

const makeVerifierWithFailedRule = (reason) => {
  const verifier = makeVerifier();
  const fakeRule = input => ({passed: false, reason: reason});
  verifier.addRule(fakeRule);
  return verifier;
};

describe('PasswordVerifier', () => {
  describe('with a failing rule', () => {
    it('has an error message based on the rule.reason', () => {
      const verifier = makeVerifierWithFailedRule('fake reason');
```

```
        const errors = verifier.verify('any input');
        expect(errors[0]).toContain('fake reason');
      });
      it('has exactly one error', () => {
        const verifier = makeVerifierWithFailedRule('fake reason');
        const errors = verifier.verify('any input');
        expect(errors.length).toBe(1);
      });
    });
    describe('with a passing rule', () => {
      it('has no errors', () => {
        const verifier = makeVerifierWithPassingRule();
        const errors = verifier.verify('any input');
        expect(errors.length).toBe(0);
      });
    });
    describe('with a failing and a passing rule', () => {
      it('has one error', () => {
        const verifier = makeVerifierWithFailedRule('fake reason');
        verifier.addRule(passingRule);
        const errors = verifier.verify('any input');
        expect(errors.length).toBe(1);
      });
      it('error text belongs to failed rule', () => {
        const verifier = makeVerifierWithFailedRule('fake reason');
        verifier.addRule(passingRule);
        const errors = verifier.verify('any input');
        expect(errors[0]).toContain('fake reason');
      });
    });
  });
});
```

The length here is about the same as in listing 2.16, but I find the code to be more readable and thus more easily maintained. We've eliminated the `beforeEach()` functions, but we didn't lose maintainability. The amount of repetition we've eliminated is negligible, but the readability has improved greatly due to the removal of the nested `beforeEach()` blocks.

Furthermore, we've reduced the risk of scroll fatigue. As a reader of the test, I don't have to scroll up and down the file to find out when an object is created or declared. I can glean all the information from the `it()`. We don't need to know *how* something is created, but we know *when* it is created and what important parameters it is initialized with. Everything is explicitly explained.

If the need arises, I can drill into specific factory methods, and I like that each `it()` is encapsulating its own state. The nested `describe()` structure is a good way to know where we are, but the state is all triggered from inside the `it()` blocks, not outside of them.

2.8   *Going full circle to test()*

The tests in listing 2.17 are self-encapsulated enough that the `describe()` blocks act only as added sugar for understanding. They are no longer needed if we don't want them. If we wanted to, we could write the tests as in the following listing.

Listing 2.18   Removing nested describes

```
test('pass verifier, with failed rule, ' +
        'has an error message based on the rule.reason', () => {
  const verifier = makeVerifierWithFailedRule('fake reason');
  const errors = verifier.verify('any input');
  expect(errors[0]).toContain('fake reason');
});
test('pass verifier, with failed rule, has exactly one error', () => {
  const verifier = makeVerifierWithFailedRule('fake reason');
  const errors = verifier.verify('any input');
  expect(errors.length).toBe(1);
});
test('pass verifier, with passing rule, has no errors', () => {
  const verifier = makeVerifierWithPassingRule();
  const errors = verifier.verify('any input');
  expect(errors.length).toBe(0);
});
test('pass verifier, with passing  and failing rule,' +
        ' has one error', () => {
  const verifier = makeVerifierWithFailedRule('fake reason');
  verifier.addRule(passingRule);
  const errors = verifier.verify('any input');
  expect(errors.length).toBe(1);
});
test('pass verifier, with passing  and failing rule,' +
        ' error text belongs to failed rule', () => {
  const verifier = makeVerifierWithFailedRule('fake reason');
  verifier.addRule(passingRule);
  const errors = verifier.verify('any input');
  expect(errors[0]).toContain('fake reason');
});
```

The factory methods provide us with all the functionality we need, without losing clarity for each specific test.

   I kind of like the terseness of listing 2.18. It's easy to understand. We might lose a bit of structure clarity here, so there are instances where I go with the `describe`-less approach, and there are places where nested `describes` make things more readable. The sweet spot of maintainability and readability for your project is probably somewhere between these two points.

2.9   *Refactoring to parameterized tests*

Let's move away from the `verifier` class to work on creating and testing a new custom rule for the verifier. Listing 2.19 shows a simple rule for an uppercase letter (I realize passwords with these requirements are no longer considered a great idea, but for demonstration purposes I'm okay with it).

Listing 2.19 Password rules

```
const oneUpperCaseRule = (input) => {
  return {
    passed: (input.toLowerCase() !== input),
    reason: 'at least one upper case needed'
  };
};
```

We could write a couple of tests as in the following listing.

Listing 2.20 Testing a rule with variations

```
describe('one uppercase rule', function () {
  test('given no uppercase, it fails', () => {
    const result = oneUpperCaseRule('abc');
    expect(result.passed).toEqual(false);
  });
  test('given one uppercase, it passes', () => {
    const result = oneUpperCaseRule('Abc');
    expect(result.passed).toEqual(true);
  });
  test('given a different uppercase, it passes', () => {
    const result = oneUpperCaseRule('aBc');
    expect(result.passed).toEqual(true);
  });
});
```

In listing 2.20 I highlighted some duplication we might have if we're trying out the same scenario with small variations in the input to the unit of work. In this case, we want to test that it should not matter where the uppercase letter is, as long as it's there. But this duplication will hurt us down the road if we ever want to change the uppercase logic, or if we need to correct the assertions in some way for that use case.

There are a few ways to create parameterized tests in JavaScript, and Jest already includes one that's built in: `test.each` (also aliased to `it.each`). The next listing shows how we could use this feature to remove duplication in our tests.

Listing 2.21 Using `test.each`

```
describe('one uppercase rule', () => {
  test('given no uppercase, it fails', () => {
    const result = oneUpperCaseRule('abc');
    expect(result.passed).toEqual(false);
  });

  test.each(['Abc',
            'aBc'])
    ('given one uppercase, it passes', (input) => {
```

Passing in an array of values that are mapped to the input parameter

Using each input parameter passed in the array

```
        const result = oneUpperCaseRule(input);
        expect(result.passed).toEqual(true);
    });
});
```

In this example, the test will repeat once for each value in the array. It's a bit of a mouthful at first, but once you've tried this approach, it becomes easy to use. It's also pretty readable.

If we want to pass in multiple parameters, we can enclose them in an array, as in the following listing.

Listing 2.22   Refactoring `test.each`

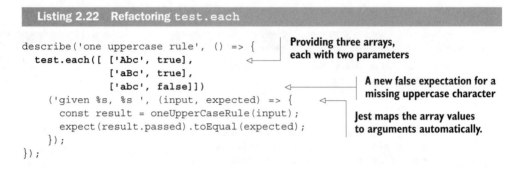

Providing three arrays, each with two parameters

A new false expectation for a missing uppercase character

Jest maps the array values to arguments automatically.

```
describe('one uppercase rule', () => {
  test.each([ ['Abc', true],
             ['aBc', true],
             ['abc', false]])
    ('given %s, %s ', (input, expected) => {
      const result = oneUpperCaseRule(input);
      expect(result.passed).toEqual(expected);
    });
});
```

We don't have to use Jest, though. JavaScript is versatile enough to allow us to roll out our own parameterized test quite easily if we want to.

Listing 2.23   Using a vanilla JavaScript `for`

```
describe('one uppercase rule, with vanilla JS for', () => {
  const tests = {
    'Abc': true,
    'aBc': true,
    'abc': false,
  };

  for (const [input, expected] of Object.entries(tests)) {
    test('given ${input}, ${expected}', () => {
      const result = oneUpperCaseRule(input);
      expect(result.passed).toEqual(expected);
    });
  }
});
```

It's up to you which one you want to use (I like to keep it simple and use `test.each`). The point is, Jest is just a tool. The pattern of parameterized tests can be implemented in multiple ways. This pattern gives us a lot of power, but also a lot of responsibility. It's really easy to abuse this technique and create tests that are harder to understand.

I usually try to make sure that the same scenario (type of input) holds for the entire table. If I were reviewing this test in a code review, I would have told the person who wrote it that this test is actually testing two different scenarios: one with *no upper-case*, and a couple with *one uppercase*. I would split those out into two different tests.

In this example, I wanted to show that it's very easy to get rid of many tests and put them all in a big `test.each`—even when it hurts readability—so be careful when running with these specific scissors.

2.10 *Checking for expected thrown errors*

Sometimes we need to design a piece of code that throws an error at the right time with the right data. What happens if we add code to the `verify` function that throws an error if there are no rules configured, as in the next listing?

Listing 2.24 Throwing an error

```
verify (input) {
  if (this.rules.length === 0) {
    throw new Error('There are no rules configured');
  }
  . . .
```

We could test it the old-fashioned way by using `try/catch`, and failing the test if we *don't* get an error.

Listing 2.25 Testing exceptions with `try/catch`

```
test('verify, with no rules, throws exception', () => {
    const verifier = makeVerifier();
    try {
        verifier.verify('any input');
        fail('error was expected but not thrown');
    } catch (e) {
        expect(e.message).toContain('no rules configured');
    }
});
```

> **Using fail()**
> Technically, `fail()` is a leftover API from the original fork of Jasmine, which Jest is based on. It's a way to trigger a test failure, but it's not in the official Jest API docs, and they would recommend that you use `expect.assertions(1)` instead. This would fail the test if you never reached the `catch()` expectation. I find that as long as `fail()` still works, it does the job quite nicely for my purposes, which are to demonstrate why you shouldn't use the `try/catch` construct in a unit test if you can help it.

This `try/catch` pattern is an effective method but very verbose and annoying to type. Jest, like most other frameworks, contains a shortcut to accomplish exactly this type of scenario, using `expect().toThrowError()`.

Listing 2.26 Using `expect().toThrowError()`

```
test('verify, with no rules, throws exception', () => {
    const verifier = makeVerifier();
    expect(() => verifier.verify('any input'))
        .toThrowError(/no rules configured/);
});
```

Using a regular expression instead of looking for the exact string

Notice that I'm using a regular expression match to check that the error string *contains* a specific string, and is not equal to it, so as to make the test a bit more future-proof if the string changes on its sides. `toThrowError` has a few variations, and you can go to https://jestjs.io/ find out all about them.

Jest snapshots

Jest has a unique feature called Snapshots. It allows you to render a component (when working in a framework like React) and then match the current rendering to a saved snapshot of that component, including all of its properties and HTML.

I won't be touching on this too much, but from what I've seen, this feature tends to be abused quite heavily. You can use it to create hard-to-read tests that look something like this:

```
it('renders',()=>{
    expect(<MyComponent/>).toMatchSnapshot();
});
```

This is obtuse (hard to reason about what is being tested) and it's testing many things that might not be related to one another. It will also break for many reasons that you might not care about, so the maintainability cost of that test will be higher over time. It's also a great excuse not to write readable and maintainable tests, because you're on a deadline but still have to show you write tests. Yes, it does serve a purpose, but it's easy to use in places where other types of tests are more relevant.

If you need a variation of this, try using `toMatchInlineSnapshot()` instead. You can find more info at https://jestjs.io/docs/en/snapshot-testing.

2.11 Setting test categories

If you'd like to run only a specific category of tests, such as only unit tests, or only integration tests, or only tests that touch a specific part of the application, Jest currently doesn't have the ability to define test case categories.

All is not lost, though. Jest has a special `--testPathPattern` command-line flag, which allows us to define how Jest will find our tests. We can trigger this command with a different path for a specific type of test we'd like to run (such as "all tests under the 'integration' folder"). You can get the full details at https://jestjs.io/docs/en/cli.

Another alternative is to create a separate jest.config.js file for each test category, each with its own `testRegex` configuration and other properties.

Listing 2.27 Creating separate jest.config.js files

```
// jest.config.integration.js
var config = require('./jest.config')
config.testRegex = "integration\\.js$"
module.exports = config

// jest.config.unit.js
var config = require('./jest.config')
config.testRegex = "unit\\.js$"
module.exports = config
```

Then, for each category, you can create a separate npm script that invokes the Jest command line with a custom config file: `jest -c my.custom.jest.config.js`.

Listing 2.28 Using separate npm scripts

```
//Package.json
. . .
"scripts": {
    "unit": "jest -c jest.config.unit.js",
    "integ": "jest -c jest.config.integration.js"
. . .
```

In the next chapter, we'll look at code that has dependencies and testability problems, and we'll start discussing the idea of fakes, spies, mocks, and stubs, and how you can use them to write tests against such code.

Summary

- Jest is a popular, open source test framework for JavaScript applications. It simultaneously acts as a *test library* to use when writing tests, an *assertion library* for asserting inside the tests, a *test runner*, and a *test reporter*.
- *Arrange-Act-Assert* (*AAA*) is a popular pattern for structuring tests. It provides a simple, uniform layout for all tests. Once you get used to it, you can easily read and understand any test.
- In the AAA pattern, the *arrange* section is where you bring the system under test and its dependencies to a desired state. In the *act* section, you call methods, pass the prepared dependencies, and capture the output value (if any). In the *assert* section, you verify the outcome.
- A good pattern for naming tests is to include in the name of the test the unit of work under test, the scenario or inputs to the unit, and the expected behavior or exit point. A handy mnemonic for this pattern is USE (unit, scenario, expectation).
- Jest provides several functions that help create more structure around multiple related tests. `describe()` is a scoping function that allows for grouping multiple tests (or groups of tests) together. A good metaphor for `describe()` is a folder

containing tests or other folders. `test()` is a function denoting an individual test. `it()` is an alias for `test()`, but it provides better readability when used in combination with `describe()`.

- `beforeEach()` helps avoid duplication by extracting code that is common for the nested `describe` and `it` functions.

- The use of `beforeEach()` often leads to scroll fatigue, when you have to look at various places to understand what a test does.

- *Factory methods* with plain tests (without any `beforeEach()`) improve readability and help avoid scroll fatigue.

- *Parameterized tests* help reduce the amount of code needed for similar tests. The drawback is that the tests become less readable as you make them more generic.

- To maintain a balance between test readability and code reuse, only parameterize input values. Create separate tests for different output values.

- Jest doesn't support test categories, but you can run groups of tests using the `--testPathPattern` flag. You can also set up `testRegex` in the configuration file.

Part 2

Core techniques

Having covered the basics in part 1, I'll now introduce the core testing and refactoring techniques necessary for writing tests in the real world.

In chapter 3, we'll examine stubs and how they help break dependencies. We'll go over refactoring techniques that make code more testable, and you'll learn about seams in the process.

In chapter 4, we'll move on to mock objects and interaction testing, we'll look at how mock objects differ from stubs, and we'll explore the concept of fakes.

In chapter 5, we'll look at isolation frameworks, also known as mocking frameworks, and at how they solve some of the repetitive coding involved in handwritten mocks and stubs. Chapter 6 deals with asynchronous code, such as promises, timers, and events, and various approaches to testing such code.

Breaking dependencies with stubs

3

This chapter covers

- Types of dependencies—mocks, stubs, and more
- Reasons to use stubs
- Functional injection techniques
- Modular injection techniques
- Object-oriented injection techniques

In the previous chapter, you wrote your first unit test using Jest, and we looked more at the maintainability of the test itself. The scenario was pretty simple, and more importantly, it was completely self-contained. The Password Verifier had no reliance on outside modules, and we could focus on its functionality without worrying about other things that might interfere with it.

In that chapter, we used the first two types of exit points for our examples: return value exit points and state-based exit points. In this chapter, we'll talk about the final type—*calling a third party*. This chapter will also present a new requirement—having your code rely on time. We'll look at two different approaches to handling it—refactoring our code and monkey-patching it without refactoring.

The reliance on outside modules or functions can and will make it harder to write a test and to make the test repeatable, and it can also cause tests to be flaky.

We call the external things that we rely on in our code *dependencies*. I'll define them more thoroughly later in the chapter. These dependencies could include things like time, async execution, using the filesystem, or using the network, or they could simply involve using something that is very difficult to configure or that may be time consuming to execute.

3.1 *Types of dependencies*

In my experience, there are two main types of dependencies that our unit of work can use:

- *Outgoing dependencies*—Dependencies that represent an *exit point* of our unit of work, such as calling a logger, saving something to a database, sending an email, notifying an API or a webhook that something has happened, etc. Notice these are all *verbs*: "calling," "sending," and "notifying." They are flowing *outward* from the unit of work in a sort of fire-and-forget scenario. Each represents an exit point, or the end of a specific logical flow in a unit of work.
- *Incoming dependencies*—Dependencies that are not exit points. These do not represent a requirement on the eventual behavior of the unit of work. They are merely there to provide test-specific specialized data or behavior to the unit of work, such as a database query's result, the contents of a file on the filesystem, a network response, etc. Notice that these are all passive pieces of data that flow *inward* to the unit of work as the result of a previous operation.

Figure 3.1 shows these side by side.

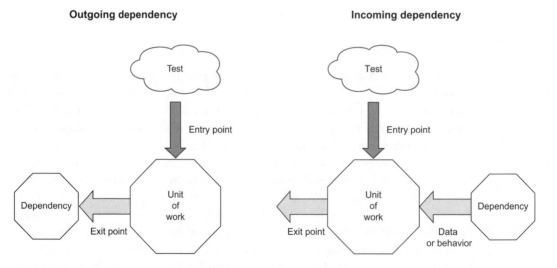

Figure 3.1   On the left, an exit point is implemented as invoking a dependency. On the right, the dependency provides indirect input or behavior and is not an exit point.

Some dependencies can be both incoming and outgoing—in some tests they will represent exit points, and in other tests they will be used to simulate data coming into the application. These shouldn't be very common, but they do exist, such as an external API that returns a success/fail response for an outgoing message.

With these types of dependencies in mind, let's look at how the book *xUnit Test Patterns* defines the various patterns for things that look like other things in tests. Table 3.1 lists my thoughts about some patterns from the book's website at http://mng.bz/n1WK.

Table 3.1 Clarifying terminology around stubs and mocks

Category	Pattern	Purpose	Uses
	Test double	Generic name for stubs and mocks	I also use the term *fake*.
Stub	Dummy object	Used to specify the values to be used in tests when the only usage is as irrelevant arguments of SUT method calls	Send as a parameter to the entry point or as the arrange part of the AAA pattern.
	Test stub	Used to verify logic independently when it depends on indirect inputs from other software components	Inject as a dependency, and configure it to return specific values or behavior into the SUT.
Mock	Test spy	Used to verify logic independently when it has indirect outputs to other software components	Override a single function on a real object, and verify that the fake function was called as expected.
	Mock object	Used to verify logic independently when it depends on indirect outputs to other software components	Inject the fake as a dependency into the SUT, and verify that the fake was called as expected.

Here's another way to think about this for the rest of this book:

- *Stubs* break incoming dependencies (indirect inputs). Stubs are fake modules, objects, or functions that provide fake behavior or data *into* the code under test. We do not assert against them. We can have many stubs in a single test.
- *Mocks* break outgoing dependencies (indirect outputs or exit points). Mocks are fake modules, objects, or functions that we assert were called in our tests. A mock represents an *exit point* in a unit test. Because of this, it is recommended that you have no more than a single mock per test.

Unfortunately, in many shops you'll hear the word "mock" thrown around as a catch-all term for both stubs and mocks. Phrases like "we'll mock this out" or "we have a mock database" can really create confusion. There is a huge difference between stubs and mocks (one should really only be used once in a test), and we should use the right terms to ensure it's clear what the other person is referring to.

When in doubt, use the term "test double" or "fake." Often, a single fake dependency can be used as a stub in one test, and it can be used as a mock in another test. We'll see an example of this later on.

XUnit test patterns and naming things

xUnit Test Patterns: Refactoring Test Code by Gerard Meszaros (Addison-Wesley, 2007) is a classic pattern reference book for unit testing. It defines patterns for things you fake in your tests in at least five ways. Once you've gotten a feel for the three types I mention here, I encourage you to take a look at the extra details that book provides.

Note that *xUnit Test Patterns* has a definition for the word "fake": "Replace a component that the system under test (SUT) depends on with a much lighter-weight implementation." For example, you might use an in-memory database instead of a full-fledged production instance.

I still consider this type of test double a "stub," and I use the word "fake" to call out anything that isn't real, much like the term "test double," but "fake" is shorter and easier on the tongue.

This might seem like a whole lot of information at once. I'll dive deep into these definitions throughout this chapter. Let's take a small bite and start with *stubs*.

3.2 Reasons to use stubs

What if we're faced with the task of testing a piece of code like the following?

Listing 3.1 `verifyPassword` **using time**

```
const moment = require('moment');
const SUNDAY = 0, SATURDAY = 6;

const verifyPassword = (input, rules) => {
    const dayOfWeek = moment().day();
    if ([SATURDAY, SUNDAY].includes(dayOfWeek)) {
        throw Error("It's the weekend!");
    }
    //more code goes here...
    //return list of errors found..
    return [];
};
```

Our password verifier has a new dependency: it can't work on weekends. Go figure. Specifically, the module has a direct dependency on moment.js, which is a very common date/time wrapper for JavaScript. Working with dates directly in JavaScript is not a pleasant experience, so we can assume many shops out there have something like this.

How does this direct use of a time-related library affect our unit tests? The unfortunate issue here is that this direct dependency forces our tests, given no direct way to affect date and time inside our application under test, to take into account the correct date and time. The following listing shows an unfortunate test that only runs on weekends.

Listing 3.2 Initial unit tests for `verifyPassword`

```
const moment = require('moment');
const {verifyPassword} = require("./password-verifier-time00");
const SUNDAY = 0, SATURDAY = 6, MONDAY = 2;

describe('verifier', () => {
    const TODAY = moment().day();

    //test is always executed, but might not do anything
    test('on weekends, throws exceptions', () => {
        if ([SATURDAY, SUNDAY].includes(TODAY)) {          ◁─── Checking the
            expect(() => verifyPassword('anything', []))        date inside
                .toThrow("It's the weekend!");                  the test
        }
    });

    //test is not even executed on week days
    if ([SATURDAY, SUNDAY].includes(TODAY)) {              ◁─── Checking the
        test('on a weekend, throws an error', () => {            date outside
            expect(() => verifyPassword('anything', []))        the test
                .toThrow("It's the weekend!");
        });
    }
});
```

The preceding listing includes two variations on the same test. One checks for the current date *inside* the test, and the other has the check *outside* the test, which means the test never even executes unless it's the weekend. This is bad.

Let's revisit one of the good test qualities mentioned in chapter 1, consistency: Every time I run a test, it is the *same exact test* that I ran before. The values being used do not change. The asserts do not change. If no code has changed (in test or production code), then the test should provide the exact same result as previous runs.

The second test sometimes doesn't even run. That's a good enough reason to use a fake to break the dependency right there. Furthermore, we can't simulate a weekend or a weekday, which gives us more than enough incentive to redesign the code under test so it's a bit more injectable for dependencies.

But wait, there's more. Tests that use time can often be flaky. They only fail sometimes, without anything but the time changing. This test is a prime candidate for this behavior, because we'll only get feedback on *one* of its two states when we run it locally. If you want to know how it behaves on a weekend, just wait a couple of days. Ugh.

Tests might become flaky due to edge cases that affect variables that are not under our control in the test. Common examples are network issues during end-to-end testing, database connectivity issues, or various server issues. When this happens, it's easy to dismiss the test failure by saying "just run it again" or "It's OK. It's just [insert variability issue here]."

3.3   *Generally accepted design approaches to stubbing*

In the next few sections, we'll discuss several common forms of injecting stubs into our units of work. First, we'll discuss basic parameterization as a first step, then we'll jump into the following approaches:

- *Functional approaches*
  - Function as parameter
  - Partial application (currying)
  - Factory functions
  - Constructor functions
- *Modular approach*
  - Module injection
- *Object-oriented approaches*
  - Class constructor injection
  - Object as parameter (aka duck typing)
  - Common interface as parameter (for this we'll use TypeScript)

We'll tackle each of these by starting with the simple case of controlling time in our tests.

3.3.1   *Stubbing out time with parameter injection*

I can think of at least two good reasons to control time based on what we've covered so far:

- To remove the variability from our tests
- To easily simulate any time-related scenario we'd like to test our code with

Here's the simplest refactoring I can think of that makes things a bit more repeatable. Let's add a `currentDay` parameter to our function to specify the current date. This will remove the need to use the moment.js module in our function, and it will put that responsibility on the caller of the function. That way, in our tests, we can determine the time in a hardcoded manner and make the test and the function repeatable and consistent. The following listing shows an example of such a refactoring.

> **Listing 3.3   `verifyPassword` with a `currentDay` parameter**

```
const verifyPassword2 = (input, rules, currentDay) => {
    if ([SATURDAY, SUNDAY].includes(currentDay)) {
        throw Error("It's the weekend!");
```

```
    }
    //more code goes here...
    //return list of errors found..
    return [];
};

const SUNDAY = 0, SATURDAY = 6, MONDAY = 1;
describe('verifier2 - dummy object', () => {
    test('on weekends, throws exceptions', () => {
        expect(() => verifyPassword2('anything',[],SUNDAY ))
            .toThrow("It's the weekend!");
    });
});
```

By adding the `currentDay` parameter, we're essentially giving control over time to the caller of the function (our test). What we're injecting is formally called a "dummy"— it's just a piece of data with no behavior—but we can call it a "stub" from now on.

This is approach is a form of *Dependency Inversion*. It seems the term "Inversion of Control" first came up in Johnson and Foote's paper "Designing Reusable Classes," published by the *Journal of Object-Oriented Programming* in 1988. The term "Dependency Inversion" is also one of the SOLID patterns described by Robert C. Martin in 2000, in his "Design Principles and Design Patterns" paper. I'll talk more about higher-level design considerations in chapter 8.

Adding this parameter is a simple refactoring, but it's quite effective. It provides a couple of nice benefits other than consistency in the test:

- We can now easily simulate any day we want.
- The code under test is not responsible for managing time imports, so it has one less reason to change if we ever use a different time library.

We're doing "dependency injection" of time into our unit of work. We've changed the design of the entry point to use a day value as a parameter. The function is now "pure" by functional programming standards in that it has no side effects. Pure functions have built-in injections of all of their dependencies, which is one of the reasons you'll find functional programming designs are typically much easier to test.

It might feel weird to call the `currentDay` parameter a stub if it's just a day integer value, but based on the definitions from *xUnit Test Patterns*, we can say that this is a "dummy" value, and as far as I'm concerned, it falls into the "stub" category. It does not have to be complex in order to be a stub. It just has to be under our control. It's a stub because we are using it to simulate some input or behavior being passed *into* the unit under test. Figure 3.2 shows this visually.

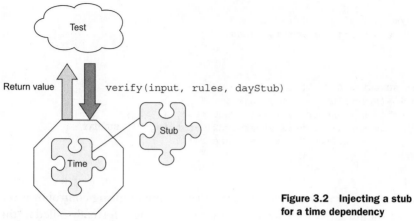

Figure 3.2   Injecting a stub
for a time dependency

3.3.2   *Dependencies, injections, and control*

Table 3.2 recaps some important terms we've discussed and are about to use throughout the rest of the chapter.

Table 3.2   Terminology used in this chapter

Dependencies	The things that make our testing lives and code maintainability difficult, since we cannot *control* them from our tests. Examples include time, the filesystem, the network, random values, and more.
Control	The ability to instruct a dependency how to behave. Whoever is *creating* the dependencies is said to be in control of them, since they have the ability to configure them before they are used in the code under test.
	In listing 3.1, our test does *not* have control over *time* because the module under test has control over it. The module has chosen to always use the *current* date and time. This forces the test to do the exact same thing, and thus we lose consistency in our tests.
	In listing 3.3, we have gained access to the dependency by *inverting the control* over it via the `currentDay` parameter. Now the test has control over the time and can decide to use a hardcoded time. The module under test has to use the time provided, which makes things much easier for our test.
Inversion of control	Designing the code to remove the responsibility of creating the dependency internally, and externalizing it instead. Listing 3.3 shows one way of doing this with *parameter injection*.
Dependency injection	The act of sending a dependency through the design interface to be used internally by a piece of code. The place where you inject the dependency is the injection point. In our case, we are using a parameter injection point. Another word for this place where we can inject things is *a seam*.
Seam	Pronounced "s-ee-m," and coined by Michael Feathers in his book *Working Effectively with Legacy Code* (Pearson, 2004).
	Seams are where two pieces of software meet and something else can be injected. They are a place where you can alter behavior in your program without editing in that place. Examples include parameters, functions, module loaders, function rewriting, and, in the object-oriented world, class interfaces, public virtual methods, and more.

Seams in production code play an important role in the maintainability and readability of unit tests. The easier it is to change and inject behavior or custom data into the code under test, the easier it will be to write, read, and later on maintain the test as the production code changes. I'll talk more about some patterns and antipatterns related to designing code in chapter 8.

3.4   *Functional injection techniques*

At this point, we might not be happy with our design choice. Adding a parameter did solve the dependency issue at the function level, but now every caller will need to know how to handle dates in some way. It feels a bit too chatty.

JavaScript enables two major styles of programming—functional and object-oriented—so I'll show approaches in both styles when it makes sense, and you can pick and choose what works best in your situation.

There isn't a single way to design something. Functional programming proponents will argue for the simplicity, clarity, and provability of the functional style, but it does come with a learning curve. For that reason alone, it is wise to learn both approaches so that you can apply whichever works best for the team you're working with. Some teams will lean more toward object-oriented designs because they feel more comfortable with that. Others will lean towards functional designs. I'd argue that the patterns remain largely the same; we just translate them to different styles.

3.4.1   *Injecting a function*

The following listing shows a different refactoring for the same problem: instead of a data object, we're expecting a function as the parameter. That function returns the date object.

Listing 3.4   Dependency injection with a function

```
const verifyPassword3 = (input, rules, getDayFn) => {
    const dayOfWeek = getDayFn();
    if ([SATURDAY, SUNDAY].includes(dayOfWeek)) {
        throw Error("It's the weekend!");
    }
    //more code goes here...
    //return list of errors found..
    return [];
};
```

The associated test is shown in the following listing.

Listing 3.5   Testing with function injection

```
describe('verifier3 - dummy function', () => {
    test('on weekends, throws exceptions', () => {
        const alwaysSunday = () => SUNDAY;
        expect(()=> verifyPassword3('anything',[], alwaysSunday))
            .toThrow("It's the weekend!");
    });
```

There's very little difference from the previous test, but using a function as a parameter is a valid way to do injection. In other scenarios, it's also a great way to enable special behavior, such as simulating special cases or exceptions in your code under test.

3.4.2   *Dependency injection via partial application*

Factory functions or methods (a subcategory of "higher-order functions") are functions that return other functions, preconfigured with some context. In our case, the context can be the list of rules and the current day function. We then get back a new function that we can trigger with only a string input, and it will use the rules and get-Day() function configured in its creation.

The code in the following listing essentially turns the factory function into the arrange part of the test, and calls the returned function into the act part. Quite lovely.

Listing 3.6   Using a higher-order factory function

```
const SUNDAY = 0, . . . FRIDAY=5, SATURDAY = 6;

const makeVerifier = (rules, dayOfWeekFn) => {
    return function (input) {
        if ([SATURDAY, SUNDAY].includes(dayOfWeekFn())) {
            throw new Error("It's the weekend!");
        }
        //more code goes here..
    };
};

describe('verifier', () => {
    test('factory method: on weekends, throws exceptions', () => {
        const alwaysSunday = () => SUNDAY;
        const verifyPassword = makeVerifier([], alwaysSunday);

        expect(() => verifyPassword('anything'))
            .toThrow("It's the weekend!");
    });
```

3.5   *Modular injection techniques*

JavaScript also allows for the idea of *modules*, which we import or require. How can we handle the idea of dependency injection when faced with a direct import of a dependency in our code under test, such as in the code from listing 3.1, shown again here?

```
const moment = require('moment');
const SUNDAY = 0; const SATURDAY = 6;

const verifyPassword = (input, rules) => {
    const dayOfWeek = moment().day();
    if ([SATURDAY, SUNDAY].includes(dayOfWeek)) {
        throw Error("It's the weekend!");
    }
```

```
    // more code goes here...
    // return list of errors found..
    return [];
};
```

How can we overcome this direct dependency that's happening? The answer is, we can't. We'll have to write the code differently to allow for the replacement of that dependency later on. We'll have to create a *seam* through which we can replace our dependencies. Here's one such example.

Listing 3.7 Abstracting the required dependencies

```
const originalDependencies = {          Wrapping moment.js
    moment: require('moment'),          with an intermediary
};                                      object
                                                        The object containing
let dependencies = { ...originalDependencies };  ◁─────  the current dependency,
                                                        either real or fake
const inject = (fakes) => {              ◁────   A function that replaces the real
    Object.assign(dependencies, fakes);          dependency with a fake one
    return function reset() {                      ◁──────  A function that resets
        dependencies = { ...originalDependencies };        the dependency back
    }                                                      to the real one
};

const SUNDAY = 0; const SATURDAY = 6;

const verifyPassword = (input, rules) => {
    const dayOfWeek = dependencies.moment().day();
    if ([SATURDAY, SUNDAY].includes(dayOfWeek)) {
        throw Error("It's the weekend!");
    }
    // more code goes here...
    // return list of errors found..
    return [];
};

module.exports = {
    SATURDAY,
    verifyPassword,
    inject
};
```

What's going on here? Three new things have been introduced:

- First, we have replaced our direct dependency on moment.js with an object: originalDependencies. It contains that module import as part of its implementation.
- Next, we have added yet another object into the mix: dependencies. This object, by default, takes on all of the real dependencies that the original-Dependencies object contains.

- Finally, the `inject` function, which we're also exposing as part of our own module, allows whoever is importing our module (both production code and tests) to override our real dependencies with custom dependencies (fakes).

  When you invoke `inject`, it returns a `reset` function that reapplies the original dependencies onto the current `dependencies` variable, thus resetting any fakes currently being used.

Here's how you can use the `inject` and `reset` functions in a test.

Listing 3.8   Injecting a fake module with `inject()`

```
const { inject, verifyPassword, SATURDAY } = require('./password-verifier-
    time00-modular');
                                                    A helper function
const injectDate = (newDay) => {      ◁
    const reset = inject({            ◁────────   Injecting a fake API
        moment: function () {                      instead of moment.js
            //we're faking the moment.js module's API here.
            return {
                day: () => newDay
            }
        }
    });
    return reset;
};

describe('verifyPassword', () => {
    describe('when its the weekend', () => {
        it('throws an error', () => {                   Providing a
            const reset = injectDate(SATURDAY);    ◁─   fake day

            expect(() => verifyPassword('any input'))
                .toThrow("It's the weekend!");

            reset();         ◁────   Resetting the
        });                           dependency
    });
});
```

Let's break down what's going on here:

1 The `injectDate` function is just a helper function meant to reduce the boilerplate code in our test. It always builds the fake structure of the moment.js API, and it sets its `getDay` function to return the `newDay` parameter.
2 The `injectDate` function calls `inject` with the new fake moment.js API. This applies the fake dependency in our unit of work to the one we have sent in as a parameter.
3 Our test calls the `inject` function with a custom, fake day.
4 At the end of the test, we call the `reset` function, which resets the unit of work's module dependencies to the original ones.

Once you've done this a couple of times, it starts making sense. But it has some caveats as well. On the pro side, it definitely takes care of the dependency issue in our tests, and it's relatively easy to use. As for the cons, there is one huge downside as far as I can see. Using this method to fake our modular dependencies forces our tests to be closely tied to the API signature of the dependencies we are faking. If these are third-party dependencies, such as moment.js, loggers, or anything else that we do not fully control, our tests will become very brittle when the time comes (as it always does) to upgrade or replace the dependencies with something that has a different API. This doesn't hurt much if it's just a test or two, but we'll usually have hundreds or thousands of tests that have to fake several common dependencies, and that sometimes means changing and fixing hundreds of files when replacing a logger with a breaking API change, for example.

I have two possible ways to prevent such a situation:

- Never import a third-party dependency that you don't control directly in your code. Always use an interim abstraction that you do control. The Ports and Adapters architecture is a good example of such an idea (other names for this architecture are Hexagonal architecture and Onion architecture). With such an architecture, faking these internal APIs should present less risk, because we can control their rate of change, thus making our tests less brittle. (We can refactor them internally without our tests caring, even if the outside world changes.)
- Avoid using module injection, and instead use one of the other ways mentioned in this book for dependency injection: function parameters, currying, and, as mentioned in the next section, constructors and interfaces. Between these, you should have plenty of choices instead of importing things directly.

3.6 Moving toward objects with constructor functions

Constructor functions are a slightly more object-oriented JavaScript-ish way of achieving the same result as a factory function, but they return something akin to an object with methods we can trigger. We then use the keyword new to call this function and get back that special object.

Here's what the same code and tests look like with this design choice.

Listing 3.9 Using a constructor function

```
const Verifier = function(rules, dayOfWeekFn)
{
    this.verify = function (input) {
        if ([SATURDAY, SUNDAY].includes(dayOfWeekFn())) {
            throw new Error("It's the weekend!");
        }
        //more code goes here..
    };
};
```

```
const {Verifier} = require("./password-verifier-time01");

test('constructor function: on weekends, throws exception', () => {
    const alwaysSunday = () => SUNDAY;
    const verifier = new Verifier([], alwaysSunday);

    expect(() => verifier.verify('anything'))
        .toThrow("It's the weekend!");
});
```

You might look at this and ask, "Why move toward objects?" The answer really depends on the context of your current project, its stack, your team's knowledge of functional programming and object-oriented background, and many other non-technical factors. It's good to have this tool in your toolbox so you can use it when it makes sense to you. Keep this in the back of your mind as you read the next few sections.

3.7   *Object-oriented injection techniques*

If a more object-oriented style is what you're leaning toward, or if you're working in an object-oriented language such as C# or Java, here are a few common patterns that are widely used in the object-oriented world for dependency injection.

3.7.1   *Constructor injection*

Constructor injection is how I would describe a design in which we can inject dependencies through the constructor of a class. In the JavaScript world, Angular is the best-known web frontend framework that uses this design for injecting "services," which is just a code word for "dependencies" in Angular-speak. This is a viable design in many other situations.

Having a stateful class is not without benefits. It can remove repetition from clients that only need to configure our class once and can then reuse the configured class multiple times.

If we had chosen to create a stateful version of Password Verifier, and we wanted to inject the date function through constructor injection, it might look like the following design.

Listing 3.10   Constructor injection design

```
class PasswordVerifier {
    constructor(rules, dayOfWeekFn) {
        this.rules = rules;
        this.dayOfWeek = dayOfWeekFn;
    }

    verify(input) {
        if ([SATURDAY, SUNDAY].includes(this.dayOfWeek())) {
            throw new Error("It's the weekend!");
        }
        const errors = [];
        //more code goes here..
```

```
        return errors;
    };
}

test('class constructor: on weekends, throws exception', () => {
    const alwaysSunday = () => SUNDAY;
    const verifier = new PasswordVerifier([], alwaysSunday);

    expect(() => verifier.verify('anything'))
        .toThrow("It's the weekend!");
});
```

This looks and feels a lot like the constructor function design in section 3.6. This is a more class-oriented design that many people will feel more comfortable with, coming from an object-oriented background. It also is more verbose. You'll see that we get more and more verbose the more object-oriented we make things. It's part of the object-oriented game. This is partly why people are choosing functional styles more and more—they are much more concise.

Let's talk a bit about the maintainability of the tests. If I wrote a second test with this class, I'd extract the creation of the class via the constructor to a nice little factory function that returns an instance of the class under test, so that if (i.e., "when") the constructor signature changes and breaks many tests at once, I only have to fix a single place to get all the tests working again, as you can see in the following listing.

> **Listing 3.11 Adding a helper factory function to our tests**

```
describe('refactored with constructor', () => {
    const makeVerifier = (rules, dayFn) => {
        return new PasswordVerifier(rules, dayFn);
    };

    test('class constructor: on weekends, throws exceptions', () => {
        const alwaysSunday = () => SUNDAY;
        const verifier = makeVerifier([],alwaysSunday);

        expect(() => verifier.verify('anything'))
            .toThrow("It's the weekend!");
    });

    test('class constructor: on weekdays, with no rules, passes', () => {
        const alwaysMonday = () => MONDAY;
        const verifier = makeVerifier([],alwaysMonday);

        const result = verifier.verify('anything');
        expect(result.length).toBe(0);
    });
});
```

Notice that this is not the same as the factory function design in section 3.4.2. This factory function resides in our *tests*; the other was in our production code. This one is for test maintainability, and it can work with object-oriented and functional production code because it hides how the function or object is being created or configured. It's an abstraction layer in our tests, so we can push the dependency on how a function or object is created or configured into a single place in our tests.

3.7.2   *Injecting an object instead of a function*

Right now, our class constructor takes in a function as the second parameter:

```
constructor(rules, dayOfWeekFn) {
    this.rules = rules;
    this.dayOfWeek = dayOfWeekFn;
}
```

Let's go one step up in our object-oriented design and use an object instead of a function as our parameter. This requires us to do a bit of legwork: refactor the code.

First, we'll create a new file called time-provider.js, which will contain our real object that has a dependency on moment.js. The object will be designed to have a single function called getDay():

```
import moment from "moment";

const RealTimeProvider = () => {
    this.getDay = () => moment().day()
};
```

Next, we'll change the parameter usage to use an object with a function:

```
const SUNDAY = 0, MONDAY = 1, SATURDAY = 6;
class PasswordVerifier {
    constructor(rules, timeProvider) {
        this.rules = rules;
        this.timeProvider = timeProvider;
    }

    verify(input) {
        if ([SATURDAY, SUNDAY].includes(this.timeProvider.getDay())) {
            throw new Error("It's the weekend!");
        }
        ...
}
```

Finally, let's give whoever needs an instance of our PasswordVerifier the ability to get it preconfigured with the real time provider by default. We'll do this with a new passwordVerifierFactory function that any production code that needs a verifier instance will need to use:

```
const passwordVerifierFactory = (rules) => {
    return new PasswordVerifier(new RealTimeProvider())
};
```

IoC containers and dependency injection

There are many other ways to glue `PasswordVerifier` and `TimeProvider` together. I've just chosen manual injection to keep things simple. Many frameworks today are able to configure the injection of dependencies into objects under test, so that we can define how an object is to be constructed. Angular is one such framework.

If you're using libraries like Spring in Java or Autofac or StructureMap in C#, you can easily configure the construction of objects with constructor injection without needing to create specialized functions. Commonly, these features are called Inversion of Control (IoC) containers or Dependency Injection (DI) containers. I'm not using them in this book to avoid unneeded details. You don't need them to create great tests.

In fact, I don't normally use IoC containers in tests. I'll almost always use custom factory functions to inject dependencies. I find that makes my tests easier to read and reason about.

Even for tests covering Angular code, we don't have to go through Angular's DI framework to inject a dependency into an object in memory; we can call that object's constructor directly and send in fake stuff. As long as we do that in a factory function, we're not sacrificing maintainability, and we're also not adding extra code to tests unless it's essential to the tests.

The following listing shows the entire piece of new code.

Listing 3.12 Injecting an object

```
import moment from "moment";

const RealTimeProvider = () => {
    this.getDay = () => moment().day()
};

const SUNDAY = 0, MONDAY=1, SATURDAY = 6;
class PasswordVerifier {
    constructor(rules, timeProvider) {
        this.rules = rules;
        this.timeProvider = timeProvider;
    }

    verify(input) {
        if ([SATURDAY, SUNDAY].includes(this.timeProvider.getDay())) {
            throw new Error("It's the weekend!");
        }
        const errors = [];
        //more code goes here..
        return errors;
    };
}

const passwordVerifierFactory = (rules) => {
    return new PasswordVerifier(new RealTimeProvider())
};
```

How can we handle this type of design in our tests, where we need to inject a fake object, instead of a fake function? We'll do this manually at first, so you can see that it's not a big deal. Later, we'll let frameworks help us, but you'll see that sometimes hand-coding fake objects can actually make your test more readable than using a framework, such as Jasmine, Jest, or Sinon (we'll cover those in chapter 5).

First, in our test file, we'll create a new fake object that has the same function signature as our real time provider, but it will be controllable by our tests. In this case, we'll just use a constructor pattern:

```
function FakeTimeProvider(fakeDay) {
    this.getDay = function () {
        return fakeDay;
    }
}
```

> **NOTE**   If you are working in a more object-oriented style, you might choose to create a simple class that inherits from a common interface. We'll cover that a bit later in the chapter.

Next, we'll construct the `FakeTimeProvider` in our tests and inject it into the `verifier` under test:

```
describe('verifier', () => {
    test('on weekends, throws exception', () => {
        const verifier =
            new PasswordVerifier([], new FakeTimeProvider(SUNDAY));

        expect(()=> verifier.verify('anything'))
            .toThrow("It's the weekend!");
    });
```

Here's what the full test file looks like.

Listing 3.13   Creating a handwritten stub object

```
function FakeTimeProvider(fakeDay) {
    this.getDay = function () {
        return fakeDay;
    }
}

describe('verifier', () => {
    test('class constructor: on weekends, throws exception', () => {
        const verifier =
            new PasswordVerifier([], new FakeTimeProvider(SUNDAY));

        expect(() => verifier.verify('anything'))
            .toThrow("It's the weekend!");
    });
});
```

This code works because JavaScript, by default, is a very permissive language. Much like Ruby or Python, you can get away with duck typing things. *Duck typing* refers to the idea that if it walks like a duck and it talks like a duck, we'll treat it like a duck. In this case, the real object and fake object both implement the same function, even though they are completely different objects. We can simply send one in place of the other, and the production code should be OK with this.

Of course, we'll only know that this is OK and that we didn't make any mistakes or miss anything regarding the function signatures at run time. If we want a bit more confidence, we can try it in a more type-safe manner.

3.7.3 *Extracting a common interface*

We can take things one step further, and, if we're using TypeScript or a strongly typed language such as Java or C#, start using interfaces to denote the roles that our dependencies play. We can create a contract of sorts that both real objects and fake objects will have to abide by at the compiler level.

First, we'll define our new interface (notice that this is now TypeScript code):

```
export interface TimeProviderInterface {
    getDay(): number;
}
```

Second, we'll define a real time provider that implements our interface in our production code like this:

```
import * as moment from "moment";
import {TimeProviderInterface} from "./time-provider-interface";

export class RealTimeProvider implements TimeProviderInterface {
    getDay(): number {
        return moment().day();
    }
}
```

Third, we'll update the constructor of our `PasswordVerifier` to take a dependency of our new `TimeProviderInterface` type, instead of having a parameter type of `RealTimeProvider`. We're abstracting away the role of a time provider and declaring that we don't care what object is being passed, as long as it answers to this role's interface:

```
export class PasswordVerifier {
    private _timeProvider: TimeProviderInterface;

    constructor(rules: any[], timeProvider: TimeProviderInterface) {
        this._timeProvider = timeProvider;
    }

    verify(input: string):string[] {
        const isWeekened = [SUNDAY, SATURDAY]
            .filter(x => x === this._timeProvider.getDay())
            .length > 0;
```

```
        if (isWeekened) {
            throw new Error("It's the weekend!")
        }
         // more logic goes here
        return [];
    }
}
```

Now that we have an interface that defines what a "duck" looks like, we can implement a duck of our own in our tests. It's going to look a lot like the previous test's code, but it will have one strong difference: it will be compiler checked to ensure the correctness of the method signatures.

Here's what our fake time provider looks like in our test file:

```
class FakeTimeProvider implements TimeProviderInterface {
    fakeDay: number;
    getDay(): number {
        return this.fakeDay;
    }
}
```

And here's our test:

```
describe('password verifier with interfaces', () => {
    test('on weekends, throws exceptions', () => {
        const stubTimeProvider = new FakeTimeProvider();
        stubTimeProvider.fakeDay = SUNDAY;
        const verifier = new PasswordVerifier([], stubTimeProvider);

        expect(() => verifier.verify('anything'))
            .toThrow("It's the weekend!");
    });
});
```

The following listing shows all the code together.

Listing 3.14   Extracting a common interface in production code

```
export interface TimeProviderInterface {  getDay(): number;  }

export class RealTimeProvider implements TimeProviderInterface {
    getDay(): number {
        return moment().day();
    }
}

export class PasswordVerifier {
    private _timeProvider: TimeProviderInterface;

    constructor(rules: any[], timeProvider: TimeProviderInterface) {
        this._timeProvider = timeProvider;
    }
```

```
    verify(input: string):string[] {
        const isWeekend = [SUNDAY, SATURDAY]
            .filter(x => x === this._timeProvider.getDay())
            .length>0;
        if (isWeekend) {
            throw new Error("It's the weekend!")
        }
        return [];
    }
}

class FakeTimeProvider implements TimeProviderInterface{
    fakeDay: number;
    getDay(): number {
        return this.fakeDay;
    }
}

describe('password verifier with interfaces', () => {
    test('on weekends, throws exceptions', () => {
        const stubTimeProvider = new FakeTimeProvider();
        stubTimeProvider.fakeDay = SUNDAY;
        const verifier = new PasswordVerifier([], stubTimeProvider);

        expect(() => verifier.verify('anything'))
            .toThrow("It's the weekend!");
    });
});
```

We've now made a full transition from a purely functional design into a strongly typed, object-oriented design. Which is best for your team and your project? There's no single answer. I'll talk more about design in chapter 8. Here, I mainly wanted to show that whatever design you end up choosing, the pattern of injection remains largely the same. It is just enabled with different vocabulary or language features.

It's the ability to inject that enables us to simulate things that would be practically impossible to test in real life. That's where the idea of stubs shines the most. We can tell our stubs to return fake values or even to simulate exceptions in our code, to see how it handles errors arising from dependencies. Injection makes this possible. Injection has also made our tests more repeatable, consistent, and trustworthy, and I'll talk about trustworthiness in the third part of this book. In the next chapter, we'll look at mock objects and see how they differ from stubs.

Summary

- *Test double* is an overarching term that describes all kinds of non-production-ready, fake dependencies in tests. There are five variations on test doubles that can be grouped into just two types: *mocks* and *stubs*.
- *Mocks* help emulate and examine *outgoing dependencies*: dependencies that represent an exit point of our unit of work. The system under test (SUT) calls outgoing

dependencies to change the state of those dependencies. *Stubs* help emulate *incoming dependencies*: the SUT makes calls to such dependencies to get input data.

- Stubs help replace an unreliable dependency with a fake, reliable one and thus avoid *test flakiness*.
- There are multiple ways to inject a stub into a unit of work:
  - *Function as parameter*—Injecting a function instead of a plain value.
  - *Partial application (currying) and factory functions*—Creating a function that returns another function with some of the context baked in. This context may include the dependency you replaced with a stub.
  - *Module injection*—Replacing a module with a fake one with the same API. This approach is fragile. You may need a lot of refactoring if the module you are faking changes its API in the future.
  - *Constructor function*—This is mostly the same as partial application.
  - *Class constructor injection*—This is a common object-oriented technique where you inject a dependency via a constructor.
  - *Object as parameter (aka duck typing)*—In JavaScript, you can inject any dependency in place of the required one as long as that dependency implements the same functions.
  - *Common interface as parameter*—This is the same as object as parameter, but it involves a check during compile time. For this approach, you need a strongly typed language like TypeScript.

Interaction testing using mock objects 4

This chapter covers
- Defining interaction testing
- Reasons to use mock objects
- Injecting and using mocks
- Dealing with complicated interfaces
- Partial mocks

In the previous chapter, we solved the problem of testing code that depends on other objects to run correctly. We used stubs to make sure that the code under test received all the inputs it needed so that we could test the unit of work in isolation.

So far, you've only written tests that work against the first two of the three types of exit points a unit of work can have: *returning a value* and *changing the state of the system* (you can read more about these types in chapter 1). In this chapter, we'll look at how you can test the third type of exit point—a call to a third-party function, module, or object. This is important, because often we'll have code that depends on things we can't control. Knowing how to check that type of code is an important skill in the world of unit testing. Basically, we'll find ways to prove that our unit of work ends up calling a function that we don't control and identify what values were sent as arguments.

The approaches we've looked at so far won't do here, because third-party functions usually don't have specialized APIs that allow us to check if they were called correctly. Instead, they internalize their operations for clarity and maintainability. So, how can you test that your unit of work interacts with third-party functions correctly? You use mocks.

4.1   *Interaction testing, mocks, and stubs*

Interaction testing is checking how a unit of work interacts with and sends messages (i.e., calls functions) to a dependency beyond its control. Mock functions or objects are used to assert that a call was made correctly to an external dependency.

Let's recall the differences between mocks and stubs as we covered them in chapter 3. The main difference is in the flow of information:

- *Mock*—Used to break outgoing dependencies. Mocks are fake modules, objects, or functions that we assert were called in our tests. A mock represents an *exit point* in a unit test. If we don't assert on it, it's not used as a mock.

  It is normal to have no more than a single mock per test, for maintainability and readability reasons. (We'll discuss this more in part 3 of this book about writing maintainable tests.)

- *Stub*—Used to break incoming dependencies. Stubs are fake modules, objects, or functions that provide fake behavior or data to the code under test. We do not assert against them, and we can have many stubs in a single test.

  Stubs represent waypoints, not exit points, because the data or behavior flows *into* the unit of work. They are points of interaction, but they do not represent an ultimate outcome of the unit of work. Instead, they are an interaction *on the way* to achieving the end result we care about, so we don't treat them as exit points.

Figure 4.1 shows these two side by side.

Let's look at a simple example of an exit point to a dependency that we do not control: calling a logger.

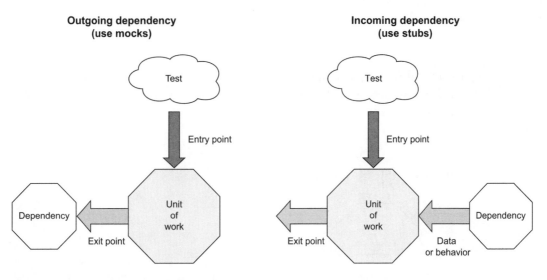

Figure 4.1 On the left, an exit point that is implemented as invoking a dependency. On the right, the dependency provides indirect input or behavior and is not an exit point.

4.2 Depending on a logger

Let's take this Password Verifier function as our starting example, and we'll assume we have a complicated logger (which is a logger that has more functions and parameters, so the interface may present more of a challenge). One of the requirements of our function is to call the logger when verification has passed or failed, as follows.

Listing 4.1 Depending directly on a complicated logger

```
// impossible to fake with traditional injection techniques
const log = require('./complicated-logger');

const verifyPassword = (input, rules) => {
  const failed = rules
    .map(rule => rule(input))
    .filter(result => result === false);
  if (failed.count === 0) {
    // to test with traditional injection techniques
    log.info('PASSED');
    return true; //
  }
  //impossible to test with traditional injection techniques
  log.info('FAIL'); //
  return false; //
};

const info = (text) => {
    console.log(`INFO: ${text}`);
};
```

Exit
point

```
const debug = (text) => {
    console.log(`DEBUG: ${text}`);
};
```

Figure 4.2 illustrates this. Our `verifyPassword` function is the entry point to the unit of work, and we have a total of two exit points: one that returns a value, and another that calls `log.info()`.

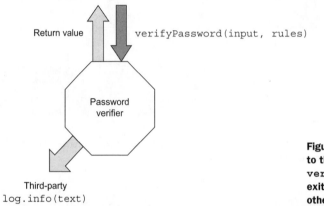

Return value   `verifyPassword(input, rules)`

Password
verifier

Third-party
`log.info(text)`

Figure 4.2   **The entry point
to the Password Verifier is the
`verifyPassword` function. One
exit point returns a value, and the
other calls `log.info()`.**

Unfortunately, we cannot verify that `logger` was called by using any traditional means, or without using some Jest tricks, which I usually use only if there's no other choice, as they tend to make tests less readable and harder to maintain (more on that later in this chapter).

Let's do what we like to do with dependencies: *abstract them*. There are many ways to create a seam in our code. Remember, *seams* are places where two pieces of code meet—we can use them to inject fake things. Table 4.1 lists the most common ways to abstract dependencies.

Table 4.1   Techniques for injecting fakes

Style	Technique
Standard	Introduce parameter
Functional	Use currying Convert to higher-order functions
Modular	Abstract module dependency
Object oriented	Inject untyped object Inject interface

4.3 Standard style: Introduce parameter refactoring

The most obvious way we can start this journey is by introducing a new parameter into
our code under test.

Listing 4.2 Mock logger parameter injection

```
const verifyPassword2 = (input, rules, logger) => {
    const failed = rules
        .map(rule => rule(input))
        .filter(result => result === false);

    if (failed.length === 0) {
        logger.info('PASSED');
        return true;
    }
    logger.info('FAIL');
    return false;
};
```

The following listing shows how we could write the simplest of tests for this, using a
simple closure mechanism.

Listing 4.3 Handwritten mock object

```
describe('password verifier with logger', () => {
    describe('when all rules pass', () => {
        it('calls the logger with PASSED', () => {
            let written = '';
            const mockLog = {
                info: (text) => {
                    written = text;
                }
            };

            verifyPassword2('anything', [], mockLog);

            expect(written).toMatch(/PASSED/);
        });
    });
});
```

Notice first that we are naming the variable mockXXX (mockLog in this example) to
denote the fact that we have a mock function or object in the test. I use this naming
convention because I want you, as a reader of the test, to know that you should expect
an assert (also known as *verification*) against that mock at the end of the test. This naming approach removes the element of surprise for the reader and makes the test much
more predictable. Only use this naming convention for things that are actually mocks.

Here's our first mock object:

```
let written = '';
const mockLog = {
```

```
    info: (text) => {
        written = text;
    }
};
```

It only has one function, which mimics the signature of the logger's `info` function. It then saves the parameter being passed to it (`text`) so that we can assert that it was called later in the test. If the `written` variable has the correct text, this proves that our function was called, which means we have proven that the exit point is invoked correctly from our unit of work.

On the `verifyPassword2` side, the refactoring we did is pretty common. It's pretty much the same as we did in the previous chapter, where we extracted a *stub* as a dependency. Stubs and mocks are often treated the same way in terms of refactoring and introducing seams in our application's code.

What did this simple refactoring into a parameter provide us with?

- We do not need to explicitly import (via `require`) the `logger` in our code under test anymore. That means that if we ever change the real dependency of the logger, the code under test will have one less reason to change.
- We now have the ability to inject *any logger* of our choosing into the code under test, as long as it lives up to the same interface (or at least has the `info` method). This means that we can provide a mock logger that does our bidding for us: the mock logger helps us verify that it was called correctly.

NOTE   The fact that our mock object only mimics a part of the `logger`'s interface (it's missing the `debug` function) is a form of duck typing. I discussed this idea in chapter 3: if it walks like a duck, and it talks like a duck, then we can use it as a fake object.

4.4 *The importance of differentiating between mocks and stubs*

Why do I care so much about what we name each thing? If we can't tell the difference between mocks and stubs, or we don't name them correctly, we can end up with tests that are testing multiple things and that are less readable and harder to maintain. Naming things correctly helps us avoid these pitfalls.

Given that a mock represents a requirement from our unit of work ("it calls the logger," "it sends an email," etc.) and that a stub represents incoming information or behavior ("the database query returns false," "this specific configuration throws an error"), we can set a simple rule of thumb: It should be OK to have multiple stubs in a test, but you don't usually want to have more than a *single mock* per test, because that would mean you're testing more than one requirement in a single test.

If we can't (or won't) differentiate between things (naming is key to that), we can end up with multiple mocks per test or asserting our stubs, both of which can have negative effects on our tests. Keeping naming consistent gives us the following benefits:

- *Readability*—Your test name will become much more generic and harder to understand. You want people to be able to read the name of the test and know everything that happens or is tested inside of it, without needing to read the test's code.

- *Maintainability*—You could, without noticing or even caring, assert against stubs if you don't differentiate between mocks and stubs. This produces little value to you and increases the coupling between your tests and internal production code. Asserting that you queried a database is a good example of this. Instead of testing that a database query returns some value, it would be much better to test that the application's behavior changes after we change the input from the database.

- *Trust*—If you have multiple mocks (requirements) in a single test, and the first mock verification fails the test, most test frameworks won't execute the rest of the test (below the failing assert line) because an exception has been thrown. This means that the other mocks aren't verified, and you won't get the results from them.

To drive the last point home, imagine a doctor who only sees 30% of their patient's symptoms, but still needs to make a decision—they might make the wrong decision about treatment. If you can't see where all the bugs are, or that two things are failing instead of just one (because one of them is hidden after the first failure), you're more likely to fix the wrong thing or to fix it in the wrong place.

XUnit Test Patterns (Addison-Wesley, 2007), by Gerard Meszaros, calls this situation *assertion roulette* (http://xunitpatterns.com/Assertion%20Roulette.html). I like this name. It's quite a gamble. You start commenting out lines of code in your test, and lots of fun ensues (and possibly alcohol).

Not everything is a mock

It's unfortunate that people still tend to use the word "mock" for anything that isn't real, such as "mock database" or "mock service." Most of the time they really mean they are using a stub.

It's hard to blame them, though. Frameworks like Mockito, jMock, and most isolation frameworks (I don't call them mocking frameworks, for the same reasons I'm discussing right now), use the word "mock" to denote both mocks and stubs.

There are newer frameworks, such as Sinon and testdouble in JavaScript, NSubstitute and FakeItEasy in .NET, and others, that have helped start a change in the naming conventions. I hope this persists.

4.5   Modular-style mocks

I covered modular dependency injection in the previous chapter, but now we're going to look at how we can use it to inject mock objects and simulate answers on them.

4.5.1 *Example of production code*

Let's look at a slightly more complicated example than we saw before. In this scenario, our `verifyPassword` function depends on two external dependencies:

- A logger
- A configuration service

The configuration service provides the logging level that is required. Usually this type of code would be moved into a special logger module, but for the purposes of this book's examples, I'm putting the logic that calls `logger.info` and `logger.debug` directly in the code under test.

Listing 4.4 A hard modular dependency

```
const { info, debug } = require("./complicated-logger");
const { getLogLevel } = require("./configuration-service");

const log = (text) => {
  if (getLogLevel() === "info") {
    info(text);
  }
  if (getLogLevel() === "debug") {
    debug(text);
  }
};

const verifyPassword = (input, rules) => {
  const failed = rules
    .map((rule) => rule(input))
    .filter((result) => result === false);

  if (failed.length === 0) {
    log("PASSED");          ◁─┐
    return true;              │  Calling the
  }                           │  logger
  log("FAIL");            ◁──┘
  return false;
};

module.exports = {
  verifyPassword,
};
```

Let's assume that we realized we have a bug when we call the logger. We've changed the way we check for failures, and now we call the logger with a PASSED result when the number of failures is positive instead of zero. How can we prove that this bug exists, or that we've fixed it, with a unit test?

Our problem here is that we are importing (or requiring) the modules directly in our code. If we want to replace the logger module, we have to either replace the file or perform some other dark magic through Jest's API. I wouldn't recommend that usually, because using these techniques leads to more pain and suffering than is usual when dealing with code.

4.5.2 Refactoring the production code in a modular injection style

We can abstract away the module dependencies into their own object and allow the user of our module to replace that object as follows.

Listing 4.5 Refactoring to a modular injection pattern

```
const originalDependencies = {                          Holding original
    log: require('./complicated-logger'),                dependencies
};

let dependencies = { ...originalDependencies };    ◁——    The layer of
                                                           indirection
const resetDependencies = () => {                       A function that resets
    dependencies = { ...originalDependencies };         the dependencies
};

const injectDependencies = (fakes) => {                 A function that overrides
    Object.assign(dependencies, fakes);                 the dependencies
};

const verifyPassword = (input, rules) => {
    const failed = rules
        .map(rule => rule(input))
        .filter(result => result === false);

    if (failed.length === 0) {
        dependencies.log.info('PASSED');
        return true;
    }
    dependencies.log.info('FAIL');
    return false;
};

module.exports = {
    verifyPassword,                          Exposing the API to the
    injectDependencies,                      users of the module
    resetDependencies
};
```

There's more production code here, and it seems more complex, but this allows us to replace dependencies in our tests in a relatively easy manner if we are forced to work in such a modular fashion.

The `originalDependencies` variable will always hold the original dependencies, so that we never lose them between tests. `dependencies` is our layer of indirection. It defaults to the original dependencies, but our tests can direct the code under test to replace that variable with custom dependencies (without knowing anything about the internals of the module). `injectDependencies` and `resetDependencies` are the public API that the module exposes for overriding and resetting the dependencies.

4.5.3   A test example with modular-style injection

The following listing shows what a test for modular injection might look like.

```
Listing 4.6   Testing with modular injection
```

```javascript
const {
  verifyPassword,
  injectDependencies,
  resetDependencies,
} = require("./password-verifier-injectable");

describe("password verifier", () => {
  afterEach(resetDependencies);

  describe("given logger and passing scenario", () => {
    it("calls the logger with PASS", () => {
      let logged = "";
      const mockLog = { info: (text) => (logged = text) };
      injectDependencies({ log: mockLog });

      verifyPassword("anything", []);

      expect(logged).toMatch(/PASSED/);
    });
  });
});
```

As long as we don't forget to use the `resetDependencies` function after each test, we can now inject modules pretty easily for test purposes. The obvious main caveat is that this approach requires each module to expose inject and reset functions that can be used from the outside. This might or might not work with your current design limitations, but if it does, you can abstract them both into reusable functions and save yourself a lot of boilerplate code.

4.6   Mocks in a functional style

Let's jump into a few of the functional styles we can use to inject mocks into our code under test.

4.6.1   Working with a currying style

Let's implement the currying technique introduced in chapter 3 to perform a more functional-style injection of our logger. In the following listing, we'll use `lodash`, a library that facilitates functional programming in JavaScript, to get currying working without too much boilerplate code.

```
Listing 4.7   Applying currying to our function
```

```javascript
const verifyPassword3 = _.curry((rules, logger, input) => {
  const failed = rules
      .map(rule => rule(input))
      .filter(result => result === false);
```

```
            if (failed.length === 0) {
                logger.info('PASSED');
                return true;
            }
            logger.info('FAIL');
            return false;
    });
```

The only change is the call to _.curry on the first line, and closing it off at the end of the code block.

The following listing demonstrates what a test for this type of code might look like.

Listing 4.8 Testing a curried function with dependency injection

```
describe("password verifier", () => {
  describe("given logger and passing scenario", () => {
    it("calls the logger with PASS", () => {
      let logged = "";
      const mockLog = { info: (text) => (logged = text) };
      const injectedVerify = verifyPassword3([], mockLog);

      // this partially applied function can be passed around
      // to other places in the code
      // without needing to inject the logger
      injectedVerify("anything");

      expect(logged).toMatch(/PASSED/);
    });
  });
});
```

Our test invokes the function with the first two arguments (injecting the rules and logger dependencies, effectively returning a partially applied function), and then invokes the returned function injectedVerify with the final input, thus showing the reader two things:

- How this function is meant to be used in real life
- What the dependencies are

Other than that, it's pretty much the same as in the previous test.

4.6.2 Working with higher-order functions and not currying

Listing 4.9 is another variation on the functional programming design. We're using a higher-order function, but without currying. You can tell that the following code does not contain currying because we always need to send in all of the parameters as arguments to the function for it to be able to work correctly.

Listing 4.9   Injecting a mock in a higher-order function

```
const makeVerifier = (rules, logger) => {
    return (input) => {                              Returning a
        const failed = rules                         preconfigured
            .map(rule => rule(input))                verifier
            .filter(result => result === false);

        if (failed.length === 0) {
            logger.info('PASSED');
            return true;
        }
        logger.info('FAIL');
        return false;
    };
};
```

This time I'm explicitly making a factory function that returns a *preconfigured verifier function* that already contains the `rules` and `logger` in its closure's dependencies.

Now let's look at the test for this. The test needs to first call the `makeVerifier` factory function and then call the function that's returned by that function (`passVerify`).

Listing 4.10   Testing using a factory function

```
describe("higher order factory functions", () => {
  describe("password verifier", () => {
    test("given logger and passing scenario", () => {
      let logged = "";
      const mockLog = { info: (text) => (logged = text) };
      const passVerify = makeVerifier([], mockLog);     Calling the
                                                        factory
                                                        function
      passVerify("any input");      Calling the
                                    resulting function
      expect(logged).toMatch(/PASSED/);
    });
  });
});
```

4.7   Mocks in an object-oriented style

Now that we've covered some functional and modular styles, let's look at the object-oriented styles. People coming from an object-oriented background will feel much more comfortable with this type of approach, and people coming from a functional background will hate it. But life is about accepting people's differences.

4.7.1   Refactoring production code for injection

Listing 4.11 shows what this type of injection might look like in a class-based design in JavaScript. Classes have constructors, and we use the constructor to force the caller of the class to provide parameters. This is not the only way to accomplish that, but it's very common and useful in an object-oriented design because it makes the requirement of those parameters explicit and practically undeniable in strongly typed languages such as Java or C, and when using TypeScript. We want to make sure whoever uses our code knows what is expected to configure it properly.

Listing 4.11 Class-based constructor injection

```
class PasswordVerifier {
  _rules;
  _logger;

  constructor(rules, logger) {
    this._rules = rules;
    this._logger = logger;
  }

  verify(input) {
    const failed = this._rules
        .map(rule => rule(input))
        .filter(result => result === false);

    if (failed.length === 0) {
      this._logger.info('PASSED');
      return true;
    }
    this._logger.info('FAIL');
    return false;
  }
}
```

This is just a standard class that takes a couple of constructor parameters and then uses them inside the verify function. The following listing shows what a test might look like.

Listing 4.12 Injecting a mock logger as a constructor parameter

```
describe("duck typing with function constructor injection", () => {
  describe("password verifier", () => {
    test("logger&passing scenario,calls logger with PASSED", () => {
      let logged = "";
      const mockLog = { info: (text) => (logged = text) };
      const verifier = new PasswordVerifier([], mockLog);
      verifier.verify("any input");

      expect(logged).toMatch(/PASSED/);
    });
  });
});
```

Mock injection is straightforward, much like with stubs, as we saw in the previous chapter. If we were to use properties rather than a constructor, it would mean that the dependencies are *optional*. With a constructor, we're explicitly saying they're not optional.

In strongly typed languages like Java or C#, it's common to extract the fake logger as a separate class, like so:

```
class FakeLogger {
  logged = "";

  info(text) {
    this.logged = text;
  }
}
```

We simply implement the `info` function in the class, but instead of logging anything, we just save the value being sent as a parameter to the function in a publicly visible variable that we can assert again later in our test.

Notice that I didn't call the fake object `MockLogger` or `StubLogger` but `FakeLogger`. This is so that I can reuse this class in multiple different tests. In some tests, it might be used as a stub, and in others it might be used as a mock object. I use the word "fake" to denote anything that isn't *real*. Another common term for this sort of thing is "test double." Fake is shorter, so I like it.

In our tests, we'll instantiate the class and send it over as a constructor parameter, and then we'll assert on the `logged` variable of the class, like so:

```
test("logger + passing scenario, calls logger with PASSED", () => {
    let logged = "";
    const mockLog = new FakeLogger();
    const verifier = new PasswordVerifier([], mockLog);
    verifier.verify("any input");

    expect(mockLog.logged).toMatch(/PASSED/);
});
```

4.7.2   *Refactoring production code with interface injection*

Interfaces play a large role in many object-oriented programs. They are one variation on the idea of *polymorphism*: allowing one or more objects to be replaced with one another as long as they implement the same interface. In JavaScript and other languages like Ruby, interfaces are not needed, since the language allows for the idea of duck typing without needing to cast an object to a specific interface. I won't touch here on the pros and cons of duck typing. You should be able to use either technique as you see fit, in the language of your choice. In JavaScript, we can turn to TypeScript to use interfaces. The compiler, or *transpiler*, we'll use can help ensure that we are using types based on their signatures correctly.

Listing 4.13 shows three code files: the first describes a new `ILogger` interface, the second describes a `SimpleLogger` that implements that interface, and the third is our `PasswordVerifier`, which uses only the `ILogger` interface to get a logger instance. `PasswordVerifier` has no knowledge of the actual type of logger being injected.

Listing 4.13   Production code gets an `ILogger` interface

```
export interface ILogger {          │  A new interface,
    info(text: string);            │  which is part of
}                                   │  production code

//this class might have dependencies on files or network
class SimpleLogger implements ILogger {        ◁────   The logger now
    info(text: string) {                                implements that
    }                                                   interface.
}

export class PasswordVerifier {
    private _rules: any[];
    private _logger: ILogger;
                                              The verifier
    constructor(rules: any[], logger: ILogger) {   now uses the
        this._rules = rules;                        interface.
        this._logger = logger;
    }

    verify(input: string): boolean {
        const failed = this._rules
            .map(rule => rule(input))
            .filter(result => result === false);

        if (failed.length === 0) {
            this._logger.info('PASSED');
            return true;
        }
        this._logger.info('FAIL');
        return false;
    }
}
```

Notice that a few things have changed in the production code. I've added a new interface to the production code, and the existing logger now implements this interface. I'm changing the design to make the logger replaceable. Also, the `PasswordVerifier` class works with the interface instead of the `SimpleLogger` class. This allows me to replace the instance of the `logger` class with a fake one, instead of having a hard dependency on the real logger.

The following listing shows what a test might look like in a strongly typed language, but with a handwritten fake object that implements the `ILogger` interface.

Listing 4.14   Injecting a handwritten mock `ILogger`

```
class FakeLogger implements ILogger {
    written: string;
    info(text: string) {
        this.written = text;
    }
}
```

```
describe('password verifier with interfaces', () => {
    test('verify, with logger, calls logger', () => {
        const mockLog = new FakeLogger();
        const verifier = new PasswordVerifier([], mockLog);

        verifier.verify('anything');

        expect(mockLog.written).toMatch(/PASS/);
    });
});
```

In this example, I've created a handwritten class called `FakeLogger`. All it does is override the one method in the `ILogger` interface and save the `text` parameter for future assertion. We then expose this value as a field in the `written` class. Once this value is exposed, we can verify that the fake logger was called by checking that field.

I've done this manually because I wanted you to see that even in object-oriented land, the patterns repeat themselves. Instead of having a mock *function*, we now have a mock *object*, but the code and test work just like the previous examples.

> ### Interface naming conventions
>
> I'm using the naming convention of prefixing the logger interface with an "I" because it's going to be used for polymorphic reasons (i.e., I'm using it to abstract a role in the system). This is not always the case for interface naming in TypeScript, such as when we use interfaces to define the structure of a set of parameters (basically using them as strongly typed structures). In that case, naming without an "I" makes sense to me.
>
> For now, think of it like this: If you're going to implement it more than once, you should prefix it with an "I" to make the expected use of the interface more explicit.

4.8   *Dealing with complicated interfaces*

What happens when the interface is more complicated, such as when it has more than one or two functions in it, or more than one or two parameters in each function?

4.8.1   *Example of a complicated interface*

Listing 4.15 is an example of such a complicated interface, and of the production code verifier that uses the complicated logger, injected as an interface. The `IComplicatedLogger` interface has four functions, each with one or more parameters. Every function would need to be faked in our tests, and that can lead to complexity and maintainability problems in our code and tests.

> ### Listing 4.15   Working with a more complicated interface (production code)

```
export interface IComplicatedLogger {        ◁──┐  A new interface, which is
    info(text: string)                           │  part of production code
    debug(text: string, obj: any)
```

```
    warn(text: string)
    error(text: string, location: string, stacktrace: string)
}

export class PasswordVerifier2 {
    private _rules: any[];
    private _logger: IComplicatedLogger;          ◁──────────────┐   The class now
                                                                  │   works with the
    constructor(rules: any[], logger: IComplicatedLogger) {  ◁───┘   new interface.
        this._rules = rules;
        this._logger = logger;
    }
...
}
```

As you can see, the new `IComplicatedLogger` interface will be part of production
code, which will make the `logger` replaceable. I'm leaving off the implementation of a
real logger, because it's not relevant for our examples. That's the benefit of abstracting away things with an interface: we don't need to reference them directly. Also
notice that the type of parameter expected in the class's constructor is that of the
`IComplicatedLogger` interface. This allows me to replace the instance of the logger
class with a fake one, just like we did before.

4.8.2   *Writing tests with complicated interfaces*

Here's what the test looks like. It has to override each and every interface function,
which creates long and annoying boilerplate code.

Listing 4.16   Test code with a complicated logger interface

```
describe("working with long interfaces", () => {
  describe("password verifier", () => {
    class FakeComplicatedLogger                    A fake logger class that
        implements IComplicatedLogger {            implements the new interface
      infoWritten = "";
      debugWritten = "";
      errorWritten = "";
      warnWritten = "";

      debug(text: string, obj: any) {
        this.debugWritten = text;
      }

      error(text: string, location: string, stacktrace: string) {
        this.errorWritten = text;
      }

      info(text: string) {
        this.infoWritten = text;
      }

      warn(text: string) {
        this.warnWritten = text;
```

```
    }
  }
  ...

  test("verify passing, with logger, calls logger with PASS", () => {
    const mockLog = new FakeComplicatedLogger();

    const verifier = new PasswordVerifier2([], mockLog);
    verifier.verify("anything");

    expect(mockLog.infoWritten).toMatch(/PASSED/);
  });

  test("A more JS oriented variation on this test", () => {
    const mockLog = {} as IComplicatedLogger;
    let logged = "";
    mockLog.info = (text) => (logged = text);

    const verifier = new PasswordVerifier2([], mockLog);
    verifier.verify("anything");

    expect(logged).toMatch(/PASSED/);
  });
 });
});
```

Here, we're declaring, again, a fake logger class (FakeComplicatedLogger) that implements the IComplicatedLogger interface. Look at how much boilerplate code we have. This will be especially true if we're working in strongly typed object-oriented languages such as Java, C#, or C++. There are ways around all this boilerplate code, which we'll touch on in the next chapter.

4.8.3   Downsides of using complicated interfaces directly

There are other downsides to using long, complicated interfaces in our tests:

- If we're saving arguments being sent in manually, it's more cumbersome to verify multiple arguments across multiple methods and calls.
- It's likely that we are depending on third-party interfaces instead of internal ones, and this will end up making our tests more brittle as time goes by.
- Even if we are depending on internal interfaces, long interfaces have more reasons to change, and now so do our tests.

What does this mean for us? I highly recommend using only fake interfaces that meet both of these conditions:

- You control the interfaces (they are not made by a third party).
- They are adapted to the needs of your unit of work or component.

4.8.4 *The interface segregation principle*

The second of the preceding conditions might need a bit of explanation. It relates to the *interface segregation principle* (ISP; https://en.wikipedia.org/wiki/Interface_segregation_principle). ISP means that if we have an interface that contains more functionality than we require, we should create a small, simpler adapter interface that contains just the functionality we need, preferably with fewer functions, better names, and fewer parameters.

This will end up making our tests much simpler. By abstracting away the real dependencies, we won't need to change our tests when the complicated interfaces change—only a single adapter class file somewhere. We'll see an example of this in chapter 5.

4.9 *Partial mocks*

It's possible, in JavaScript and in most other languages and associated test frameworks, to take over existing objects and functions and "spy" on them. By spying on them, we can later check if they were called, how many times, and with which arguments.

This essentially can turn *parts* of a real object into mock functions, while keeping the rest of the object as a real object. This can create more complicated tests that are more brittle, but it can sometimes be a viable option, especially if you're dealing with legacy code (see chapter 12 for more on legacy code).

4.9.1 *A functional example of a partial mock*

The following listing shows what such a test might look like. We create the real logger, and then we simply override one of its existing real functions using a custom function.

Listing 4.17 A partial mock example

```
describe("password verifier with interfaces", () => {
  test("verify, with logger, calls logger", () => {
    const testableLog: RealLogger = new RealLogger();      // Instantiating a real logger
    let logged = "";
    testableLog.info = (text) => (logged = text);          // Mocking one of its functions

    const verifier = new PasswordVerifier([], testableLog);
    verifier.verify("any input");

    expect(logged).toMatch(/PASSED/);
  });
});
```

In this test, I'm instantiating a `RealLogger`, and in the next line I'm replacing one of its existing functions with a fake one. More specifically, I'm using a mock function that allows me to track its latest invocation parameter using a custom variable.

The important part here is that the `testableLog` variable is a *partial mock*. That means that at least some of its internal implementation is not fake and might have real dependencies and logic in it.

Sometimes it makes sense to use partial mocks, especially when you're working with legacy code and you might need to isolate some existing code from its dependencies. I'll touch more on that in chapter 12.

4.9.2   *An object-oriented partial mock example*

One object-oriented version of a partial mock uses inheritance to override functions from real classes so that we can verify they were called. The following listing shows how we can do this using inheritance and overrides in JavaScript.

Listing 4.18   An object-oriented partial mock example

```
class TestableLogger extends RealLogger {        ◁——  Inheriting from
  logged = "";                                         the real logger
  info(text) {
    this.logged = text;          Overriding one
  }                              of its functions
  // the error() and debug() functions
  // are still "real"
}

describe("partial mock with inheritance", () => {
  test("verify with logger, calls logger", () => {
    const mockLog: TestableLogger = new TestableLogger();

    const verifier = new PasswordVerifier([], mockLog);
    verifier.verify("any input");

    expect(mockLog.logged).toMatch(/PASSED/);
  });
});
```

I inherit from the real logger class in my tests and then use the inherited class, not the original class, in my tests. This technique is commonly called Extract and Override, and you can find more about this in Michael Feathers' book *Working Effectively with Legacy Code* (Pearson, 2004).

Note that I've named the fake logger class "TestableXXX" because it's a testable version of real production code, containing a mix of fake and real code, and this convention helps me make this explicit for the reader. I also put the class right alongside my tests. My production code doesn't need to know that this class exists. This Extract and Override style requires that my class in production code allows inheritance and that the function allows overriding. In JavaScript this is less of an issue, but in Java and C# these are explicit design choices that need to be made (although there are frameworks that allow us to circumvent this rule; we'll discuss them in the next chapter).

In this scenario, we're inheriting from a class that we're not testing directly (Real-Logger). We use that class to test another class (PasswordVerifier). However, this technique can be used quite effectively to isolate and stub or mock single functions from classes that you're directly testing. We'll touch more on that later in the book when we talk about legacy code and refactoring techniques.

Summary

- *Interaction testing* is a way to check how a unit of work interacts with its outgoing dependencies: what calls were made and with which parameters. Interaction testing relates to the third type of exit points: a third-party module, object, or system. (The first two types are a return value and a state change.)
- To do interaction testing, you should use *mocks*, which are test doubles that replace outgoing dependencies. *Stubs* replace incoming dependencies. You should verify interactions with mocks in tests, but not with stubs. Unlike with mocks, interactions with stubs are implementation details and shouldn't be checked.
- It's OK to have multiple stubs in a test, but you don't usually want to have more than a single mock per test, because that means you're testing more than one requirement in a single test.
- Just like with stubs, there are multiple ways to inject a mock into a unit of work:
  - *Standard*—By introducing a parameter
  - *Functional*—Using a partial application or factory functions
  - *Modular*—Abstracting the module dependency
  - *Object-oriented*—Using an untyped object (in languages like JavaScript) or a typed interface (in TypeScript)
- In JavaScript, a complicated interface can be implemented partially, which helps reduce the amount of boilerplate. There's also the option of using *partial mocks*, where you inherit from a real class and replace only some of its methods with fakes.

Isolation frameworks

5

This chapter covers

- Defining isolation frameworks and how they help
- Two main flavors of frameworks
- Faking modules with Jest
- Faking functions with Jest
- Object-oriented fakes with substitute.js

In the previous chapters, we looked at writing mocks and stubs manually and saw the challenges involved, especially when the interface we'd like to fake requires us to create long, error prone, repetitive code. We kept having to declare custom variables, create custom functions, or inherit from classes that use those variables and basically make things a bit more complicated than they need to be (most of the time).

In this chapter, we'll look at some elegant solutions to these problems in the form of an *isolation framework*—a reusable library that can create and configure fake objects *at run time*. These objects are referred to as *dynamic stubs* and *dynamic mocks*.

I call them isolation frameworks because they allow you to isolate the unit of work from its dependencies. You'll find that many resources will refer to them as "mocking frameworks," but I try to avoid that because they can be used for both mocks and stubs. In this chapter, we'll take a look at a few of the JavaScript frameworks available and how we can use them in modular, functional, and object-oriented designs. You'll see how you can use such frameworks to test various things and to create stubs, mocks, and other interesting things.

But the specific frameworks I'll present here aren't the point. While using them, you'll see the values that their APIs promote in your tests (readability, maintainability, robust and long-lasting tests, and more), and you'll find out what makes an isolation framework good and, alternatively, what can make it a drawback for your tests.

5.1 Defining isolation frameworks

I'll start with a basic definition that may sound a bit bland, but it needs to be generic in order to include the various isolation frameworks out there:

> *An isolation framework is a set of programmable APIs that allow the dynamic creation, configuration, and verification of mocks and stubs, either in object or function form. When using an isolation framework, these tasks are often simpler, quicker, and produce shorter code than hand-coded mocks and stubs.*

Isolation frameworks, when used properly, can save developers from the need to write repetitive code to assert or simulate object interactions, and if applied in the right places, they can help make tests last many years without requiring a developer to come back and fix them after every little production code change. If they're applied badly, they can cause confusion and full-on abuse of these frameworks, to the point where we either can't read or can't trust our own tests, so be wary. I'll discuss some dos and don'ts in part 3 of this book.

5.1.1 Choosing a flavor: Loose vs. typed

Because JavaScript supports multiple paradigms of programming design, we can split the frameworks in our world into two main flavors:

- *Loose JavaScript isolation frameworks*—These are vanilla JavaScript-friendly loose-typed isolation frameworks (such as Jest and Sinon). These frameworks usually also lend themselves better to more functional styles of code because they require less ceremony and boilerplate code to do their work.
- *Typed JavaScript isolation frameworks*—These are more object-oriented and Type-Script-friendly isolation frameworks (such as substitute.js). They're very useful when dealing with whole classes and interfaces.

Which flavor you end up choosing to use in your project will depend on a few things, like taste, style, and readability, but the main question to start with is, what type of dependencies will you mostly need to fake?

- *Module dependencies (imports, requires)*—Jest and other loosely typed frameworks should work well.
- *Functional (single and higher-order functions, simple parameters and values)*—Jest and other loosely typed frameworks should work well.

- *Full objects, object hierarchies, and interfaces*—Look into the more object-oriented frameworks, such as substitute.js.

Let's go back to our Password Verifier and see how we can fake the same types of dependencies we did in previous chapters, but this time using a framework.

5.2   *Faking modules dynamically*

For people who are trying to test code with direct dependencies on modules using `require` or `import`, isolation frameworks such as Jest or Sinon present the powerful ability to fake an entire module dynamically, with very little code. Since we started with Jest as our test framework, we'll stick with it for the examples in this chapter.

Figure 5.1 illustrates a Password Verifier with two dependencies:

- A configuration service that helps decide what the logging level is (`INFO` or `ERROR`)
- A logging service that we call as the exit point of our unit of work, whenever we verify a password

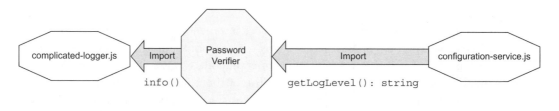

Figure 5.1   Password Verifier has two dependencies: an incoming one to determine the logging level, and an outgoing one to create a log entry.

The arrows represent the flow of behavior through the unit of work. Another way to think about the arrows is through the terms *command* and *query*. We are querying the configuration service (to get the log level), but we are sending commands to the logger (to log).

> ### Command/query separation
> There is a school of design that falls under the ideas of command/query separation. If you'd like to learn more about these terms, I highly recommend reading Martin Fowler's 2005 article on the topic, at https://martinfowler.com/bliki/CommandQuerySeparation .html. This pattern is very beneficial as you navigate your way around different design ideas, but we won't be touching on this too much in this book.

The following listing shows a Password Verifier that has a hard dependency on a logger module.

Listing 5.1   Code with hardcoded modular dependencies

```
const { info, debug } = require("./complicated-logger");
const { getLogLevel } = require("./configuration-service");

const log = (text) => {
  if (getLogLevel() === "info") {
    info(text);
  }
  if (getLogLevel() === "debug") {
    debug(text);
  }
};

const verifyPassword = (input, rules) => {
  const failed = rules
    .map((rule) => rule(input))
    .filter((result) => result === false);

  if (failed.length === 0) {
    log("PASSED");
    return true;
  }
  log("FAIL");
  return false;
};
```

In this example we're forced to find a way to do two things:

- Simulate (stub) values returned from the `configuration` service's `getLogLevel` function.
- Verify (mock) that the `logger` module's `info` function was called.

Figure 5.2 shows a visual representation of this.

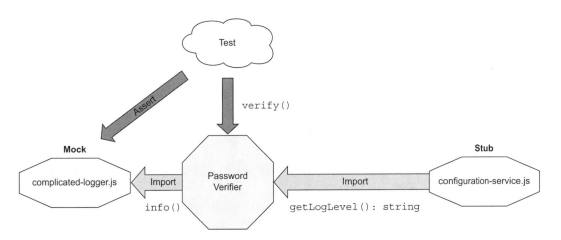

Figure 5.2   The test stubs an incoming dependency (the configuration service) and mocks the outgoing dependency (the logger).

Jest presents us with a few ways to accomplish both simulation and verification, and one of the cleaner ways it presents is using `jest.mock([module name])` at the top of the spec file, followed by us requiring the fake modules in our tests so that we can configure them.

Listing 5.2   Faking the module APIs directly with `jest.mock()`

```
jest.mock("./complicated-logger");
jest.mock("./configuration-service");                  Faking the modules

const { stringMatching } = expect;
const { verifyPassword } = require("./password-verifier");       Getting the fake
const mockLoggerModule = require("./complicated-logger");        instances of the
const stubConfigModule = require("./configuration-service");     modules

describe("password verifier", () => {          Telling Jest to reset any fake
  afterEach(jest.resetAllMocks);         ◁──── module behavior between tests

  test('with info log level and no rules,
        it calls the logger with PASSED', () => {             Configuring the
    stubConfigModule.getLogLevel.mockReturnValue("info");  ◁── stub to return a
                                                              fake "info" value.
    verifyPassword("anything", []);

    expect(mockLoggerModule.info)                        Asserting that the mock
      .toHaveBeenCalledWith(stringMatching(/PASS/));      was called correctly
  });

  test('with debug log level and no rules,
        it calls the logger with PASSED', () => {             Changing the
    stubConfigModule.getLogLevel.mockReturnValue("debug");  ◁── stub config

    verifyPassword("anything", []);

    expect(mockLoggerModule.debug)                       Asserting on the mock
      .toHaveBeenCalledWith(stringMatching(/PASS/));      logger as done previously
  });
});
```

By using Jest here, I've saved myself a bunch of typing, and the tests still look pretty readable.

5.2.1   *Some things to notice about Jest's API*

Jest uses the word "mock" almost everywhere, whether we're stubbing things or mocking them, which can be a bit confusing. It'd be great if it had the word "stub" aliased to "mock" to make things more readable.

Also, due to the way JavaScript "hoisting" works, the lines faking the modules (via `jest.mock`) will need to be at the top of the file. You can read more about this in Ashutosh Verma's "Understanding Hoisting in JavaScript" article here: http://mng .bz/j11r.

Also note that Jest has many other APIs and abilities, and its worth exploring them if you're interested in using it. Head over to https://jestjs.io/ to get the full picture— it's beyond the scope of this book, which is mostly about patterns, not tools.

A few other frameworks, among them Sinon (https://sinonjs.org), also support faking modules. Sinon is quite pleasant to work with, as far as isolation frameworks go, but like many other frameworks in the JavaScript world, and much like Jest, it contains too many ways of accomplishing the same task, and that can often be confusing. Still, faking modules by hand can be quite annoying without these frameworks.

5.2.2 *Consider abstracting away direct dependencies*

The good news about the `jest.mock` API, and others like it, is that it meets a very real need for developers who are stuck trying to test modules that have baked-in dependencies that are not easily changeable (i.e., code they cannot control). This issue is very prevalent in legacy code situations, which I'll discuss in chapter 12.

The bad news about the `jest.mock` API is that it also allows us to mock the code that we do control and that might have benefited from abstracting away the real dependencies behind simpler, shorter, internal APIs. This approach, also known as *onion architecture* or *hexagonal architecture* or *ports and adapters,* is very useful for the long-term maintainability of our code. You can read more about this type of architecture in Alistair Cockburn's article, "Hexagonal Architecture," at https://alistair.cockburn.us/hexagonal-architecture/.

Why are direct dependencies potentially problematic? By using those APIs directly, we're also forced into faking the module APIs directly in our tests instead of their abstractions. We're gluing the design of those direct APIs to the implementation of the tests, which means that if (or really, when) those APIs change, we'll also need to change many of our tests.

Here's a quick example. Imagine your code depends on a well-known JavaScript logging framework (such as Winston) and depends on it directly in hundreds or thousands of places in the code. Then imagine that Winston releases a breaking upgrade. Lots of pain will ensue, which could have been addressed much earlier, before things got out of hand. One simple way to accomplish this would be with a simple abstraction to a single adapter file, which is the only one holding a reference to that logger. That abstraction can expose a simpler, internal logging API that we do control, so we can prevent large-scale breakage across our code. I'll return to this subject in chapter 12.

5.3 *Functional dynamic mocks and stubs*

We covered modular dependencies, so let's turn to faking simple functions. We've done that plenty of times in the previous chapters, but we've always done it by hand. That works great for stubs, but for mocks it gets annoying fast.

The following listing shows the manual approach we used before.

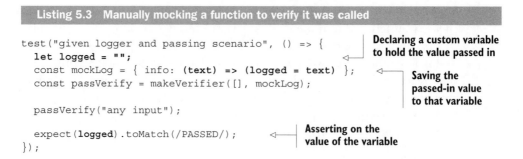

Listing 5.3 Manually mocking a function to verify it was called

```
test("given logger and passing scenario", () => {
  let logged = "";                                          ◁──── Declaring a custom variable
  const mockLog = { info: (text) => (logged = text) };   ◁──     to hold the value passed in
  const passVerify = makeVerifier([], mockLog);                  Saving the
                                                                 passed-in value
  passVerify("any input");                                       to that variable

  expect(logged).toMatch(/PASSED/);          ◁──── Asserting on the
});                                                 value of the variable
```

It works—we're able to verify that the logger function was called, but that's a lot of work that can become very repetitive. Enter isolation frameworks like Jest. `jest.fn()` is the simplest way to get rid of such code. The following listing shows how we can use it.

Listing 5.4 Using `jest.fn()` for simple function mocks

```
test('given logger and passing scenario', () => {
  const mockLog = { info: jest.fn() };
  const verify = makeVerifier([], mockLog);

  verify('any input');

  expect(mockLog.info)
    .toHaveBeenCalledWith(stringMatching(/PASS/));
});
```

Compare this code with the previous example. It's subtle, but it saves plenty of time. Here we're using `jest.fn()` to get back a function that is automatically tracked by Jest, so that we can query it later using Jest's API via `toHaveBeenCalledWith()`. It's small and cute, and it works well any time you need to track calls to a specific function. The `stringMatching` function is an example of a *matcher*. A matcher is usually defined as a utility function that can assert on the value of a parameter being sent into a function. The Jest docs use the term a bit more liberally, but you can find the full list of matchers in the Jest documentation at https://jestjs.io/docs/en/expect.

To summarize, `jest.fn()` works well for single-function-based mocks and stubs. Let's move on to a more object-oriented challenge.

5.4   *Object-oriented dynamic mocks and stubs*

As we've just seen, `jest.fn()` is an example of a single-function faking utility function. It works well in a functional world, but it breaks down a bit when we try to use it on full-blown API interfaces or classes that contain multiple functions.

5.4.1   *Using a loosely typed framework*

I mentioned before that there are two categories of isolation frameworks. To start, we'll use the first (loosely typed, function-friendly) kind. The following listing is an example of trying to tackle the `IComplicatedLogger` we looked at in the previous chapter.

Listing 5.5   The `IComplicatedLogger` interface

```
export interface IComplicatedLogger {
    info(text: string, method: string)
    debug(text: string, method: string)
    warn(text: string, method: string)
    error(text: string, method: string)
}
```

Creating a handwritten stub or mock for this interface may be very time consuming, because you'd need to remember the parameters on a per-method basis, as the next listing shows.

Listing 5.6   Handwritten stubs creating lots of boilerplate code

```
describe("working with long interfaces", () => {
  describe("password verifier", () => {
    class FakeLogger implements IComplicatedLogger {
      debugText = "";
      debugMethod = "";
      errorText = "";
      errorMethod = "";
      infoText = "";
      infoMethod = "";
      warnText = "";
      warnMethod = "";

      debug(text: string, method: string) {
        this.debugText = text;
        this.debugMethod = method;
      }

      error(text: string, method: string) {
        this.errorText = text;
        this.errorMethod = method;
      }
      ...
    }


    test("verify, w logger & passing, calls logger with PASS", () => {
      const mockLog = new FakeLogger();
      const verifier = new PasswordVerifier2([], mockLog);

      verifier.verify("anything");

      expect(mockLog.infoText).toMatch(/PASSED/);
    });
  });
});
```

What a mess. Not only is this handwritten fake time consuming and cumbersome to write, what happens if you want it to return a specific value somewhere in the test, or simulate an error from a function call on the logger? We can do it, but the code gets ugly fast.

Using an isolation framework, the code for doing this becomes trivial, more readable, and much shorter. Let's use `jest.fn()` for the same task and see where we end up.

Listing 5.7   Mocking individual interface functions with `jest.fn()`

```
import stringMatching = jasmine.stringMatching;

describe("working with long interfaces", () => {
  describe("password verifier", () => {
    test("verify, w logger & passing, calls logger with PASS", () => {
      const mockLog: IComplicatedLogger = {
        info: jest.fn(),
        warn: jest.fn(),
        debug: jest.fn(),
        error: jest.fn(),
      };

      const verifier = new PasswordVerifier2([], mockLog);
      verifier.verify("anything");

      expect(mockLog.info)
        .toHaveBeenCalledWith(stringMatching(/PASS/));
    });
  });
});
```

Setting up the mock using Jest

Not too shabby. Here we simply outline our own object and attach a `jest.fn()` function to each of the functions in the interface. This saves a lot of typing, but it has one important caveat: whenever the interface changes (a function is added, for example), we'll have to go back to the code that defines this object and add that function. With plain JavaScript, this would be less of an issue, but it can still create some complications if the code under test uses a function we didn't define in the test.

In any case, it might be wise to push the creation of such a fake object into a factory helper method, so that the creation only exists in a single place.

5.4.2   *Switching to a type-friendly framework*

Let's switch to the second category of frameworks and try substitute.js (www.npmjs .com/package/@fluffy-spoon/substitute). We have to choose one, and I like the C# version of this framework a lot and used it in the previous edition of this book.

With substitute.js (and the assumption of working with TypeScript), we can write code like the following.

Listing 5.8   Using substitute.js to fake a full interface

```
import { Substitute, Arg } from "@fluffy-spoon/substitute";

describe("working with long interfaces", () => {
  describe("password verifier", () => {
```

```
test("verify, w logger & passing, calls logger w PASS", () => {
  const mockLog = Substitute.for<IComplicatedLogger>();

  const verifier = new PasswordVerifier2([], mockLog);
  verifier.verify("anything");

  mockLog.received().info(
    Arg.is((x) => x.includes("PASSED")),
    "verify"
  );
});
});
});
```

> Generating the fake object

> Verifying the fake object was called

In the preceding listing, we generate the fake object, which absolves us of caring about any functions other than the one we're testing against, even if the object's signature changes in the future. We then use `.received()` as our verification mechanism, as well as another argument matcher, `Arg.is`, this time from substitute.js's API, which works just like string matches from Jasmine. The added benefit here is that if new functions are added to the object's signature, we will be less likely to need to change the test, and there's no need to add those functions to any tests that use the same object signature.

Isolation frameworks and the Arrange-Act-Assert pattern

Notice that the way you use the isolation framework matches nicely with the Arrange-Act-Assert structure, which we discussed in chapter 1. You start by arranging a fake object, you act on the thing you're testing, and then you assert on something at the end of the test.

It wasn't always this easy, though. In the olden days (around 2006), most of the open source isolation frameworks didn't support the idea of Arrange-Act-Assert and instead used a concept called Record-Replay (we're talking about Java and C#). Record-Replay was a nasty mechanism where you'd have to tell the isolation API that its fake object was in *record* mode, and then you'd have to call the methods on that object as you expected them to be called from production code. Then you'd have to tell the isolation API to switch into *replay* mode, and only *then* could you send your fake object into the heart of your production code. An example can be seen on the Baeldung site at www.baeldung.com/easymock.

Compared to today's ability to write tests that use the far more readable Arrange-Act-Assert model, this tragedy cost many developers millions of combined hours in painstaking test reading to figure out exactly where tests failed.

If you have the first edition of this book, you can see an example of Record-Replay when I showed Rhino Mocks (which initially had the same design).

OK, that was mocks. What about stubs?

5.5   *Stubbing behavior dynamically*

Jest has a very simple API for simulating return values for modular and functional dependencies: mockReturnValue() and mockReturnValueOnce().

Listing 5.9   Stubbing a value from a fake function with jest.fn()

```
test("fake same return values", () => {
  const stubFunc = jest.fn()
    .mockReturnValue("abc");

  //value remains the same
  expect(stubFunc()).toBe("abc");
  expect(stubFunc()).toBe("abc");
  expect(stubFunc()).toBe("abc");
});

test("fake multiple return values", () => {
  const stubFunc = jest.fn()
    .mockReturnValueOnce("a")
    .mockReturnValueOnce("b")
    .mockReturnValueOnce("c");

  //value remains the same
  expect(stubFunc()).toBe("a");
  expect(stubFunc()).toBe("b");
  expect(stubFunc()).toBe("c");
  expect(stubFunc()).toBe(undefined);
});
```

Notice that, in the first test, we're setting a *permanent* return value for the duration of the test. This is my preferred method of writing tests if I can use it, because it makes the tests simple to read and maintain. If we do need to simulate multiple values, we can use mockReturnValueOnce.

If you need to simulate an error or do anything more complicated, you can use mockImplementation() and mockImplementationOnce():

```
yourStub.mockImplementation(() => {
  throw new Error();
});
```

5.5.1   *An object-oriented example with a mock and a stub*

Let's add another ingredient into our Password Verifier equation.

- Let's say that the Password Verifier is *not* active during a special maintenance window, when software is being updated.
- When a maintenance window is active, calling verify() on the verifier will cause it to call logger.info() with "under maintenance."
- Otherwise it will call logger.info() with a "passed" or "failed" result.

For this purpose (and for the purpose of showing an object-oriented design decision), we'll introduce a `MaintenanceWindow` interface that will be injected into the constructor of our Password Verifier, as illustrated in figure 5.3.

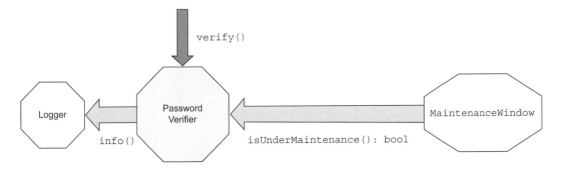

Figure 5.3 Using the `MaintenanceWindow` interface

The following listing shows the code for the Password Verifier using the new dependency.

Listing 5.10 Password Verifier with a `MaintenanceWindow` dependency

```
export class PasswordVerifier3 {
  private _rules: any[];
  private _logger: IComplicatedLogger;
  private _maintenanceWindow: MaintenanceWindow;

  constructor(
    rules: any[],
    logger: IComplicatedLogger,
    maintenanceWindow: MaintenanceWindow
  ) {
    this._rules = rules;
    this._logger = logger;
    this._maintenanceWindow = maintenanceWindow;
  }

  verify(input: string): boolean {
    if (this._maintenanceWindow.isUnderMaintenance()) {
      this._logger.info("Under Maintenance", "verify");
      return false;
    }
    const failed = this._rules
      .map((rule) => rule(input))
      .filter((result) => result === false);

    if (failed.length === 0) {
      this._logger.info("PASSED", "verify");
      return true;
    }
```

```
      this._logger.info("FAIL", "verify");
      return false;
   }
}
```

The `MaintenanceWindow` interface is injected as a constructor parameter (i.e., using constructor injection), and it's used to determine where to execute or not execute the password verification and send the proper message to the logger.

5.5.2 Stubs and mocks with substitute.js

Now we'll use substitute.js instead of Jest to create a stub of the `MaintenanceWindow` interface and a mock of the `IComplicatedLogger` interface. Figure 5.4 illustrates this.

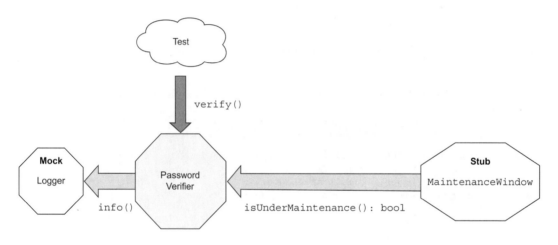

Figure 5.4 A `MaintenanceWindow` **dependency**

Creating stubs and mocks with substitute.js works the same way: we use the `Substitute.for<T>` function. We can configure stubs with the `.returns` function and verify mocks with the `.received` function. Both of these are part of the fake object that is returned from `Substitute.for<T>()`.

Here's what stub creation and configuration looks like:

```
const stubMaintWindow = Substitute.for<MaintenanceWindow>();
stubMaintWindow.isUnderMaintenance().returns(true);
```

Mock creation and verification looks like this:

```
const mockLog = Substitute.for<IComplicatedLogger>();
. . .
/// later down in the end of the test…
mockLog.received().info("Under Maintenance", "verify");
```

The following listing shows the full code for a couple of tests that use a mock and a stub.

Listing 5.11   Testing Password Verifier with substitute.js

```
import { Substitute } from "@fluffy-spoon/substitute";

const makeVerifierWithNoRules = (log, maint) =>
  new PasswordVerifier3([], log, maint);

describe("working with substitute part 2", () => {
  test("verify, during maintenance, calls logger", () => {
    const stubMaintWindow = Substitute.for<MaintenanceWindow>();
    stubMaintWindow.isUnderMaintenance().returns(true);
    const mockLog = Substitute.for<IComplicatedLogger>();
    const verifier = makeVerifierWithNoRules(mockLog, stubMaintWindow);

    verifier.verify("anything");

    mockLog.received().info("Under Maintenance", "verify");
  });

  test("verify, outside maintanance, calls logger", () => {
    const stubMaintWindow = Substitute.for<MaintenanceWindow>();
    stubMaintWindow.isUnderMaintenance().returns(false);
    const mockLog = Substitute.for<IComplicatedLogger>();
    const verifier = makeVerifierWithNoRules(mockLog, stubMaintWindow);

    verifier.verify("anything");

    mockLog.received().info("PASSED", "verify");
  });
});
```

We can successfully and relatively easily simulate values in our tests with dynamically created objects. I encourage you to research the flavor of an isolation framework you'd like to use. I've only used substitute.js as an example in this book. It's not the only framework out there.

This test requires no handwritten fakes, but notice that it's already starting to take a toll on the readability for the test reader. Functional designs are usually much slimmer than this. In an object-oriented setting, sometimes this is a necessary evil. However, we could easily refactor the creation of various helpers, mocks, and stubs to helper functions as we refactor our code, so that the test can be simpler and shorter to read. More on that in part 3 of this book.

5.6   Advantages and traps of isolation frameworks

Based on what we've covered in this chapter, we've seen distinct advantages to using isolation frameworks:

- *Easier modular faking*—Module dependencies can be hard to get around without some boilerplate code, which isolation frameworks help us eliminate. This point can also be counted as a negative, as explained earlier, because it encourages us to have code strongly coupled to third-party implementations.

- *Easier simulation of values or errors*—Writing mocks manually can be difficult across a complicated interface. Frameworks help a lot.
- *Easier fake creation*—Isolation frameworks can be used to create both mocks and stubs more easily.

Although there are many advantages to using isolation frameworks, there are also possible dangers. Let's now talk about a few things to watch out for.

5.6.1   *You don't need mock objects most of the time*

The biggest trap that isolation frameworks lead you into is making it easy to fake anything, and encouraging you to think you need mock objects in the first place. I'm not saying you won't need stubs, but mock objects shouldn't be the standard operating procedure for most unit tests. Remember that a unit of work can have three different types of exit points: return values, state change, and calling a third-party dependency. Only one of these types can benefit from a mock object in your test. The others don't.

I find that, in my own tests, mock objects are present in perhaps 2%–5% of my tests. The rest of the tests are usually return-value or state-based tests. For functional designs, the number of mock objects should be near zero, except for some corner cases.

If you find yourself defining a test and verifying that an object or function was called, think carefully whether you can prove the same functionality without a mock object, but instead by verifying a return value or a change in the behavior of the overall unit of work from the outside (for example, verifying that a function throws an exception when it didn't before). Chapter 6 of *Unit Testing Principles, Practices, and Patterns* by Vladimir Khorikov (Manning, 2020) contains a detailed description of how to refactor interaction-based tests into simpler, more reliable tests that check a return value instead.

5.6.2   *Unreadable test code*

Using a mock in a test makes the test a little less readable, but still readable enough that an outsider can look at it and understand what's going on. Having many mocks, or many expectations, in a single test can ruin the readability of the test so it's hard to maintain, or even to understand what's being tested.

If you find that your test becomes unreadable or hard to follow, consider removing some mocks or some mock expectations, or separating the test into several smaller tests that are more readable.

5.6.3   *Verifying the wrong things*

Mock objects allow you to verify that methods were called on your interfaces or that functions were called, but that doesn't necessarily mean that you're testing the right thing. A lot of people new to tests end up verifying things just because they can, not because it makes sense. Examples may include the following:

- Verifying that an internal function calls another internal function (not an exit point).
- Verifying that a stub was called (an incoming dependency should not be verified; it's the overspecification antipattern, as we'll discuss in section 5.6.5).
- Verifying that something was called simply because someone told you to write a test, and you're not sure what should really be tested. (This is a good time to verify that you're understanding the requirements correctly.)

5.6.4 Having more than one mock per test

It's considered good practice to test only one concern per test. Testing more than one concern can lead to confusion and problems maintaining the test. Having two mocks in a test is the same as testing several end results of the same unit of work (multiple exit points).

For each exit point, consider writing a separate test, as it could be considered a separate requirement. Chances are that your test names will also become more focused and readable when you only test one concern. If you can't name your test because it does too many things and the name becomes very generic (e.g., "XWorksOK"), it's time to separate it into more than one test.

5.6.5 Overspecifying the tests

If your test has too many expectations (`x.received().X()`, `x.received().Y()`, and so on), it may become very fragile, breaking on the slightest of production code changes, even though the overall functionality still works. Testing interactions is a double-edged sword: test them too much, and you start to lose sight of the big picture—the overall functionality; test them too little, and you'll miss the important interactions between units of work.

Here are some ways to balance this effect:

- *Use stubs instead of mocks when you can*—If more than 5% of your tests use mock objects, you might be overdoing it. Stubs can be everywhere. Mocks, not so much. You only need to test one scenario at a time. The more mocks you have, the more verifications will take place at the end of the test, but usually only one will be the important one. The rest will be noise against the current test scenario.
- *Avoid using stubs as mocks if possible*—Use a stub only for faking simulated values into the unit of work under test or to throw exceptions. Don't verify that methods were called on stubs.

Summary

- Isolation, or mocking, frameworks allow you to dynamically create, configure, and verify mocks and stubs, either in object or function form. Isolation frameworks save a lot of time compared to handwritten fakes, especially in modular dependency situations.

- There are two flavors of isolation frameworks: loosely typed (such as Jest and Sinon) and strongly typed (such as substitute.js). Loosely typed frameworks require less boilerplate and are good for functional-style code; strongly typed frameworks are useful when dealing with classes and interfaces.

- Isolation frameworks can replace whole modules, but try to abstract away direct dependencies and fake those abstractions instead. This will help you reduce the amount of refactoring needed when the module's API changes.

- It's important to lean toward return-value or state-based testing as opposed to interaction testing whenever you can, so that your tests assume as little as possible about internal implementation details.

- Mocks should be used only when there's no other way to test the implementation, because they eventually lead to tests that are harder to maintain if you're not careful.

- Choose the way you work with isolation frameworks based on the codebase you are working on. In legacy projects, you may need to fake whole modules, as it might be the only way to add tests to such projects. In greenfield projects, try to introduce proper abstractions on top of third-party modules. It's all about picking the right tool for the job, so be sure to look at the big picture when considering how to approach a specific problem in testing.

Unit testing
asynchronous code

When we're dealing with regular synchronous code, waiting for actions to finish is *implicit.* We don't worry about it, and we don't really think about it too much. When dealing with asynchronous code, however, waiting for actions to finish becomes an *explicit* activity that is under our control. Asynchronicity makes code, and the tests for that code, potentially trickier because we have to be explicit about waiting for actions to complete.

Let's start with a simple fetching example to illustrate the issue.

6.1   *Dealing with async data fetching*

Let's say we have a module that checks whether our website at example.com is alive. It does this by fetching the context from the main URL and checking for a specific word, "illustrative," to determine if the website is up. We'll look at two different and very simple implementations of this functionality. The first uses a `callback` mechanism, and the second uses an `async/await` mechanism.

Figure 6.1 illustrates their entry and exit points for our purposes. Note that the callback arrow is pointed differently, to make it more obvious that it's a different type of exit point.

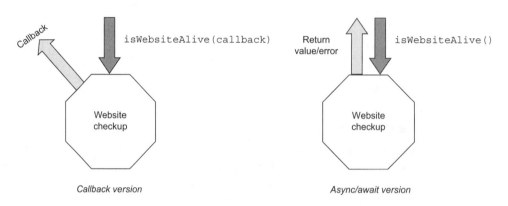

Figure 6.1 `IsWebsiteAlive()` **callback vs. the** `async/await` **version**

The initial code is shown in the following listing. We're using `node-fetch` to get the URL's content.

Listing 6.1 `IsWebsiteAlive()` callback and await versions

```
//Callback version
const fetch = require("node-fetch");
const isWebsiteAliveWithCallback = (callback) => {
  const website = "http://example.com";
  fetch(website)
    .then((response) => {
      if (!response.ok) {
        //how can we simulate this network issue?
        throw Error(response.statusText);          ◁──  Throwing a custom
      }                                                  error to handle
      return response;                                   problems in our code
    })
    .then((response) => response.text())
    .then((text) => {
      if (text.includes("illustrative")) {
        callback({ success: true, status: "ok" });
      } else {
        //how can we test this path?
```

```
        callback({ success: false, status: "text missing" });
      }
    })
    .catch((err) => {
      //how can we test this exit point?
      callback({ success: false, status: err });
    });
};


// Await version
const isWebsiteAliveWithAsyncAwait = async () => {
  try {
    const resp = await fetch("http://example.com");
    if (!resp.ok) {
      //how can we simulate a non ok response?
      throw resp.statusText;
    }
    const text = await resp.text();
    const included = text.includes("illustrative");
    if (included) {
      return { success: true, status: "ok" };
    }
    // how can we simulate different website content?
    throw "text missing";
  } catch (err) {
    return { success: false, status: err };
  }
};
```

Throwing a custom
error to handle
problems in our code

Wrapping the error
into a response

NOTE   In the preceding code, I'm assuming you know how promises work in JavaScript. If you need more information, I recommend reading the Mozilla documentation on promises at http://mng.bz/W11a.

In this example, we are converting any errors from connectivity failures or missing text on the web page to either a callback or a return value to denote a failure to the user of our function.

6.1.1   An initial attempt with an integration test

Since everything is hardcoded in listing 6.1, how would you test this? Your initial reaction might involve writing an integration test. The following listing shows how we could write an integration test for the callback version.

Listing 6.2   An initial integration test

```
test("NETWORK REQUIRED (callback): correct content, true", (done) => {
  samples.isWebsiteAliveWithCallback((result) => {
    expect(result.success).toBe(true);
    expect(result.status).toBe("ok");
    done();
  });
});
```

To test a function whose exit point is a callback function, we pass it our own callback function in which we can

- Check the correctness of the passed-in values
- Tell the test runner to stop waiting through whatever mechanism is given to us by the test framework (in this case, that's the `done()` function)

6.1.2   *Waiting for the act*

Because we're using callbacks as exit points, our test has to explicitly wait until the parallel execution completes. That parallel execution could be on the JavaScript event loop or it could be in a separate thread, or even in a separate process if you're using another language.

In the Arrange-Act-Assert pattern, the act part is the thing we need to wait out. Most test frameworks will allow us to do so with special helper functions. In this case, we can use the optional `done` callback that Jest provides to signal that the test needs to wait until we explicitly call `done()`. If `done()` isn't called, our test will time out and fail after the default 5 seconds (which is configurable, of course).

Jest has other means for testing asynchronous code, a couple of which we'll cover later in the chapter.

6.1.3   *Integration testing of async/await*

What about the `async/await` version? We could technically write a test that looks almost exactly like the previous one, since `async/await` is just syntactic sugar over promises.

Listing 6.3   Integration test with callbacks and `.then()`

```
test("NETWORK REQUIRED (await): correct content, true", (done) => {
  samples.isWebsiteAliveWithAsyncAwait().then((result) => {
    expect(result.success).toBe(true);
    expect(result.status).toBe("ok");
    done();
  });
});
```

However, a test that uses callbacks such as `done()` and `then()` is much less readable than one using the Arrange-Act-Assert pattern. The good news is there's no need to complicate our lives by forcing ourselves to use callbacks. We can use the `await` syntax in our test as well. This will force us to put the `async` keyword in front of the test function, but, overall, our test becomes simpler and more readable, as you can see here.

Listing 6.4   Integration test with `async/await`

```
test("NETWORK REQUIRED2 (await): correct content, true", async () => {
  const result = await samples.isWebsiteAliveWithAsyncAwait();
  expect(result.success).toBe(true);
  expect(result.status).toBe("ok");
});
```

Having asynchronous code that allows us to use the `async/await` syntax turns our test into *almost* a run-of-the-mill value-based test. The entry point is also the exit point, as we saw in figure 6.1.

Even though the call is simplified, the call is still asynchronous underneath, which is why I still call this an integration test. What are the caveats for this type of test? Let's discuss.

6.1.4 Challenges with integration tests

The tests we've just written aren't horrible as far as integration tests go. They're relatively short and readable, but they still suffer from what any integration test suffers from:

- *Lengthy run time*—Compared to unit tests, integration tests are orders of magnitude slower, sometimes taking seconds or even minutes.
- *Flaky*—Integration tests can present inconsistent results (different timings based on where they run, inconsistent failures or successes, etc.)
- *Tests possibly irrelevant code and environment conditions*—Integration tests test multiple pieces of code that might be unrelated to what we care about. (In our case, it's the `node-fetch` library, network conditions, firewall, external website functionality, etc.)
- *Longer investigations*—When an integration test fails, it requires more time for investigation and debugging because there are many possible reasons for a failure.
- *Simulation is harder*—It is harder than it needs to be to simulate a negative test with an integration test (simulating wrong website content, website down, network down, etc.)
- *Harder to trust results*—We might believe the failure of an integration test is due to an external issue when in fact it's a bug in our code. I'll talk about trust more in the next chapter.

Does all this mean you shouldn't write integration tests? No, I believe you should absolutely have integration tests, but you don't need to have that many of them to get enough confidence in your code. Whatever integration tests don't cover should be covered by lower-level tests, such as unit, API, or component tests. I'll discuss this strategy at length in chapter 10, which focuses on testing strategies.

6.2 Making our code unit-test friendly

How can we test the code with a unit test? I'll show you some patterns that I use to make the code more unit testable (i.e., to more easily inject or avoid dependencies, and to check exit points):

- *Extract Entry Point pattern*—Extracting the parts of the production code that are pure logic into their own functions, and treating those functions as entry points for our tests
- *Extract Adapter pattern*—Extracting the thing that is inherently asynchronous and abstracting it away so that we can replace it with something that is synchronous

6.2.1   *Extracting an entry point*

In this pattern, we take a specific unit of async work and split it into two pieces:

- The async part (which stays intact).
- The callbacks that are invoked when the async execution finishes. These are extracted as new functions, which eventually become entry points for a purely logical unit of work that we can invoke with pure unit tests.

Figure 6.2 depicts this idea: In the *before* diagram, we have a single unit of work that contains asynchronous code mixed with logic that processes the async results internally and returns a result via a callback or promise mechanism. In step 1, we extract the logic into its own function (or functions) that contains only the results of the async work as inputs. In step 2, we externalize those functions so that we can use them as entry points for our unit tests.

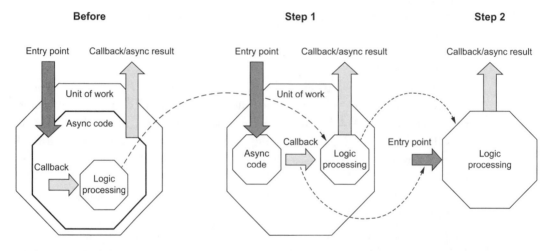

Figure 6.2   Extracting the internal processing logic into a separate unit of work helps simplify the tests, because we are able to verify the new unit of work synchronously and without involving external dependencies.

This provides us with the important ability to test the logical processing of the async callbacks (and to simulate inputs easily). At the same time, we can choose to write a higher-level integration test against the original unit of work to gain confidence that the async orchestration works correctly as well.

If we do integration tests only for all our scenarios, we would end up in a world of many long-running and flaky tests. In the new world, we're able to have most of our tests be fast and consistent, and to have a small layer of integration tests on top to make sure all the orchestration works in between. This way we don't sacrifice speed and maintainability for confidence.

EXAMPLE OF EXTRACTING A UNIT OF WORK

Let's apply this pattern to the code from listing 6.1. Figure 6.3 shows the steps we'll follow:

1. The *before* state contains processing logic that is baked into the `isWebsiteAlive()` function.
2. We'll extract any logical code that happens at the edge of the fetch results and put it in two separate functions: one for handling the success case, and the other for the error case.
3. We'll then externalize these two functions so that we can invoke them directly from unit tests.

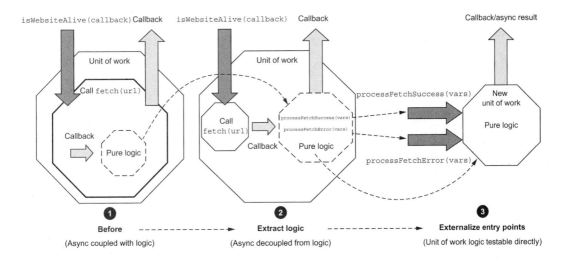

Figure 6.3 Extracting the success and error-handling logic from `isWebsiteAlive()` to test that logic separately

The following listing shows the refactored code.

Listing 6.5 Extracting entry points with `callback`

```
//Entry Point
const isWebsiteAlive = (callback) => {
  fetch("http://example.com")
    .then(throwOnInvalidResponse)
    .then((resp) => resp.text())
    .then((text) => {
      processFetchSuccess(text, callback);
    })
    .catch((err) => {
      processFetchError(err, callback);
    });
};
```

```
const throwOnInvalidResponse = (resp) => {
  if (!resp.ok) {
    throw Error(resp.statusText);
  }
  return resp;
};

//Entry Point
const processFetchSuccess = (text, callback) => {      ◁
  if (text.includes("illustrative")) {
    callback({ success: true, status: "ok" });
  } else {
    callback({ success: false, status: "missing text" });
  }
};

//Entry Point
const processFetchError = (err, callback) => {      ◁
  callback({ success: false, status: err });
};
```

**New entry
points (units
of work)**

As you can see, the original unit we started with now has three entry points instead of
the single one we started with. The new entry points can be used for unit testing, while
the original one can still be used for integration testing, as shown in figure 6.4.

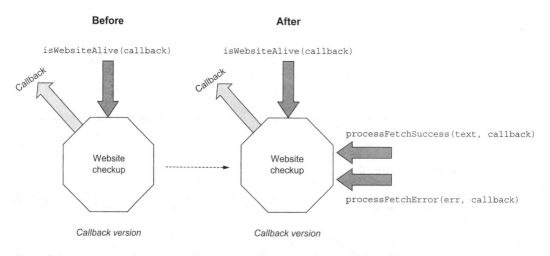

**Figure 6.4   New entry points introduced after extracting the two new functions. The new functions can now be
tested with simpler unit tests instead of the integration tests that were required before the refactoring.**

We'd still want an integration test for the original entry point, but not more than one
or two of those. Any other scenario can be simulated using the purely logical entry
points, quickly and painlessly.

Now we're free to write unit tests that invoke the new entry points, like this.

Listing 6.6 Unit tests with extracted entry points

```
describe("Website alive checking", () => {
  test("content matches, returns true", (done) => {
    samples.processFetchSuccess("illustrative", (err, result) => {
      expect(err).toBeNull();
      expect(result.success).toBe(true);
      expect(result.status).toBe("ok");
      done();
    });
  });
  test("website content does not match, returns false", (done) => {
    samples.processFetchSuccess("bad content", (err, result) => {
      expect(err.message).toBe("missing text");
      done();
    });
  });
  test("When fetch fails, returns false", (done) => {
   samples.processFetchError("error text", (err,result) => {
      expect(err.message).toBe("error text");
      done();
    });
  });
});
```

Invoking
the new
entry
points

Notice that we are invoking the new entry points directly, and we're able to simulate various conditions easily. Nothing is asynchronous in these tests, but we still need the `done()` function, since the callbacks might not be invoked at all, and we'll want to catch that.

We still need at least one integration test that gives us confidence that the asynchronous orchestration works between our entry points. That's where the original integration test can help, but we don't need to write all our test scenarios as integration tests anymore (more on this in chapter 10).

EXTRACTING AN ENTRY POINT WITH AWAIT

The same pattern we just applied can work well for standard `async/await` function structures. Figure 6.5 illustrates that refactoring.

By providing the `async/await` syntax, we can go back to writing code in a linear fashion, without using callback arguments. The `isWebsiteAlive()` function starts looking almost exactly the same as regular synchronous code, only returning values and throwing errors when needed.

Listing 6.7 shows how that looks in our production code.

Before   **After**

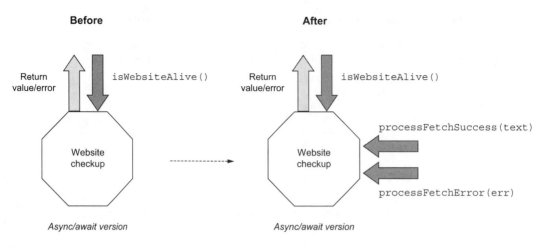

Return
value/error   isWebsiteAlive()

Website
checkup

Return
value/error   isWebsiteAlive()

processFetchSuccess(text)

Website
checkup

processFetchError(err)

Async/await version   *Async/await version*

Figure 6.5   Extracting entry points with `async/await`

Listing 6.7   The function written with `async/await` instead of callbacks

```
//Entry Point
const isWebsiteAlive = async () => {
  try {
    const resp = await fetch("http://example.com");
    throwIfResponseNotOK(resp);
    const text = await resp.text();
    return processFetchContent(text);
  } catch (err) {
    return processFetchError(err);
  }
};

const throwIfResponseNotOK = (resp) => {
  if (!resp.ok) {
    throw resp.statusText;
  }
};

//Entry Point
const processFetchContent = (text) => {
  const included = text.includes("illustrative");
  if (included) {
    return { success: true, status: "ok" };
  }
  return { success: false, status: "missing text" };
};

//Entry Point
const processFetchError = (err) => {
  return { success: false, status: err };
};
```

**Returning a
value instead
of calling a
callback**

Notice that, unlike the callback examples, we're using `return` or `throw` to denote success or failure. This is a common pattern of writing code using `async/await`.

Our tests are simplified as well, as shown in the following listing.

Listing 6.8 Testing entry points extracted from `async/await`

```
describe("website up check", () => {
  test("on fetch success with good content, returns true", () => {
    const result = samples.processFetchContent("illustrative");
    expect(result.success).toBe(true);
    expect(result.status).toBe("ok");
  });

  test("on fetch success with bad content, returns false", () => {
    const result = samples.processFetchContent("text not on site");
    expect(result.success).toBe(false);
    expect(result.status).toBe("missing text");
  });

  test("on fetch fail, throws ", () => {
    expect(() => samples.processFetchError("error text"))
      .toThrowError("error text");
  });
});
```

Again, notice that we don't need to add any kind of `async/await`-related keywords or to be explicit about waiting for execution, because we've separated the logical unit of work from the asynchronous pieces that make our lives more complicated.

6.2.2 *The Extract Adapter pattern*

The Extract Adapter pattern takes the opposite view from the previous pattern. We look at the asynchronous piece of code just like we look at any dependency we've discussed in the previous chapters—as something we'd like to replace in our tests to gain more control. Instead of extracting the logical code into its own set of entry points, we'll extract the asynchronous code (our *dependency*) and abstract it away under an adapter, which we can later inject, just like any other dependency. Figure 6.6 shows this.

It's also common to create a special interface for the adapter that is simplified for the needs of the consumer of the dependency. Another name for this approach is the *interface segregation principle*. In this case, we'll create a `network-adapter` module that hides the real fetching functionality and has its own custom functions, as shown in figure 6.7.

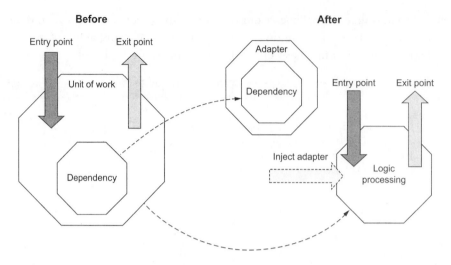

Figure 6.6   Extracting a dependency and wrapping it with an adapter helps us simplify that dependency and replace it with a fake in tests.

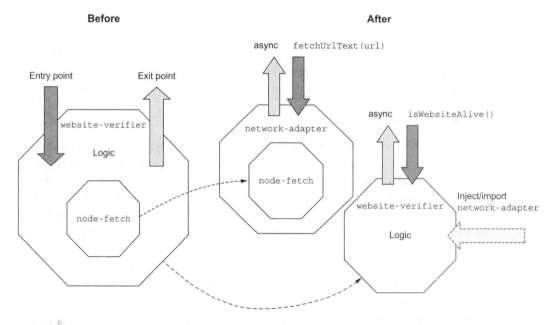

Figure 6.7   Wrapping the `node-fetch` module with our own `network-adapter` module helps us expose only the functionality our application needs, expressed in the language most suitable for the problem at hand.

> ### Interface segregation principle
>
> The term *interface segregation principle* was coined by Robert Martin. Imagine a database dependency with dozens of functions hidden behind an adapter whose interface might only contain a couple of functions with custom names and parameters. The adapter serves to hide the complexity and simplify both the consumer's code and the tests that simulate it. For more information on interface segregation, see the Wikipedia article about it: https://en.wikipedia.org/wiki/Interface_segregation_principle.

The following listing shows what the `network-adapter` module looks like.

Listing 6.9 The `network-adapter` code

```
const fetch = require("node-fetch");

const fetchUrlText = async (url) => {
  const resp = await fetch(url);
  if (resp.ok) {
    const text = await resp.text();
    return { ok: true, text: text };
  }
  return { ok: false, text: resp.statusText };
};
```

Note that the `network-adapter` module is the only module in the project that imports `node-fetch`. If that dependency changes at some point in the future, this increases the chances that only the current file would need to change. We've also simplified the function both by name and by functionality. We're hiding the need to fetch the status and the text from the URL, and we're abstracting them both under a single easier-to-use function.

Now we get to choose how to use the adapter. First, we can use it in the modular style. Then we'll use a functional approach and an object-oriented one with a strongly typed interface.

MODULAR ADAPTER

The following listing shows a modular use of `network-adapter` by our initial `isWebsite-Alive()` function.

Listing 6.10 `isWebsiteAlive()` using the `network-adapter` module

```
const network = require("./network-adapter");

const isWebsiteAlive = async () => {
  try {
    const result = await network.fetchUrlText("http://example.com");
    if (!result.ok) {
      throw result.text;
    }
```

```
      const text = result.text;
      return processFetchSuccess(text);
    } catch (err) {
      throw processFetchFail(err);
    }
  }
};
```

In this version, we are directly importing the `network-adapter` module, which we'll fake in our tests later on.

The unit tests for this module are shown in the following listing. Because we're using a modular design, we can fake the module using `jest.mock()` in our tests. We'll also inject the module in later examples, don't worry.

Listing 6.11 Faking `network-adapter` with `jest.mock`

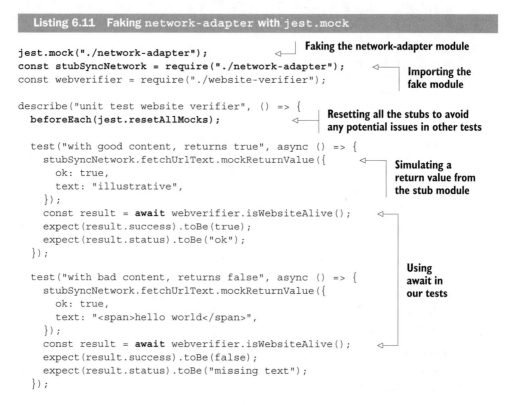

```
jest.mock("./network-adapter");                          Faking the network-adapter module
const stubSyncNetwork = require("./network-adapter");     Importing the
const webverifier = require("./website-verifier");        fake module

describe("unit test website verifier", () => {
  beforeEach(jest.resetAllMocks);                         Resetting all the stubs to avoid
                                                          any potential issues in other tests
  test("with good content, returns true", async () => {
    stubSyncNetwork.fetchUrlText.mockReturnValue({        Simulating a
      ok: true,                                           return value from
      text: "illustrative",                               the stub module
    });
    const result = await webverifier.isWebsiteAlive();
    expect(result.success).toBe(true);
    expect(result.status).toBe("ok");
  });

  test("with bad content, returns false", async () => {   Using
    stubSyncNetwork.fetchUrlText.mockReturnValue({         await in
      ok: true,                                            our tests
      text: "<span>hello world</span>",
    });
    const result = await webverifier.isWebsiteAlive();
    expect(result.success).toBe(false);
    expect(result.status).toBe("missing text");
  });
});
```

Notice that we are using `async/await` again, because we are back to using the original entry point we started with at the beginning of the chapter. But just because we're using `await` doesn't mean our tests are running asynchronously. Our test code, and the production code it invokes, actually runs linearly, with an async-friendly signature. We'll need to use `async/await` for the functional and object-oriented designs as well, because the entry point requires it.

I've named our fake network `stubSyncNetwork` to make the synchronous nature of the test clearer. Otherwise, it's hard to tell just by looking at the test whether the code it invokes runs linearly or asynchronously.

FUNCTIONAL ADAPTER

In the functional design pattern, the design of the `network-adapter` module stays the same, but we enable its injection into our `website-verifier` differently. As you can see in the next listing, we add a new parameter to our entry point.

Listing 6.12 A functional injection design for `isWebsiteAlive()`

```
const isWebsiteAlive = async (network) => {
  const result = await network.fetchUrlText("http://example.com");
  if (result.ok) {
    const text = result.text;
    return onFetchSuccess(text);
  }
  return onFetchError(result.text);
};
```

In this version, we're expecting the `network-adapter` module to be injected through a common parameter to our function. In a functional design, we can use higher-order functions and currying to configure a pre-injected function with our own network dependency. In our tests, we can simply send in a fake network via this parameter. As far as the design of the injection goes, almost nothing else has changed from previous samples, other than the fact that we don't import the `network-adapter` module anymore. Reducing the amount of imports and requires can help maintainability in the long run.

Our tests are simpler in the following listing, with less boilerplate code.

Listing 6.13 Unit test with functional injection of `network-adapter`

```
const webverifier = require("./website-verifier");

const makeStubNetworkWithResult = (fakeResult) => {      ◁─┐  A new helper function
  return {                                                  │  to create a custom
    fetchUrlText: () => {                                   │  object that matches
      return fakeResult;                                    │  the important parts of
    },                                                      │  the network-adapter's
  };                                                        │  interface
};
describe("unit test website verifier", () => {
  test("with good content, returns true", async () => {
    const stubSyncNetwork = makeStubNetworkWithResult({
      ok: true,
      text: "illustrative",
    });
    const result = await webverifier.isWebsiteAlive(stubSyncNetwork);   ◁─┐
    expect(result.success).toBe(true);                                    │
    expect(result.status).toBe("ok");                          Injecting the
  });                                                          custom object
                                                                          │

  test("with bad content, returns false", async () => {
    const stubSyncNetwork = makeStubNetworkWithResult({
```

```
    ok: true,
    text: "unexpected content",
  });
  const result = await webverifier.isWebsiteAlive(stubSyncNetwork);    ◁─────┐
  expect(result.success).toBe(false);
  expect(result.status).toBe("missing text");                        Injecting the
});                                                                 custom object
  ...
```

Notice that we don't need a lot of the boilerplate at the top of the file, as we did in the modular design. We don't need to fake the module indirectly (via `jest.mock`), we don't need to re-import it for our tests (via `require`), and we don't need to reset Jest's state using `jest.resetAllMocks`. All we need to do is call our new `makeStubNetwork-WithResult` helper function from each test to generate a new fake network adapter, and then inject the fake network by sending it as a parameter to our entry point.

OBJECT-ORIENTED, INTERFACE-BASED ADAPTER

We've taken a look at the modular and functional designs. Let's now turn our attention to the object-oriented side of the equation. In the object-oriented paradigm, we can take the parameter injection we've done before and promote it into a constructor injection pattern. We'll start with the network adapter and its interfaces (public API and results signature) in the following listing.

Listing 6.14 `NetworkAdapter` and its interfaces

```
export interface INetworkAdapter {
  fetchUrlText(url: string): Promise<NetworkAdapterFetchResults>;
}
export interface NetworkAdapterFetchResults {
  ok: boolean;
  text: string;
}

ch6-async/6-fetch-adapter-interface-oo/network-adapter.ts

export class NetworkAdapter implements INetworkAdapter {
  async fetchUrlText(url: string):
       Promise<NetworkAdapterFetchResults> {
    const resp = await fetch(url);
    if (resp.ok) {
      const text = await resp.text();
      return Promise.resolve({ ok: true, text: text });
    }
    return Promise.reject({ ok: false, text: resp.statusText });
  }
}
```

In the next listing, we create a `WebsiteVerifier` class that has a constructor that receives an `INetworkAdapter` parameter.

Listing 6.15 `WebsiteVerifier` class with constructor injection

```
export interface WebsiteAliveResult {
  success: boolean;
  status: string;
}

export class WebsiteVerifier {
  constructor(private network: INetworkAdapter) {}

  isWebsiteAlive = async (): Promise<WebsiteAliveResult> => {
    let netResult: NetworkAdapterFetchResults;
    try {
      netResult = await this.network.fetchUrlText("http://example.com");
      if (!netResult.ok) {
        throw netResult.text;
      }
      const text = netResult.text;
      return this.processNetSuccess(text);
    } catch (err) {
      throw this.processNetFail(err);
    }
  };

  processNetSuccess = (text): WebsiteAliveResult => {
    const included = text.includes("illustrative");
    if (included) {
      return { success: true, status: "ok" };
    }
    return { success: false, status: "missing text" };
  };

  processNetFail = (err): WebsiteAliveResult => {
    return { success: false, status: err };
  };
}
```

The unit tests for this class can instantiate a fake network adapter and inject it through a constructor. In the following listing, we'll use substitute.js to create a fake object that fits the new interface.

Listing 6.16 Unit tests for the object-oriented `WebsiteVerifier`

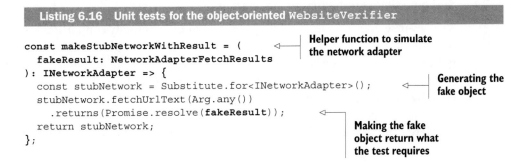

```
const makeStubNetworkWithResult = (          ◁──┤ Helper function to simulate
  fakeResult: NetworkAdapterFetchResults          the network adapter
): INetworkAdapter => {
  const stubNetwork = Substitute.for<INetworkAdapter>();   ◁──┤ Generating the
  stubNetwork.fetchUrlText(Arg.any())                          fake object
    .returns(Promise.resolve(fakeResult));   ◁──┐
  return stubNetwork;                              Making the fake
};                                                object return what
                                                  the test requires
```

```
describe("unit test website verifier", () => {
  test("with good content, returns true", async () => {
    const stubSyncNetwork = makeStubNetworkWithResult({
      ok: true,
      text: "illustrative",
    });
    const webVerifier = new WebsiteVerifier(stubSyncNetwork);

    const result = await webVerifier.isWebsiteAlive();
    expect(result.success).toBe(true);
    expect(result.status).toBe("ok");
  });

  test("with bad content, returns false", async () => {
    const stubSyncNetwork = makeStubNetworkWithResult({
      ok: true,
      text: "unexpected content",
    });
    const webVerifier = new WebsiteVerifier(stubSyncNetwork);

    const result = await webVerifier.isWebsiteAlive();
    expect(result.success).toBe(false);
    expect(result.status).toBe("missing text");
  });
```

This type of Inversion of Control (IOC) and Dependency Injection (DI) works well. In the object-oriented world, constructor injection with interfaces is very common and can, in many instances, provide a valid and maintainable solution for separating your dependencies from your logic.

6.3   *Dealing with timers*

Timers, such as `setTimeout`, represent a very JavaScript-specific problem. They are part of the domain and are used, for better or worse, in many pieces of code. Instead of extracting adapters and entry points, sometimes it's just as useful to disable these functions and work around them. We'll look at two patterns for getting around timers:

- Directly monkey-patching the function
- Using Jest and other frameworks to disable and control them

6.3.1   *Stubbing timers out with monkey-patching*

Monkey-patching is a way for a program to extend or modify supporting system software locally (affecting only the running instance of the program). Programming languages and runtimes such as JavaScript, Ruby, and Python can accommodate monkey-patching pretty easily. It's much more difficult to do with more strongly typed and compile-time languages such as C# and Java. I discuss monkey-patching in more detail in the appendix.

Here's one way to do it in JavaScript. We'll start with the following piece of code that uses the `setTimeout` method.

Listing 6.17 Code with `setTimeout` we'd like to monkey-patch

```
const calculate1 = (x, y, resultCallback) => {
  setTimeout(() => { resultCallback(x + y); },
    5000);
};
```

We can monkey-patch the `setTimeout` function to be synchronous by literally setting that function's prototype in memory, as follows.

Listing 6.18 A simple monkey-patching pattern

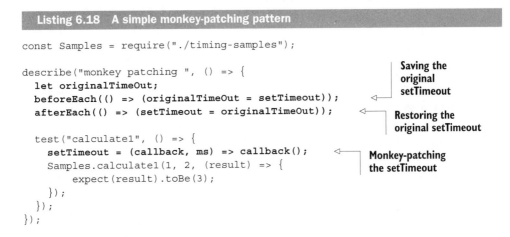

```
const Samples = require("./timing-samples");

describe("monkey patching ", () => {
  let originalTimeOut;
  beforeEach(() => (originalTimeOut = setTimeout));     ← Saving the
  afterEach(() => (setTimeout = originalTimeOut));      ← original
                                                          setTimeout
                                                       ← Restoring the
  test("calculate1", () => {                             original setTimeout
    setTimeout = (callback, ms) => callback();         ← Monkey-patching
    Samples.calculate1(1, 2, (result) => {               the setTimeout
        expect(result).toBe(3);
    });
  });
});
```

Since everything is synchronous, we don't need to use `done()` to wait for a callback invocation. We are replacing `setTimeout` with a purely synchronous implementation that invokes the received callback immediately.

The only downside to this approach is that it requires a bunch of boilerplate code and is generally more error prone, since we need to remember to clean up correctly. Let's look at what frameworks like Jest provide us with to handle these situations.

6.3.2 Faking setTimeout with Jest

Jest provides us with three major functions for handling most types of timers in JavaScript:

- `jest.useFakeTimers`—Stubs out all the various timer functions, such as `setTimetout`
- `jest.resetAllTimers`–Resets all fake timers to the real ones
- `jest.advanceTimersToNextTimer`–Triggers any fake timer so that any callbacks are triggered

Together, these functions take care of most of the boilerplate code for us.

Here's the same test we just did in listing 6.18, this time using Jest's helper functions.

Listing 6.19 Faking `setTimeout` with Jest

```
describe("calculate1 - with jest", () => {
  beforeEach(jest.clearAllTimers);
  beforeEach(jest.useFakeTimers);

  test("fake timeout with callback", () => {
    Samples.calculate1(1, 2, (result) => {
      expect(result).toBe(3);
    });
    jest.advanceTimersToNextTimer();
  });
});
```

Notice that, once again, we don't need to call `done()`, since everything is synchronous. At the same time, we have to use `advanceTimersToNextTimer` because, without it, our fake `setTimeout` would be stuck forever. `advanceTimersToNextTimer` is also useful for scenarios such as when the module being tested schedules a `setTimeout` whose callback schedules another `setTimeout` recursively (meaning the scheduling never stops). In these scenarios, it's useful to be able to run forward in time, step by step.

With `advanceTimersToNextTimer`, you could potentially advance all timers by a specified number of steps to simulate the passage of steps that will trigger the next timer callback waiting in line.

The same pattern also works well with `setInterval`, as shown next.

Listing 6.20 A function that uses `setInterval`

```
const calculate4 = (getInputsFn, resultFn) => {
  setInterval(() => {
    const { x, y } = getInputsFn();
    resultFn(x + y);
  }, 1000);
};
```

In this case, our function takes in two callbacks as parameters: one to provide the inputs to calculate, and the other to call back with the calculation result. It uses `setInterval` to continuously get more inputs and calculate their results.

The following listing shows a test that will advance our timer, trigger the interval twice, and expect the same result from both invocations.

Listing 6.21 Advancing fake timers in a unit test

```
describe("calculate with intervals", () => {
  beforeEach(jest.clearAllTimers);
  beforeEach(jest.useFakeTimers);

  test("calculate, incr input/output, calculates correctly", () => {
    let xInput = 1;
    let yInput = 2;
    const inputFn = () => ({ x: xInput++, y: yInput++ });
```

Incrementing a variable to verify the number of callbacks

```
      const results = [];
      Samples.calculate4(inputFn, (result) => results.push(result));

      jest.advanceTimersToNextTimer();        Invoking
      jest.advanceTimersToNextTimer();        setInterval twice

      expect(results[0]).toBe(3);
      expect(results[1]).toBe(5);
  });
});
```

In this example, we verify that the new values are being calculated and stored correctly. Notice that we could have written the same test with only a single invocation and a single expect, and we would have gotten close to the same amount of confidence that this more elaborate test provides, but I like to put in additional validation when I need more confidence.

6.4 Dealing with common events

I can't talk about async unit testing and not discuss the basic events flow. Hopefully the topic of async unit testing now seems relatively straightforward, but I want to go over the events part explicitly.

6.4.1 Dealing with event emitters

To make sure we're all on the same page, here's a clear and concise definition of event emitters from DigitalOcean's "Using Event Emitters in Node.js" tutorial (http://mng .bz/844z):

> *Event emitters are objects in Node.js that trigger an event by sending a message to signal that an action was completed. JavaScript developers can write code that listens to events from an event emitter, allowing them to execute functions every time those events are triggered. In this context, events are composed of an identifying string and any data that needs to be passed to the listeners.*

Consider the `Adder` class in the following listing, which emits an event every time it adds something.

Listing 6.22 A simple event-emitter-based `Adder`

```
const EventEmitter = require("events");

class Adder extends EventEmitter {
  constructor() {
    super();
  }

  add(x, y) {
    const result = x + y;
    this.emit("added", result);
    return result;
```

```
    }
}
```

The simplest way to write a unit test that verifies that the event is emitted is to literally subscribe to the event in our test and verify that it triggers when we call the `add` function.

Listing 6.23   Testing an event emitter by subscribing to it

```
describe("events based module", () => {
  describe("add", () => {
    it("generates addition event when called", (done) => {
      const adder = new Adder();
      adder.on("added", (result) => {
        expect(result).toBe(3);
        done();
      });
      adder.add(1, 2);
    });
  });
});
```

By using `done()`, we are verifying that the event actually was emitted. If we didn't use `done()`, and the event wasn't emitted, our test would pass because the subscribed code never executed. By adding `expect(x).toBe(y)`, we are also verifying the values sent in the event parameters, as well as implicitly testing that the event was triggered.

6.4.2   *Dealing with click events*

What about those pesky UI events, such as `click`? How can we test that we have bound them correctly via our scripts? Consider the simple web page and associated logic in listings 6.24 and 6.25.

Listing 6.24   A simple web page with JavaScript `click` functionality

```
<!DOCTYPE html>
<html lang="en">
<head>
    <meta charset="UTF-8">
    <title>File to Be Tested</title>
    <script src="index-helper.js"></script>
</head>
<body>
    <div>
        <div>A simple button</div>
        <Button data-testid="myButton" id="myButton">Click Me</Button>
        <div data-testid="myResult" id="myResult">Waiting...</div>
    </div>
</body>
</html>
```

Listing 6.25 The logic for the web page in JavaScript

```javascript
window.addEventListener("load", () => {
  document
    .getElementById("myButton")
    .addEventListener("click", onMyButtonClick);

  const resultDiv = document.getElementById("myResult");
  resultDiv.innerText = "Document Loaded";
});

function onMyButtonClick() {
  const resultDiv = document.getElementById("myResult");
  resultDiv.innerText = "Clicked!";
}
```

We have a very simple piece of logic that makes sure our button sets a special message when clicked. How can we test this?

Here's an antipattern: we could subscribe to the click event in our tests and make sure it is triggered, but this would provide no value to us. What we care about is that the click has actually done something useful, other than triggering.

Here's a better way: we can trigger the click event and make sure it has changed the correct value inside the page—this will provide real value. Figure 6.8 shows this.

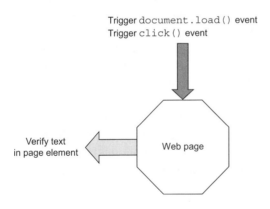

Figure 6.8 Click as an entry point, and element as an exit point

The following listing shows what our test might look like.

Listing 6.26 Triggering a click event, and testing an element's text

```javascript
/**
 * @jest-environment jsdom       ⟵  Applying the browser-simulating
 */                                   jsdom environment just for this file
//(the above is required for window events)
const fs = require("fs");
const path = require("path");
require("./index-helper.js");
```

```
const loadHtml = (fileRelativePath) => {
  const filePath = path.join(__dirname, "index.html");
  const innerHTML = fs.readFileSync(filePath);
  document.documentElement.innerHTML = innerHTML;
};

const loadHtmlAndGetUIElements = () => {
  loadHtml("index.html");
  const button = document.getElementById("myButton");
  const resultDiv = document.getElementById("myResult");
  return { window, button, resultDiv };
};

describe("index helper", () => {
  test("vanilla button click triggers change in result div", () => {
    const { window, button, resultDiv } = loadHtmlAndGetUIElements();
    window.dispatchEvent(new Event("load"));        ◁──┐ Simulating the
                                                        document.load event
    button.click();     ◁── Triggering the click

    expect(resultDiv.innerText).toBe("Clicked!");   ◁──┐ Verifying that an element
  });                                                    in our document has
});                                                      actually changed
```

In this example, I've extracted two utility methods, `loadHtml` and `loadHtmlAndGetUI-Elements`, so that I can write cleaner, more readable tests, and so I'll have fewer issues changing my tests if UI item locations or IDs change in the future.

In the test itself, we're simulating the `document.load` event, so that our custom script under test can start running and then triggering the `click`, as if the user had clicked the button. Finally, the test verifies that an element in our document has actually changed, which means our code successfully subscribed to the event and did its work.

Notice that we don't actually care about the underlying logic inside the index helper file. We just rely on observed state changes in the UI, which acts as our final exit point. This allows less coupling in our tests, so that if our code under test changes, we are less likely to need to change the test, unless the observable (publicly notice-able) functionality has truly changed.

6.5   Bringing in the DOM testing library

Our test has a lot of boilerplate code, mostly for finding elements and verifying their contents. I recommend looking into the open source DOM Testing Library written by Kent C. Dodds (https://github.com/kentcdodds/dom-testing-library-with-anything). This library has variants applicable to most frontend JavaScript frameworks today, such as React, Angular, and Vue.js. We'll be using the vanilla version of it named DOM Testing Library.

What I like about this library is that it aims to allow us to write tests closer to the point of view of the user interacting with our web page. Instead of using IDs for ele-ments, we query by element text; firing events is a bit cleaner; and querying and waiting for elements to appear or disappear is cleaner and hidden under syntactic sugar. It's quite useful once you use it in multiple tests.

Here's what our test looks like with this library.

Listing 6.27   Using the DOM Testing Library in a simple test

```
const { fireEvent, findByText, getByText }        │ Importing some of the
    = require("@testing-library/dom");            │ library APIs to be used

const loadHtml = (fileRelativePath) => {
  const filePath = path.join(__dirname, "index.html");    │ Library APIs require
  const innerHTML = fs.readFileSync(filePath);            │ the document element
  document.documentElement.innerHTML = innerHTML;         │ as the basis for most
  return document.documentElement;           ◁───────────┘ of the work.
};

const loadHtmlAndGetUIElements = () => {
  const docElem = loadHtml("index.html");
  const button = getByText(docElem, "click me", { exact: false });
  return { window, docElem, button };
};

describe("index helper", () => {
  test("dom test lib button click triggers change in page", () => {
    const { window, docElem, button } = loadHtmlAndGetUIElements();
    fireEvent.load(window);            ◁──┐  Using the library's fireEvent API
                                          │  to simplify event dispatching
    fireEvent.click(button);           ◁──┘

    //wait until true or timeout in 1 sec
    expect(findByText(docElem,"clicked", { exact: false })).toBeTruthy();  ◁──┐
  });                                                                         │
});                    This query will wait until the item is ───────────────┘
                       found or will timeout within 1 second.
```

Notice how the library allows us to use the regular text of the page items to get the items, instead of their IDs or test IDs. This is part of the way the library pushes us to work so things feel more natural and from the user's point of view. To make the test more sustainable over time, we're using the `exact: false` flag so that we don't have to worry about uppercasing issues or missing letters at the start or end of strings. This removes the need to change the test for small text changes that are less important.

Summary

- Testing asynchronous code directly results in flaky tests that take a long time to execute. To fix these issues, you can take two approaches: extract an entry point or extract an adapter.
- Extracting an entry point is when you extract the pure logic into separate functions and treat those functions as entry points for your tests. The extracted entry point can either accept a callback as an argument or return a value. Prefer return values over callbacks for simplicity.

- Extracting an adapter involves extracting a dependency that is inherently asynchronous and abstracting it away so that you can replace it with something that is synchronous. The adapter may be of different types:
  - *Modular*—When you stub the whole module (file) and replace specific functions in it.
  - *Functional*—When you inject a function or value into the system under test. You can replace the injected value with a stub in tests.
  - *Object-oriented*—When you use an interface in the production code and create a stub that implements that interface in the test code.
- Timers (such as `setTimeout` and `setInterval`) can be replaced either directly with monkey-patching or by using Jest or another framework to disable and control them.
- Events are best tested by verifying the end result they produce—changes in the HTML document the user can see. You can do this either directly or by using libraries such as the DOM Testing Library.

Part 3

The test code

This part covers techniques for managing and organizing unit tests and for ensuring that the quality of unit tests in real-world projects is high.

Chapter 7 covers test trustworthiness. It explains how to write tests that will reliably report the presence or absence of bugs. We'll also look at the differences between true and false test failures.

In chapter 8, we'll look at the main pillar of good unit tests—maintainability—and we'll explore techniques to support it. For tests to be useful in the long run, they shouldn't require much effort to maintain; otherwise, they will inevitably become abandoned.

Trustworthy tests

No matter how you organize your tests, or how many you have, they're worth very little if you can't trust them, maintain them, or read them. The tests that you write should have three properties that together make them good:

- *Trustworthiness*—Developers will want to run trustworthy tests, and they'll accept the test results with confidence. Trustworthy tests don't have bugs, and they test the right things.
- *Maintainability*—Unmaintainable tests are nightmares because they can ruin project schedules, or they may be sidelined when the project is put on a more aggressive schedule. Developers will simply stop maintaining and fixing tests that take too long to change or that need to change often on very minor production code changes.
- *Readability*—This refers not only to being able to read a test but also figuring out the problem if the test seems to be wrong. Without readability, the other

two pillars fall pretty quickly. Maintaining tests becomes harder, and you can't trust them anymore because you don't understand them.

This chapter and the next two present a series of practices related to each of these pillars that you can use when doing test reviews. Together, the three pillars ensure your time is well used. Drop one of them, and you run the risk of wasting everyone's time.

Trust is the first of the three pillars that I like to evaluate good unit tests on, so it's fitting that we start with it. If we don't trust the tests, what's the point in running them? What's the point in fixing them or fixing the code if they fail? What's the point of maintaining them?

7.1 *How to know you trust a test*

What does "trust" mean for a software developer in the context of a test? Perhaps it's easier to explain based on what we do or don't do when a test fails or passes.

You might not trust a test if

- It fails and you're not worried (you believe it's a false positive).
- You feel like it's fine to ignore the results of this test, either because it passes every once in a while or because you feel it's not relevant or buggy.
- It passes and you are worried (you believe it's a false negative).
- You still feel the need to manually debug or test the software "just in case."

You might trust the test if

- The test fails and you're genuinely worried that something broke. You don't move on, assuming the test is wrong.
- The test passes and you feel relaxed, not feeling the need to test or debug manually.

In the next few sections, we'll look at test failures as a way to identify untrustworthy tests, and we'll look at passing tests' code and see how to detect untrustworthy test code. Finally, we'll cover a few generic practices that can enhance trustworthiness in tests.

7.2 *Why tests fail*

Ideally, your tests (any tests, not just unit tests) should only be failing for *a good reason*. That good reason is, of course, that a real bug was uncovered in the underlying production code.

Unfortunately, tests can fail for a multitude of reasons. We can assume that a test failing for any reason other than that one good reason should trigger an "untrustworthy" warning, but not all tests fail the same way, and recognizing the reasons tests may fail can help us build a roadmap for what we'd like to do in each case.

Here are some reasons that tests fail:

- A real bug has been uncovered in the production code
- A buggy test gives a false failure
- The test is out of date due to a change in functionality

- The test conflicts with another test
- The test is flaky

Except for the first point here, all these reasons are the test telling you it should not be trusted in its current form. Let's go through them.

7.2.1 A real bug has been uncovered in the production code

The first reason a test will fail is when there is a bug in the production code. That's good! That's why we have tests. Let's move on to the other reasons tests fail.

7.2.2 A buggy test gives a false failure

A test will fail if the test is buggy. The production code might be correct, but that doesn't matter if the test itself has a bug that causes the test to fail. It could be that you're asserting on the wrong expected result of an exit point, or that you're using the system under test incorrectly. It could be that you're setting up the context for the test wrong or that you misunderstand what you were supposed to test.

Either way, a buggy test can be quite dangerous, because a bug in a test can also cause it to *pass* and leave you unsuspecting of what's really going on. We'll talk more about tests that don't fail but should later in the chapter.

How to recognize a buggy test

You have a failing test, but you might have already debugged the production code and couldn't find any bug there. This is when you should start suspecting the failing test. There's no way around it. You're going to have to slowly debug the test code.

Here are some potential causes of false failures:

- Asserting on the wrong thing or on the wrong exit point
- Injecting a wrong value into the entry point
- Invoking the entry point incorrectly

It could also be some other small mistake that happens when you write code at 2 A.M. (That's not a sustainable coding strategy, by the way. Stop doing that.)

What do you do once you've found a buggy test?

When you find a buggy test, don't panic. This might be the millionth time you've found one, so you might be panicking and thinking "our tests suck." You might also be right about that. But that doesn't mean you should panic. Fix the bug, and run the test to see if it now passes.

If the test passes, don't be happy too soon! Go to the production code and place an obvious bug that should be caught by the newly fixed test. For example, change a Boolean to always be `true`. Or `false`. Then run the test again, and make sure it fails. If it doesn't, you might still have a bug in your test. Fix the test until it can find the production bug and you can see it fail.

Once you are sure the test is failing for an obvious production code issue, fix the production code issue you just made and run the test again. It should pass. If the test is now passing, you're done. You've now seen the test passing when it should and failing when it should. Commit the code and move on.

If the test is still failing, it might have another bug. Repeat the whole process again until you verify that the test fails and passes when it should. If the test is still failing, you might have come across a real bug in production code. In which case, good for you!

HOW TO AVOID BUGGY TESTS IN THE FUTURE

One of the best ways I know to detect and prevent buggy tests is to write your code in a test-driven manner. I explained a bit about this technique in chapter 1 of this book. I also practice this technique in real life.

Test-driven development (TDD) allows us to see both states of a test: both that it fails when it should (that's the initial state we start in) and that it passes when it should (when the production code under test is written to make the test pass). If the test continues to fail, we've found a bug in the production code. If the test starts out passing, we have a bug in the test.

Another great way to reduce the likelihood of bugs in tests is to remove logic from them. More on this in section 7.3.

7.2.3   *The test is out of date due to a change in functionality*

A test can fail if it's no longer compatible with the current feature that's being tested. Say you have a login feature, and in an earlier version, you needed to provide a username and a password to log in. In the new version, a two-factor authentication scheme replaced the old login. The existing test will start failing because it's not providing the right parameters to the login functions.

WHAT CAN YOU DO NOW?

You now have two options:

- Adapt the test to the new functionality.
- Write a new test for the new functionality, and remove the old test because it has now become irrelevant.

AVOIDING OR PREVENTING THIS IN THE FUTURE

Things change. I don't think it's possible to not have out-of-date tests at some point in time. We'll deal with change in the next chapter, relating to the maintainability of tests and how well tests can handle changes in the application.

7.2.4   *The test conflicts with another test*

Let's say you have two tests: one of them is failing and one is passing. Let's also say they cannot pass together. You'll usually only see the failing test, because the passing one is, well, passing.

For instance, a test may fail because it suddenly conflicts with a new behavior. On the other hand, a conflicting test may expect a new behavior but doesn't find it. The simplest example is when the first test verifies that calling a function with two parameters produces "3," whereas the second test expects the same function to produce "4."

WHAT CAN YOU DO NOW?

The root cause is that one of the tests has become irrelevant, which means it needs to be removed. Which one should be removed? That's a question we'd need to ask a product owner, because the answer is related to which behavior is correct and expected from the application.

AVOIDING THIS IN THE FUTURE

I feel this is a healthy dynamic, and I'm fine with not avoiding it.

7.2.5   The test is flaky

A test can fail inconsistently. Even if the production code under test hasn't changed, a test can suddenly fail without any apparent reason, then pass again, then fail again. We call a test like that "flaky."

Flaky tests are a special beast, and I'll deal with them in section 7.5.

7.3   Avoiding logic in unit tests

The chances of having bugs in your tests increase almost exponentially as you include more and more logic in them. I've seen plenty of tests that should have been simple become dynamic, random-number-generating, thread-creating, file-writing monsters that are little test engines in their own right. Sadly, because they were "tests," the writer didn't consider that they might have bugs or didn't write them in a maintainable manner. Those test monsters take more time to debug and verify than they save.

But all monsters start out small. Often, an experienced developer in the company will look at a test and start thinking, "What if we made the function loop and create random numbers as input? We'd surely find lots more bugs that way!" And you will, especially in your tests.

Test bugs are one of the most annoying things for developers, because you'll almost never search for the cause of a failing test in the test itself. I'm not saying that tests with logic don't have any value. In fact, I'm likely to write such tests myself in some special situations. But I try to avoid this practice as much as possible.

If you have any of the following inside a unit test, your test contains logic that I usually recommend be reduced or removed completely:

- `switch`, `if`, or `else` statements
- `foreach`, `for`, or `while` loops
- Concatenations (+ sign, etc.)
- `try`, `catch`

7.3.1   Logic in asserts: Creating dynamic expected values

Here's a quick example of a concatenation to start us off.

> **Listing 7.1   A test with logic in it**

```
describe("makeGreeting", () => {
  it("returns correct greeting for name", () => {
```

```
    const name = "abc";
    const result = trust.makeGreeting(name);
    expect(result).toBe("hello" + name);          ◁——⊣  Logic in the
});                                                       assertion part
```

To understand the problem with this test, the following listing shows the code being tested. Notice that the + sign makes an appearance in both.

Listing 7.2   Code under test

```
const makeGreeting = (name) => {
  return "hello" + name;        ◁——⊣  The same logic as in
};                                      the production code
```

Notice how the algorithm (very simple, but still an algorithm) of connecting a name with a "hello" string is repeated in both the test and the code under test:

```
expect(result).toBe("hello" + name);      ◁————  Our test
return "hello" + name;               ◁——⊣  The code under test
```

My issue with this test is that the algorithm under test is repeated in the test itself. This means that if there is a bug in the algorithm, the test also contains *the same bug*. The test will not catch the bug, but instead will expect the incorrect result from the code under test.

In this case, the incorrect result is that we're missing a space character between the concatenated words, but hopefully you can see how the same issue could become much more complex with a more complex algorithm.

This is a trust issue. We can't trust this test to tell us the truth, since its logic is a repeat of the logic being tested. The test might pass when the bug exists in the code, so we can't trust the test's result.

> **WARNING**   Avoid dynamically creating the expected value in your asserts; use hardcoded values when possible.

A more trustworthy version of this test can be rewritten as follows.

Listing 7.3   A more trustworthy test

```
it("returns correct greeting for name 2", () => {
  const result = trust.makeGreeting("abc");
  expect(result).toBe("hello abc");        ◁——⊣  Using a hardcoded value
});
```

Because the inputs in this test are so simple, it's easy to write a hardcoded expected value. This is what I usually recommend—make the test inputs so simple that it is trivial to create a hardcoded version of the expected value. Note that this is mostly true of unit tests. For higher-level tests, this is a bit harder to do, which is another reason why higher-level tests should be considered a bit riskier; they often create expected results dynamically, which you should try to avoid any time you can.

"But Roy," you might say, "Now we are repeating ourselves—the string `"abc"` is repeated twice. We were able to avoid this in the previous test." When push comes to shove, trust should trump maintainability. What good is a highly maintainable test that I cannot trust? You can read more about code duplication in tests in Vladimir Khorikov's article, "DRY vs. DAMP in Unit Tests," (https://enterprisecraftsmanship .com/posts/dry-damp-unit-tests/).

7.3.2 *Other forms of logic*

Here's the opposite case: creating the inputs dynamically (using a loop) forces us to dynamically decide what the expected output should be. Suppose we have the following code to test.

Listing 7.4 A name-finding function

```
const isName = (input) => {
  return input.split(" ").length === 2;
};
```

The following listing shows a clear antipattern for a test.

Listing 7.5 Loops and ifs in a test

```
describe("isName", () => {
  const namesToTest = ["firstOnly", "first second", ""];      ⟵  Declaring
                                                                   multiple inputs
  it("correctly finds out if it is a name", () => {
    namesToTest.forEach((name) => {
      const result = trust.isName(name);
      if (name.includes(" ")) {
        expect(result).toBe(true);              Production code
      } else {                                  logic leaking into
        expect(result).toBe(false);             the test
      }
    });
  });
});
```

Notice how we're using multiple inputs for the test. This forces us to loop over those inputs, which in itself complicates the test. Remember, loops can have bugs too.

Additionally, because we have different scenarios for the values (with and without spaces) we need an `if/else` to know what the assertion is expecting, and the `if/else` can have bugs too. We are also repeating a part of the production algorithm, which brings us back to the previous concatenation example and its problems.

Finally, our test name is too generic. We can only title it as "it works" because we have to account for multiple scenarios and expected outcomes. That's bad for readability.

This is an all-around bad test. It's better to separate this into two or three tests, each with its own scenario and name. This would allow us to use hardcoded inputs and assertions and to remove any loops and `if/else` logic from the code. Anything more complex causes the following problems:

- The test is harder to read and understand.
- The test is hard to recreate. For example, imagine a multithreaded test or a test with random numbers that suddenly fails.
- The test is more likely to have a bug or to verify the wrong thing.
- Naming the test may be harder because it does multiple things.

Generally, monster tests replace original simpler tests, and that makes it harder to find bugs in the production code. If you must create a monster test, it should be added as a new test and not be a replacement for existing tests. Also, it should reside in a project or folder explicitly titled to hold tests other than unit tests. I call these "integration tests" or "complex tests" and try to keep their number to an acceptable minimum.

7.3.3 *Even more logic*

Logic can be found not only in tests but also in test helper methods, handwritten fakes, and test utility classes. Remember, every piece of logic you add in these places makes the code that much harder to read and increases the chances of a bug in a utility method that your tests use.

If you find that you need to have complicated logic in your test suite for some reason (though that's generally something I do with integration tests, not unit tests), at least make sure you have a couple of tests against the logic of your utility methods in the test project. This will save you many tears down the road.

7.4 *Smelling a false sense of trust in passing tests*

We've now covered failed tests as a means of detecting tests we shouldn't trust. What about all those quiet, green tests we have lying all over the place? Should we trust them? What about a test that we need to do a code review for, before it's pushed into a main branch? What should we look for?

Let's use the term "false-trust" to describe trusting a test that you really shouldn't, but you don't know it yet. Being able to review tests and find possible false-trust issues has immense value because, not only can you fix those tests yourself, you're affecting the trust of everyone else who's ever going to read or run those tests. Here are some reasons I reduce my trust in tests, even if they are passing:

- The test contains no asserts.
- I can't understand the test.
- Unit tests are mixed with flaky integration tests.
- The test verifies multiple concerns or exit points.
- The test keeps changing.

7.4.1 Tests that don't assert anything

We all agree that a test that doesn't actually verify that something is true or false is less than helpful, right? Less than helpful because it also costs in maintenance time, refactoring, and reading time, and sometimes unnecessary noise if it needs changing due to API changes in production code.

If you see a test with no asserts, consider that there may be hidden asserts in a function call. This causes a readability problem if the function is not named to explain this. Sometimes people also write a test that exercises a piece of code simply to make sure that the code does not throw an exception. This does have some value, and if that's the test you choose to write, make sure that the name of the test indicates this with a term such as "does not throw." To be even more specific, many test APIs support the ability to specify that something does not throw an exception. This is how you can do this in Jest:

```
expect(() => someFunction()).not.toThrow(error)
```

If you do have such tests, make sure there's a very small number of them. I don't recommend it as a standard, but only for really special cases.

Sometimes people simply forget to write an assert due to lack of experience. Consider adding the missing assert or removing the test if it brings no value. People may also actively write tests to achieve some imagined test coverage goal set by management. Those tests usually serve no real value except to get management off people's backs so they can do real work.

> **TIP** Code coverage shouldn't ever be a goal on its own. It doesn't mean "code quality." In fact, it often causes developers to write meaningless tests that will cost even more time to maintain. Instead, measure "escaped bugs," "time to fix," and other metrics that we'll discuss in chapter 11.

7.4.2 Not understanding the tests

This is a huge issue, and I'll deal with it in depth in chapter 9. There are several possible issues:

- Tests with bad names
- Tests that are too long or have convoluted code
- Tests containing confusing variable names
- Tests containing hidden logic or assumptions that cannot be understood easily
- Test results that are inconclusive (neither failed nor passed)
- Test messages that don't provide enough information

If you don't understand the test that's failing or passing, you don't know if you should be worried or not.

7.4.3   *Mixing unit tests and flaky integration tests*

They say that one rotten apple spoils the bunch. The same is true for flaky tests mixed in with nonflaky tests. Integration tests are much more likely to be flaky than unit tests because they have more dependencies. If you find that you have a mix of integration and unit tests in the same folder or test execution command, you should be suspicious.

Humans like to take the path of least resistance, and it's no different when it comes to coding. Suppose that a developer runs all the tests and one of them fails—if there's a way to blame a missing configuration or a network issue instead of spending time investigating and fixing a real problem, they will. That's *especially* true if they're under serious time pressure or they're overcommitted to delivering things they're already late on.

The easiest thing is to accuse any failing test of being a flaky test. Because flaky and nonflaky tests are mixed up with each other, that's a simple thing to do, and it's a good way to ignore the issue and work on something more fun. Because of this human factor, it's best to remove the option to blame a test for being flaky. What should you do to prevent this? Aim to have a *safe green zone* by keeping your integration and unit tests in separate places.

A safe green test area should contain only nonflaky, fast tests, where developers know that they can get the latest code version, they can run all the tests in that namespace or folder, and the tests should all be green (given no changes to production code). If some tests in the safe green zone don't pass, a developer is much more likely to be concerned.

An added benefit to this separation is that developers are more likely to run the unit tests more often, now that the run time is faster without the integration tests. It's better to have some feedback than no feedback, right? The automated build pipeline should take care of running any of the "missing" feedback tests that developers can't or won't run on their local machines.

7.4.4   *Testing multiple exit points*

An *exit point* (I'll also refer to it as a *concern*) is explained in chapter 1. It's a single end result from a unit of work: a return value, a change to system state, or a call to a third-party object.

Here's a simple example of a function that has two exit points, or two concerns. It both returns a value and triggers a passed-in callback function:

```
const trigger = (x, y, callback) => {
  callback("I'm triggered");
  return x + y;
};
```

We could write a test that checks both of these exit points at the same time.

Listing 7.6 Checking two exit points in the same test

```
describe("trigger", () => {
  it("works", () => {
    const callback = jest.fn();
    const result = trigger(1, 2, callback);
    expect(result).toBe(3);
    expect(callback).toHaveBeenCalledWith("I'm triggered");
  });
});
```

The first reason testing more than one concern in a test can backfire is that your test name suffers. I'll discuss readability in chapter 9, but here's a quick note on naming: naming tests is hugely important for both debugging and documentation purposes. I spend a lot of time thinking about good names for tests, and I'm not ashamed to admit it.

Naming a test may seem like a simple task, but if you're testing more than one thing, giving the test a good name that indicates what's being tested is difficult. Often you end up with a very generic test name that forces the reader to read the test code. When you test just one concern, naming the test is easy. But wait, there's more.

More disturbingly, in most unit test frameworks, a failed assert throws a special type of exception that's caught by the test framework runner. When the test framework catches that exception, it means the test has failed. Most exceptions in most languages, by design, don't let the code continue. So if this line,

```
expect(result).toBe(3);
```

fails the assert, this line will not execute at all:

```
expect(callback).toHaveBeenCalledWith("I'm triggered");
```

The test method exits on the same line where the exception is thrown. Each of these asserts can and should be considered different requirements, and they can also, and in this case likely should, be implemented separately and incrementally, one after the other.

Consider assert failures as symptoms of a disease. The more symptoms you can find, the easier the disease will be to diagnose. After a failure, subsequent asserts aren't executed, and you'll miss seeing other possible symptoms that could provide valuable data (symptoms) that would help you narrow your focus and discover the underlying problem. Checking multiple concerns in a single unit test adds complexity with little value. You should run additional concern checks in separate, self-contained unit tests so that you can see what really fails.

Let's break it up into two separate tests.

Listing 7.7 Checking the two exit points in separate tests

```
describe("trigger", () => {
  it("triggers a given callback", () => {
    const callback = jest.fn();
```

```
    trigger(1, 2, callback);
    expect(callback).toHaveBeenCalledWith("I'm triggered");
  });

  it("sums up given values", () => {
    const result = trigger(1, 2, jest.fn());
    expect(result).toBe(3);
  });
});
```

Now we can clearly separate the concerns, and each one can fail separately.

Sometimes it's perfectly okay to assert multiple things in the same test, as long as they are not multiple concerns. Take the following function and its associated test as an example. makePerson is designed to build a new person object with some properties.

Listing 7.8   Using multiple asserts to verify a single exit point

```
const makePerson = (x, y) => {
  return {
    name: x,
    age: y,
    type: "person",
  };
};

describe("makePerson", () => {
  it("creates person given passed in values", () => {
    const result = makePerson("name", 1);
    expect(result.name).toBe("name");
    expect(result.age).toBe(1);
  });
});
```

In our test, we are asserting on both name and age together, because they are part of the same concern (building the person object). If the first assert fails, we likely don't care about the second assert because something might have gone terribly wrong while building the object in the first place.

> **TIP**   Here's a test break-up hint: If the first assert fails, do you still care what the result of the next assert is? If you do, you should probably separate the test into two tests.

7.4.5   *Tests that keep changing*

If a test is using the current date and time as part of its execution or assertions, then we can claim that every time the test runs, it's a different test. The same can be said of tests that use random numbers, machine names, or anything that depends on grabbing a current value from outside the test's environment. There's a big chance its results won't be consistent, and that means they can be flaky. For us, as developers, flaky tests reduce our trust in the failed results of the test (as I'll discuss in the next section).

Another huge potential issue with dynamically generated values is that if we don't know ahead of time what the input into the system might be, we also have to compute the expected *output* of the system, and that can lead to a buggy test that depends on repeating production logic, as mentioned in section 7.3.

7.5 *Dealing with flaky tests*

I'm not sure who came up with the term *flaky tests*, but it does fit the bill. It's used to describe tests that, given no changes to the code, return inconsistent results. This might happen frequently or very rarely, but it does happen.

Figure 7.1 illustrates where flakiness comes from. The figure is based on the number of real dependencies the tests have. Another way to think about this is how many moving parts the tests have. For this book, we're mostly concerning ourselves with the

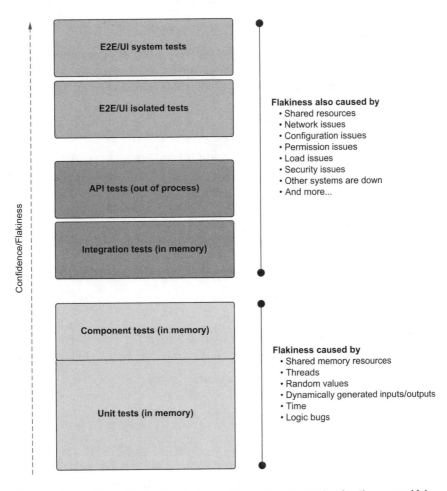

Figure 7.1 **The higher the level of the tests, the more real dependencies they use, which gives us confidence in the overall system correctness but results in more flakiness.**

bottom third of this diagram: unit and component tests. However, I want to touch on the higher-level flakiness so I can give you some pointers on what to research.

At the lowest level, our tests have full control over all of their dependencies and therefore have no moving parts, either because they're faking them or because they run purely in memory and can be configured. We did this in chapters 3 and 4. Execution paths in the code are fully deterministic because all the initial states and expected return values from various dependencies have been predetermined. The code path is almost static—if it returns the wrong expected result, then something important might have changed in the production code's execution path or logic.

As we go up the levels, our tests shed more and more stubs and mocks and start using more and more real dependencies, such as databases, networks, configuration, and more. This, in turn, means more moving parts that we have less control over and that might change our execution path, return unexpected values, or fail to execute at all.

At the highest level, there are no fake dependencies. Everything our tests rely on is real, including any third-party services, security and network layers, and configuration. These types of tests usually require us to set up an environment that is as close to a production scenario as possible, if they're not running right on the production environments.

The higher up we go in the test diagram, we should get higher confidence that our code works, unless we don't trust the tests' results. Unfortunately, the higher up we go in the diagram, the more chances there are for our tests to become flaky because of how many moving parts are involved.

We might assume that tests at the lowest level shouldn't have any flakiness issues because there shouldn't be any moving parts that cause flakiness. That's theoretically true, but in reality people still manage to add moving parts in lower-level tests: using the current date and time, the machine name, the network, the filesystem, and more can cause a test to be flaky.

A test fails sometimes without us touching production code. For example:

- A test fails every third run.
- A test fails once every unknown number of times.
- A test fails when various external conditions fail, such as network or database availability, other APIs not being available, environment configuration, and more.

To add to that salad of pain, each dependency the test uses (network, filesystem, threads, etc.) usually adds time to the test run. Calls to the network and the database take time. The same goes for waiting for threads to finish, reading configurations, and waiting for asynchronous tasks.

It also takes longer to figure out why a test is failing. Debugging a test or reading through huge amounts of logs is heartbreakingly time consuming and will drain your soul slowly into the abyss of "time to update my resume" land.

7.5.1 What can you do once you've found a flaky test?

It's important to realize that flaky tests can be costly to an organization. You should aim to have zero flaky tests as a long-term goal. Here are some ways to reduce the costs associated with handling flaky tests:

- *Define*—Agree on what "flaky" means to your organization. For example, run your test suite 10 times without any production code changes, and count all the tests that were not consistent in their results (i.e., ones that did not fail all 10 times or did not pass all 10 times).
- Place any test deemed flaky in a special category or folder of tests that can be run separately. I recommend removing all flaky tests from the regular delivery build so they do not create noise, and quarantining them in their own little pipeline temporarily. Then, go over each of the flaky tests and play my favorite flaky game, "fix, convert, or kill":
  - *Fix*—Make the test not flaky by controlling its dependencies, if possible. For example, if it requires data in the database, insert the data into the database as part of the test.
  - *Convert*—Remove flakiness by converting the test into a lower-level test by removing and controlling one or more of its dependencies. For example, simulate a network endpoint with a stub instead of using a real one.
  - *Kill*—Seriously consider whether the value the test brings is enough to continue to run it and pay the maintenance costs it creates. Sometimes old flaky tests are better off dead and buried. Sometimes they are already covered by newer, better tests, and the old tests are pure technical debt that we can get rid of. Sadly, many engineering managers are reluctant to remove these old tests because of the sunken cost fallacy—there was so much effort put into them that it would be a waste to delete them. However, at this point, it might cost you more to keep the test than to delete it, so I recommend seriously considering this option for many of your flaky tests.

7.5.2 Preventing flakiness in higher-level tests

If you're interested in preventing flakiness in higher-level tests, your best bet is to make sure that your tests are repeatable on any environment after any deployment. That could involve the following:

- Roll back any changes your tests have made to external shared resources.
- Do not depend on other tests changing external state.
- Gain some control over external systems and dependencies by ensuring you have the ability to recreate them at will (do an internet search on "infrastructure as code"), creating dummies of them that you can control, or creating special test accounts on them and pray that they stay safe.

On this last point, controlling external dependencies can be difficult or impossible when using external systems managed by other companies. When that's true, it's worth considering these options:

- Remove some of the higher-level tests if some low-level tests already cover those scenarios.
- Convert some of the higher-level tests to a set of lower-level tests.
- If you're writing new tests, consider a pipeline-friendly testing strategy with test recipes (such as the one I'll explain in chapter 10).

Summary

- If you don't trust a test when it's failing, you might ignore a real bug, and if you don't trust a test when it's passing, you'll end up doing lots of manual debugging and testing. Both of these outcomes are supposed to be reduced by having good tests, but if we don't reduce them, *and* we spend all this time writing tests that we don't trust, what's the point in writing them in the first place?
- Tests might fail for multiple reasons: a real bug found in production code, a bug in the test resulting in a false failure, a test being out of date due to a change in functionality, a test conflicting with another test, or test flakiness. Only the first reason is a valid one. All the others tell us the test shouldn't be trusted.
- Avoid complexity in tests, such as creating dynamic expected values or duplicating logic from the underlying production code. Such complexity increases the chances of introducing bugs in tests and the time it takes to understand them.
- If a test doesn't have any asserts, you can't understand what's it's doing, it runs alongside flaky tests (even if this test itself isn't flaky), it verifies multiple exit points, or it keeps changing, it can't be fully trusted.
- Flaky tests are tests that fail unpredictably. The higher the level of the test, the more real dependencies it uses, which gives us confidence in the overall system's correctness but results in more flakiness. To better identify flaky tests, put them in a special category or folder that can be run separately.
- To reduce test flakiness, either fix the tests, convert flaky higher-level tests into less flaky lower-level ones, or delete them.

Maintainability

8

This chapter covers

- Root causes of failing tests
- Common avoidable changes to test code
- Improving the maintainability of tests that aren't currently failing

Tests can enable us to develop faster, unless they make us go slower due to all the changes needed. If we can avoid changing existing tests when we change production code, we can start to hope that our tests are helping rather than hurting our bottom line. In this chapter, we'll focus on the maintainability of tests.

Unmaintainable tests can ruin project schedules and are often set aside when the project is put on a more aggressive schedule. Developers will simply stop maintaining and fixing tests that take too long to change or that need to change often as the result of very minor production code changes.

If maintainability is a measure of how often we are forced to change tests, we'd like to minimize the number of times that happens. This forces us to ask these questions if we ever want to get down to the root causes:

- When do we notice that a test fails and therefore might require a change?
- Why do tests fail?

- Which test failures force us to change the test?
- When do we choose to change a test even if we are not forced to?

This chapter presents a series of practices related to maintainability that you can use when doing test reviews.

8.1   *Changes forced by failing tests*

A failing test is usually the first sign of potential trouble for maintainability. Of course, we could have found a real bug in production code, but when that's not the case, what other reasons do tests have to fail? I'll refer to genuine failures as *true failures*, and failures that happen for reasons other than finding a bug in the underlying production code as *false failures*.

If we wanted to measure test maintainability, we could start by measuring the number of false test failures, and the reason for each failure, over time. We already discussed one such reason in chapter 7: when a test contains a bug. Let's now discuss other possible reasons for false failures.

8.1.1   *The test is not relevant or conflicts with another test*

A conflict may arise when the production code introduces a new feature that's in direct conflict with one or more existing tests. Instead of the test discovering a bug, it may discover conflicting or new requirements. There might also be a passing test that targets the new expectation for how the production code should work.

Either the existing failing test is no longer relevant, or the new requirement is wrong. Assuming that the requirement is correct, you can probably go ahead and delete the no-longer-relevant test.

Note that there's a common exception to the "remove the test" rule: when you're working with *feature toggles*. We'll touch on feature toggles in chapter 10 when we discuss testing strategies.

8.1.2   *Changes in the production code's API*

A test can fail if the production code under test changes so that a function or object being tested now needs to be used differently, even though it may still have the same functionality. Such false failures fall in the bucket of "let's avoid this as much as possible."

Consider the `PasswordVerifier` class in listing 8.1, which requires two constructor parameters:

- An array of `rules` (each is a function that takes an input and returns a Boolean)
- An `ILogger` interface

Listing 8.1   A Password Verifier with two constructor parameters

```
export class PasswordVerifier {
    ...
    constructor(rules: ((input) => boolean)[], logger: ILogger) {
        this._rules = rules;
```

```
        this._logger = logger;
    }

    ...

}
```

We could write a couple of tests like the following.

Listing 8.2   Tests without factory functions

```
describe("password verifier 1", () => {
  it("passes with zero rules", () => {
    const verifier = new PasswordVerifier([], { info: jest.fn() });   ◁──┐
    const result = verifier.verify("any input");
    expect(result).toBe(true);
  });
                                                      Test using
                                                      the code's
  it("fails with single failing rule", () => {        existing API
    const failingRule = (input) => false;
    const verifier =
      new PasswordVerifier([failingRule], { info: jest.fn() });   ◁──┘
    const result = verifier.verify("any input");
    expect(result).toBe(false);
  });
});
```

If we look at these tests from a maintainability point of view, there are several potential changes we will likely need to make in the future.

CODE USUALLY LIVES FOR A LONG TIME

Consider that the code you're writing will live in the codebase for at least 4–6 years and sometimes a decade. Over that time, what is the likelihood that the design of `PasswordVerifier` will change? Even simple things, like the constructor accepting more parameters, or the parameter types changing, become more likely over a longer timeframe.

Let's list a few changes that could happen to our Password Verifier in the future:

- We may add or remove a parameter in the constructor for `PasswordVerifier`.
- One of the parameters for `PasswordVerifier` may change to a different type.
- The number of `ILogger` functions or their signatures may change over time.
- The usage pattern changes so we don't need to instantiate a new `Password-Verifier`, but just use the functions in it directly.

If any of these things happen, how many tests would we need to change? Right now we'd need to change all the tests that instantiate `PasswordVerifier`. Could we prevent the need for some of these changes?

Let's pretend the future is here and our fears have come true—someone changed the production code's API. Let's say the constructor signature has changed to use `IComplicatedLogger` instead of `ILogger`, as follows.

Listing 8.3   A breaking change in a constructor

```
export class PasswordVerifier2 {
  private _rules: ((input: string) => boolean)[];
  private _logger: IComplicatedLogger;

  constructor(rules: ((input) => boolean)[],
      logger: IComplicatedLogger) {
    this._rules = rules;
    this._logger = logger;
  }
...
}
```

As it stands, we would have to change any test that directly instantiates `PasswordVerifier`.

FACTORY FUNCTIONS DECOUPLE CREATION OF OBJECT UNDER TEST

A simple way to avoid this pain in the future is to decouple or abstract away the creation of the code under test so that the changes to the constructor only need to be dealt with in a centralized location. A function whose sole purpose is to create and preconfigure an instance of an object is usually called a *factory* function or method. A more advanced version of this (which we won't cover here) is the Object Mother pattern.

Factory functions can help us mitigate this issue. The next two listings show how we could have initially written the tests before the signature change, and how we could easily adapt to the signature change in that case. In listing 8.4, the creation of `Password-Verifier` has been extracted into its own centralized factory function. I've done the same for the `fakeLogger`—it's now also created using its own separate factory function. If any of the changes we listed before happens in the future, we'll only need to change our factory functions; the tests will usually not need to be touched.

Listing 8.4   Refactoring to factory functions

```
describe("password verifier 1", () => {
  const makeFakeLogger = () => {            A centralized point for
    return { info: jest.fn() };             creating a fakeLogger
  };

  const makePasswordVerifier = (
    rules: ((input) => boolean)[],          A centralized point
    fakeLogger: ILogger = makeFakeLogger()) => {    for creating a
      return new PasswordVerifier(rules, fakeLogger);   PasswordVerifier
  };

  it("passes with zero rules", () => {
    const verifier = makePasswordVerifier([]);    Using the factory
                                                  function to create
    const result = verifier.verify("any input");  PasswordVerifier

    expect(result).toBe(true);
  });
```

In the following listing, I've refactored the tests based on the signature change. Notice that the change doesn't involve changing the tests, but only the factory functions. That's the type of manageable change I can live with in a real project.

Listing 8.5 Refactoring factory methods to fit a new signature

```
describe("password verifier (ctor change)", () => {
  const makeFakeLogger = () => {
    return Substitute.for<IComplicatedLogger>();
  };

  const makePasswordVerifier = (
    rules: ((input) => boolean)[],
    fakeLogger: IComplicatedLogger = makeFakeLogger()) => {
    return new PasswordVerifier2(rules, fakeLogger);
  };

  // the tests remain the same
});
```

8.1.3 Changes in other tests

A lack of test isolation is a huge cause of test blockage—I've seen this while consulting and working on unit tests. The basic concept you should keep in mind is that a test should always run in its own little world, isolated from other tests even if they verify the same functionality.

The test that cried "fail"

One project I was involved in had unit tests behaving strangely, and they got even stranger as time went on. A test would fail and then suddenly pass for a couple of days straight. A day later, it would fail, seemingly randomly, and other times it would pass even if code was changed to remove or change its behavior. It got to the point where developers would tell each other, "Ah, it's OK. If it sometimes passes, that means it passes."

Properly investigated, it turned out that the test was calling out a different (and flaky) test as part of its code, and when the other test failed, it would break the first test.

It took us three days to untangle the mess, after spending a month trying various workarounds for the situation. When we finally had the test working correctly, we discovered that we had a bunch of real bugs in our code that we were ignoring because the test had its own bugs and issues. The story of the boy who cried wolf holds true even in development.

When tests aren't isolated well, they can step on each other's toes, making you regret deciding to try unit testing and promising yourself never again. I've seen this happen. Developers don't bother looking for problems in the tests, so when there's a problem, it can take a lot of time to find out what's wrong. The easiest symptom is what I call "constrained test order."

CONSTRAINED TEST ORDER

A *constrained test order* happens when a test assumes that a previous test executed first, or did not execute first, because it relies on some shared state that is set up or reset by the other test. For example, if one test changes a shared variable in memory or some external resource like a database, and another test depends on that variable's value after the first tests' execution, we have a dependency between the tests based on order.

Couple that with the fact that most test runners don't (and won't, and maybe shouldn't!) guarantee that tests will run in a specific order. This means that if you ran all your tests today, and all your tests a week later with a new version of the test runner, the tests might not run in the same order as before.

To illustrate the problem, let's look at a simple scenario. Figure 8.1 shows a `Special-App` object that uses a `UserCache` object. The user cache holds a single instance (a singleton) that is shared as a caching mechanism for the application, and, incidentally, also for the tests. Listing 8.6 shows the implementation of `SpecialApp`, the user cache, and the `IUserDetails` interface.

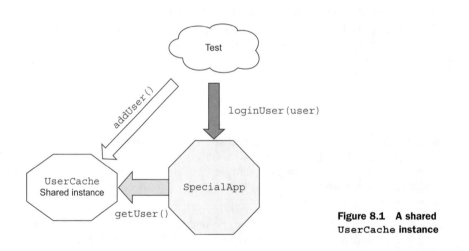

Figure 8.1   A shared `UserCache` instance

Listing 8.6   A shared user cache and associated interfaces

```
export interface IUserDetails {
  key: string;
  password: string;
}

export interface IUserCache {
  addUser(user: IUserDetails): void;
  getUser(key: string);
  reset(): void;
}
```

```
export class UserCache implements IUserCache {
  users: object = {};
  addUser(user: IUserDetails): void {
    if (this.users[user.key] !== undefined) {
      throw new Error("user already exists");
    }
    this.users[user.key] = user;
  }

  getUser(key: string) {
    return this.users[key];
  }

  reset(): void {
    this.users = {};
  }
}

let _cache: IUserCache;
export function getUserCache() {
  if (_cache === undefined) {
    _cache = new UserCache();
  }
  return _cache;
}
```

The following listing shows the `SpecialApp` implementation.

Listing 8.7 The `SpecialApp` implementation

```
export class SpecialApp {
  loginUser(key: string, pass: string): boolean {
    const cache: IUserCache = getUserCache();
    const foundUser: IUserDetails = cache.getUser(key);
    if (foundUser?.password === pass) {
      return true;
    }
    return false;
  }
}
```

This is a simplistic implementation for this example, so don't worry about `SpecialApp` too much. Let's look at the tests.

Listing 8.8 Tests that need to run in a specific order

```
describe("Test Dependence", () => {
  describe("loginUser with loggedInUser", () => {
    test("no user, login fails", () => {
      const app = new SpecialApp();
      const result = app.loginUser("a", "abc");    │ Requires the user
      expect(result).toBe(false);                  │ cache to be empty
    });
```

```
test("can only cache each user once", () => {
  getUserCache().addUser({
    key: "a",                              ◁———  Adds a user
    password: "abc",                              to the cache
  });

  expect(() =>
    getUserCache().addUser({
      key: "a",
      password: "abc",
    })
  ).toThrowError("already exists");
});

test("user exists, login succeeds", () => {
  const app = new SpecialApp();
  const result = app.loginUser("a", "abc");    │ Requires the cache
  expect(result).toBe(true);                   │ to contain the user
});
  });
});
```

Notice that the first and third tests both rely on the second test. The first test requires
that the second test has not executed yet, because it needs the user cache to be empty.
On the other hand, the third test relies on the second test to fill up the cache with the
expected user. If we run only the third test using Jest's `test.only` keyword, the test
would fail:

```
test.only("user exists, login succeeds", () => {
  const app = new SpecialApp();
  const result = app.loginUser("a", "abc");
  expect(result).toBe(true);
});
```

This antipattern usually happens when we try to reuse parts of tests without extracting
helper functions. We end up expecting a different test to run first, saving us from
doing some of the setup. This works, until it doesn't.

We can refactor this in a few steps:

- Extract a helper function for adding a user.
- Reuse this function for multiple tests.
- Reset the user cache between tests.

The following listing shows how we could refactor the tests to avoid this problem.

Listing 8.9 **Refactoring tests to remove order dependence**

```
const addDefaultUser = () =>          ◁———  Extracted user-
  getUserCache().addUser({                  creation helper
    key: "a",                               function
    password: "abc",
  });                                                    │ Extracted factory
const makeSpecialApp = () => new SpecialApp();    ◁——————│ function
```

```
describe("Test Dependence v2", () => {
  beforeEach(() => getUserCache().reset());
  describe("user cache", () => {
    test("can only add cache use once", () => {
      addDefaultUser();

      expect(() => addDefaultUser())
        .toThrowError("already exists");
    });
  });

  describe("loginUser with loggedInUser", () => {
    test("user exists, login succeeds", () => {
      addDefaultUser();
      const app = makeSpecialApp();

      const result = app.loginUser("a", "abc");
      expect(result).toBe(true);
    });

    test("user missing, login fails", () => {
      const app = makeSpecialApp();

      const result = app.loginUser("a", "abc");
      expect(result).toBe(false);
    });
  });
});
```

Resets user cache between tests

New nested describe functions

Calls reusable helper functions

There are several things going on here. First, we extracted two helper functions: a `makeSpecialApp` factory function and an `addDefaultUser` helper function that we can reuse. Next, we created a very important `beforeEach` function that resets the user cache before each test. Whenever I have a shared resource like that, I almost always have a `beforeEach` or `afterEach` function that resets it to its original condition before or after the test runs.

The first and the third tests now run in their own little nested `describe` structure. They also both use the `makeSpecialApp` factory function, and one of them is using `addDefaultUser` to make sure it does not require any other test to run first. The second test also runs in its own nested `describe` function and reuses the `addDefaultUser` function.

8.2   Refactoring to increase maintainability

Up until now, I've discussed test failures that force us to make changes. Let's now discuss changes that we *choose* to make, to make tests easier to maintain over time.

8.2.1   Avoid testing private or protected methods

This section applies more to object-oriented languages as well as TypeScript. Private or protected methods are usually private for a good reason in the developer's mind. Sometimes it's to hide implementation details, so that the implementation can change later without changing the observable behavior. It could also be for security-related or IP-related reasons (obfuscation, for example).

When you test a private method, you're testing against a contract internal to the system. Internal contracts are dynamic, and they can change when you refactor the system. When they change, your test could fail because some internal work is being done differently, even though the overall functionality of the system remains the same. For testing purposes, the public contract (the observable behavior) is all you need to care about. Testing the functionality of private methods may lead to breaking tests, even though the observable behavior is correct.

Think of it this way: no private method exists in a vacuum. Somewhere down the line, something has to call it, or it will never get triggered. Usually there's a public method that ends up invoking this private one, and if not, there's always a public method up the chain of calls that gets invoked. This means that any private method is always part of a bigger unit of work, or use case in the system, that starts out with a public API and ends with one of the three end results: return value, state change, or third-party call (or all three).

So if you see a private method, find the public use case in the system that will exercise it. If you test only the private method and it works, that doesn't mean that the rest of the system is using this private method correctly or handles the results it provides correctly. You might have a system that works perfectly on the inside, but all that nice inside stuff is used incorrectly from the public APIs.

Sometimes, if a private method is worth testing, it might be worth making it public, static, or at least internal, and defining a public contract against any code that uses it. In some cases, the design may be cleaner if you put the method in a different class altogether. We'll look at those approaches in a moment.

Does this mean there should eventually be no private methods in the codebase? No. With test-driven design, you usually write tests against methods that are public, and those public methods are later refactored into calling smaller, private methods. All the while, the tests against the public methods continue to pass.

MAKING METHODS PUBLIC

Making a method public isn't necessarily a bad thing. In a more functional world, it's not even an issue. This practice may seem to go against the object-oriented principles many of us were raised on, but that's not always the case.

Consider that wanting to test a method could mean that the method has a known behavior or contract against the calling code. By making it public, you're making this official. By keeping the method private, you tell all the developers who come after you that they can change the implementation of the method without worrying about unknown code that uses it.

EXTRACTING METHODS TO NEW CLASSES OR MODULES

If your method contains a lot of logic that can stand on its own, or it uses specialized state variables in the class or module that are relevant only to the method in question, it may be a good idea to extract the method into a new class or its own module with a specific role in the system. You can then test that class separately. Michael Feathers' *Working Effectively with Legacy Code* (Pearson, 2004) has some good examples of this technique, and *Clean Code* by Robert Martin (Pearson, 2008) can help you figure out when this is a good idea.

MAKING STATELESS PRIVATE METHODS PUBLIC AND STATIC

If your method is completely stateless, some people choose to refactor the method by making it static (in languages that support this feature). That makes it much more testable but also states that the method is a sort of utility method that has a known public contract specified by its name.

8.2.2   Keep tests DRY

Duplication in your unit tests can hurt you, as a developer, just as much as, if not more than, duplication in production code. That's because any change in a piece of code that has duplicates will force you to change all the duplicates as well. When you're dealing with tests, there's more risk of the developer just avoiding this trouble and deleting or ignoring tests instead of fixing them.

The DRY (don't repeat yourself) principle should be in effect in test code just as in production code. Duplicated code means there's more code to change when one aspect you test against changes. Changing a constructor or changing the semantics of using a class can have a major effect on tests that have a lot of duplicated code.

As we've seen in previous examples in this chapter, using helper functions can help to reduce duplication in tests.

> **WARNING**   Removing duplication can also go too far and hurt readability. We'll talk about that in the next chapter, on readability.

8.2.3   Avoid setup methods

I'm not a fan of the `beforeEach` function (also called a *setup* function) that happens once before each test and is often used to remove duplication. I much prefer using helper functions. Setup functions are too easy to abuse. Developers tend to use them for things they weren't meant for, and tests become less readable and less maintainable as a result.

Many developers abuse setup methods in several ways:

- Initializing objects in the setup method that are used in only some tests in the file
- Having setup code that's lengthy and hard to understand
- Setting up mocks and fake objects within the setup method

Also, setup methods have limitations, which you can get around by using simple helper methods:

- Setup methods can only help when you need to initialize things.
- Setup methods aren't always the best candidates for duplication removal. Removing duplication isn't always about creating and initializing new instances

of objects. Sometimes it's about removing duplication in assertion logic or calling out code in a specific way.

- Setup methods can't have parameters or return values.
- Setup methods can't be used as factory methods that return values. They're run before the test executes, so they must be more generic in the way they work. Tests sometimes need to request specific things or call shared code with a parameter for the specific test (for example, retrieving an object and setting its property to a specific value).
- Setup methods should only contain code that applies to all the tests in the current test class, or the method will be harder to read and understand.

I've almost entirely stopped using setup methods for the tests I write. Test code should be nice and clean, just like production code, but if your production code looks horrible, please don't use that as a crutch to write unreadable tests. Use factory and helper methods, and make the world a better place for the generation of developers that will have to maintain your code in 5 or 10 years.

> **NOTE**   We looked at an example of moving from using `beforeEach` to helper functions in section 8.2.3 (listing 8.9) and also in chapter 2.

8.2.4   *Use parameterized tests to remove duplication*

Another great option for replacing setup methods, if all your tests look the same, is to use parameterized tests. Different test frameworks in different languages support parameterized tests—if you're using Jest, you can use the built-in `test.each` or `it.each` functions.

Parameterization helps move the setup logic that would otherwise remain duplicated or would reside in the `beforeEach` block to the test's arrange section. It also helps avoid duplication of the assertion logic, as shown in the following listing.

Listing 8.10   Parameterized tests with Jest

```
const sum = numbers => {
    if (numbers.length > 0) {
        return parseInt(numbers);
    }
    return 0;
};

describe('sum with regular tests', () => {
    test('sum number 1', () => {
        const result = sum('1');
        expect(result).toBe(1);
    });
    test('sum number 2', () => {
        const result = sum('2');
        expect(result).toBe(2);
    });
});
```

Duplicated setup and assertion logic

```
                    describe('sum with parameterized tests', () => {
                        test.each([
                            ['1', 1],
                            ['2', 2]
                        ])('add ,for %s, returns that number', (input, expected) => {
                            const result = sum(input);
                            expect(result).toBe(expected);
                        }
                    )
                });
```

Test data used for setup and assertion (annotation pointing to the test.each array)

Setup and assertion without duplication (annotation pointing to the sum/expect lines)

In the first `describe` block, we have two tests that repeat each other with different input values and expected outputs. In the second `describe` block, we're using `test.each` to provide an array of arrays, where each subarray lists all the values needed for the test function.

Parameterized tests can help reduce a lot of duplication between tests, but we should be careful to only use this technique in cases where we repeat the exact same scenario and only change the input and output.

8.3 Avoid overspecification

An overspecified test is one that contains assumptions about how a specific unit under test (production code) should implement its internal behavior, instead of only checking that the observable behavior (exit points) is correct.

Here are ways unit tests are often overspecified:

- A test asserts purely internal state in an object under test.
- A test uses multiple mocks.
- A test uses stubs as mocks.
- A test assumes a specific order or exact string matches when that isn't required.

Let's look at some examples of overspecified tests.

8.3.1 Internal behavior overspecification with mocks

A very common antipattern is to verify that an internal function in a class or module is called, instead of checking the exit point of the unit of work. Here's a password verifier that calls an internal function, which the test shouldn't care about.

Listing 8.11 Production code that calls a protected function

```
export class PasswordVerifier4 {
    private _rules: ((input: string) => boolean)[];
    private _logger: IComplicatedLogger;

    constructor(rules: ((input) => boolean)[],
        logger: IComplicatedLogger) {
        this._rules = rules;
        this._logger = logger;
    }
```

```
verify(input: string): boolean {
  const failed = this.findFailedRules(input);        ◁──┐ Call to the
                                                          internal
  if (failed.length === 0) {                              function
    this._logger.info("PASSED");
    return true;
  }
  this._logger.info("FAIL");
  return false;
}

protected findFailedRules(input: string) {           ◁──┐ Internal
  const failed = this._rules                              function
    .map((rule) => rule(input))
    .filter((result) => result === false);
  return failed;
}
}
```

Notice that we're calling the protected findFailedRules function to get a result from it, and then doing a calculation on the result.

Here's our test.

Listing 8.12   An overspecified test verifying a call to a protected function

```
describe("verifier 4", () => {
  describe("overspecify protected function call", () => {
    test("checkfailedFules is called", () => {
      const pv4 = new PasswordVerifier4(
        [], Substitute.for<IComplicatedLogger>()
      );
      const failedMock = jest.fn(() => []);          │ Mocking the
      pv4["findFailedRules"] = failedMock;           │ internal function

      pv4.verify("abc");

      expect(failedMock).toHaveBeenCalled();    ◁──┐ Verifying the
    });                                              internal function
  });                                                call. Don't do this.
});
```

The antipattern here is that we're proving something that isn't an exit point. We're checking that the code calls some internal function, but what does that really prove? We're not checking that the calculation was correct on the result; we're simply testing for the sake of testing.

If the function is returning a value, usually that's a strong indication that we shouldn't mock that function because the function call itself does not represent the exit point. The exit point is the value returned from the verify() function. We shouldn't care whether the internal function even exists.

By verifying against a mock of a protected function that is not an exit point, we are coupling our test implementation to the internal implementation of the code under test, for no real benefit. When the internal calls change (and they will) we will also have to change all the tests associated with these calls, and that will not be a positive experience. You can read more about mocks and their relation to test fragility in chapter 5 of *Unit Testing Principles, Practices, and Patterns* by Vladimir Khorikov (Manning, 2020).

WHAT SHOULD WE DO INSTEAD?

Look for the exit point. The real exit point depends on the type of test we wish to perform:

- *Value-based test*—For a value-based test, which I would highly recommend you lean toward when possible, we look for a return value from the called function. In this case, the `verify` function returns a value, so it's the perfect candidate for a value-based test: `pv4.verify("abc")`.
- *State-based test*—For a state-based test, we look for a sibling function (a function that exists at the same level of scope as the entry point) or a sibling property that is affected by calling the `verify()` function. For example, `firstname()` and `lastname()` could be considered sibling functions. That is where we should be asserting. In this codebase, nothing is affected by calling `verify()` that is visible at the same level, so it is not a good candidate for state-based testing.
- *Third-party test*—For a third-party test, we would have to use a mock, and that would require us to find out where the fire-and-forget location is inside the code. The `findFailedRules` function isn't that, because it is actually delivering information back to our `verify()` function. In this case, there's no real third-party dependency that we have to take over.

8.3.2   *Exact outputs and ordering overspecification*

A common antipattern is when a test overspecifies the order and the structure of a collection of returned values. It's often easier to specify the whole collection, along with each of its items, in the assertion, but with this approach, we implicitly take on the burden of fixing the test when any little detail of the collection changes. Instead of using a single huge assertion, we should separate different aspects of the verification into smaller, explicit asserts.

The following listing shows a `verify()` function that takes on multiple inputs and returns a list of result objects.

Listing 8.13   A verifier that returns a list of outputs

```
interface IResult {
  result: boolean;
  input: string;
}

export class PasswordVerifier5 {
  private _rules: ((input: string) => boolean)[];
```

```
  constructor(rules: ((input) => boolean)[]) {
    this._rules = rules;
  }

  verify(inputs: string[]): IResult[] {
    const failedResults =
      inputs.map((input) => this.checkSingleInput(input));
    return failedResults;
  }

  private checkSingleInput(input: string): IResult {
    const failed = this.findFailedRules(input);
    return {
      input,
      result: failed.length === 0,
    };
  }
}
```

This `verify()` function returns an array of `IResult` objects with an `input` and `result` in each. The following listing shows a test that makes an implicit check on both the ordering of the results and the structure of each result, as well as checking the value of the results.

Listing 8.14   Overspecifying order and schema of the result

```
test("overspecify order and schema", () => {
  const pv5 =
    new PasswordVerifier5([input => input.includes("abc")]);

  const results = pv5.verify(["a", "ab", "abc", "abcd"]);

  expect(results).toEqual([
    { input: "a", result: false },        ┐
    { input: "ab", result: false },       │  A single
    { input: "abc", result: true },       │  huge assert
    { input: "abcd", result: true },      ┘
  ]);
});
```

How might this test change in the future? Here are quite a few reasons for it to change:

- When the length of the `results` array changes
- When each `result` object gains or removes a property (even if the test doesn't care about those properties)
- When the order of the results changes (even if it might not be important for the current test)

If any of these changes happens in the future, but your test is just focused on checking the logic of the verifier and the structure of its output, there's going to be a lot of pain involved in maintaining this test.

We can reduce some of that pain by verifying only the parts that matter to us.

Listing 8.15   Ignoring the schema of the results

```
test("overspecify order but ignore schema", () => {
  const pv5 =
    new PasswordVerifier5([(input) => input.includes("abc")]);

  const results = pv5.verify(["a", "ab", "abc", "abcd"]);

  expect(results.length).toBe(4);
  expect(results[0].result).toBe(false);
  expect(results[1].result).toBe(false);
  expect(results[2].result).toBe(true);
  expect(results[3].result).toBe(true);
});
```

Instead of providing the full expected output, we can simply assert on the values of specific properties in the output. However, we're still stuck if the order of the results changes. If we don't care about the order, we can simply check if the output contains a specific result, as follows.

Listing 8.16   Ignoring order and schema

```
test("ignore order and schema", () => {
  const pv5 =
    new PasswordVerifier5([(input) => input.includes("abc")]);

  const results = pv5.verify(["a", "ab", "abc", "abcd"]);

  expect(results.length).toBe(4);
  expect(findResultFor("a")).toBe(false);
  expect(findResultFor("ab")).toBe(false);
  expect(findResultFor("abc")).toBe(true);
  expect(findResultFor("abcd")).toBe(true);
});
```

Here we are using `findResultFor()` to find the specific result for a given input. Now the order of the results can change, or extra values can be added, but our test will only fail if the calculation of the true or false results changes.

Another common antipattern people tend to repeat is to assert against hardcoded strings in the unit's return value or properties, when only a specific part of a string is necessary. Ask yourself, "Can I check if a string *contains* something rather than *equals* something?" Here's a password verifier that gives us a message describing how many rules were broken during a verification.

Listing 8.17   A verifier that returns a string message

```
export class PasswordVerifier6 {
  private _rules: ((input: string) => boolean)[];
  private _msg: string = "";
```

```
constructor(rules: ((input) => boolean)[]) {
  this._rules = rules;
}

getMsg(): string {
  return this._msg;
}

verify(inputs: string[]): IResult[] {
  const allResults =
    inputs.map((input) => this.checkSingleInput(input));
  this.setDescription(allResults);
  return allResults;
}

private setDescription(results: IResult[]) {
  const failed = results.filter((res) => !res.result);
  this._msg = `you have ${failed.length} failed rules.`;
}
```

The following listing shows two tests that use getMsg().

Listing 8.18   Overspecifying a string using equality

```
describe("verifier 6", () => {
  test("over specify string", () => {
    const pv5 =
      new PasswordVerifier6([(input) => input.includes("abc")]);

    pv5.verify(["a", "ab", "abc", "abcd"]);

    const msg = pv5.getMsg();
    expect(msg).toBe("you have 2 failed rules.");      ◁—┤ Overly specific
  });                                                        string expectation

  //Here's a better way to write this test
  test("more future proof string checking", () => {
    const pv5 =
      new PasswordVerifier6([(input) => input.includes("abc")]);

    pv5.verify(["a", "ab", "abc", "abcd"]);

    const msg = pv5.getMsg();
    expect(msg).toMatch(/2 failed/);      ◁—┤ A better way to assert
  });                                           against a string
});
```

The first test checks that the string exactly equals another string. This backfires often, because strings are a form of user interface. We tend to change them slightly and embellish them over time. For example, do we care that there is a period at the end of the string? Our test requires us to care, but the meat of the assert is the correct number being shown (especially since strings change in different computer languages or cultures, but numbers usually stay the same).

The second test simply looks for the "2 failed" string inside the message. This makes the test more future-proof: the string might change slightly, but the core message remains without forcing us to change the test.

Summary

- Tests grow and change with the system under test. If we don't pay attention to maintainability, our tests may require so many changes from us that it might not be worth changing them. We may instead end up deleting them, and throwing away all the hard work that went into creating them. For tests to be useful in the long run, they should fail only for reasons we truly care about.

- A *true failure* is when a test fails because it finds a bug in production code. A *false failure* is when a test fails for any other reason.

- To estimate test maintainability, we can measure the number of false test failures and the reason for each failure, over time.

- A test may falsely fail for multiple reasons: it conflicts with another test (in which case, you should just remove it); changes in the production code's API (this can be mitigated by using factory and helper methods); changes in other tests (such tests should be decoupled from each other).

- Avoid testing private methods. Private methods are implementation details, and the resulting tests are going to be fragile. Tests should verify *observable behavior*— behavior that is relevant for the end user. Sometimes, the need to test a private method is a sign of a missing abstraction, which means the method should be made public or even be extracted into a separate class.

- Keep tests DRY. Use helper methods to abstract nonessential details of arrange and assert sections. This will simplify your tests without coupling them to each other.

- Avoid setup methods such as the `beforeEach` function. Once again, use helper methods instead. Another option is to parameterize your tests and therefore move the content of the `beforeEach` block to the test's arrange section.

- Avoid overspecification. Examples of overspecification are asserting the private state of the code under test, asserting against calls on stubs, or assuming the specific order of elements in a result collection or exact string matches when that isn't required.

Part 4

Design and process

These final chapters cover the problems you'll face and the techniques you'll need when introducing unit testing to an existing organization or codebase.

In chapter 9, we'll talk about test readability. We'll discuss naming conventions for tests and input values for them. We'll also cover best practices for test structuring and writing better assertion messages.

Chapter 10 explains how to develop a testing strategy. We'll look at which test levels you should prefer when testing a new feature, discuss common antipatterns in test levels, and talk about the test recipe strategy.

In chapter 11, we'll deal with the tough issue of implementing unit testing in an organization, and we'll cover techniques that can make your job easier. This chapter provides answers to some tough questions that are common when first implementing unit testing.

In chapter 12, we'll look at common problems associated with legacy code and examine some tools for working with it.

Readability

This chapter covers
- Naming conventions for unit tests
- Writing readable tests

Without readability, the tests you write are almost meaningless to whoever reads them later on. Readability is the connecting thread between the person who wrote the test and the poor soul who must read it a few months or years later. Tests are stories you tell the next generation of programmers on a project. They allow a developer to see exactly what an application is made of and where it started.

This chapter is all about making sure the developers who come after you will be able to maintain the production code and the tests that you write. They'll need to understand what they're doing and where they should be doing it.

There are several facets to readability:

- Naming unit tests
- Naming variables
- Separating asserts from actions
- Setting up and tearing down

Let's go through these one by one.

9.1   *Naming unit tests*

Naming standards are important because they give you comfortable rules and templates that outline what you should explain about the test. No matter how I order them, or what specific framework or language I am using, I try to make sure these three important pieces of information are present in the name of the test or in the structure of the file in which the test exists:

- The entry point to the unit of work (or the name of the feature being tested)
- The scenario under which you're testing the entry point
- The expected behavior of the exit point of the unit of work

The name of the entry point (or unit of work) is essential, so that you can easily understand the starting scope of the logic being tested. Having this as the first part of the test name also allows for easy navigation and as-you-type completion (if your IDE supports it) in the test file.

The scenario under which it's being tested gives you the "with" part of the name: "When I call entry point X *with* a null value, then it should do Y."

The expected behavior from the exit point of the unit of work is where the test specifies in plain English what the unit of work should do or return, or how it should behave, based on the current scenario: "When I call entry point X with a null value, then *it should* do Y as visible from this exit point of the unit of work."

These three elements have to exist somewhere close to the eyes of the person reading the test. Sometimes they can all be encapsulated in the test's function name, and sometimes you can include them with nested `describe` structures. Sometimes you can simply use a string description as a parameter or annotation for the test.

Some examples are shown in the following listing, all with the same pieces of information, but laid out differently.

> **Listing 9.1   Same information, different variations**

```
test('verifyPassword, with a failing rule, returns error based on
    rule.reason', () => { … }

describe('verifyPassword', () => {
  describe('with a failing rule', () => {
    it('returns error based on the rule.reason', () => { … }

verifyPassword_withFailingRule_returnsErrorBasedonRuleReason()
```

You can, of course, come up with other ways to structure this. (Who says you have to use underscores? That's just my own preference for reminding me and others that there are three pieces of information.). The key point to take away is that if you remove one of these pieces of information, you're forcing the person reading the test to read the code inside the test to find out the answer, wasting precious time.

The following listing shows examples of tests with missing information.

Listing 9.2 Test names with missing information

What is the thing under test?   **When is this supposed to happen?**

```
test(failing rule, returns error based on rule.reason', () => { ... }

test('verifyPassword, returns error based on rule.reason', () => { ... }

test('verifyPassword, with a failing rule', () => { ... }
```
What's supposed to happen then?

Your main goal with readability is to release the next developer from the burden of reading the test code in order to understand what the test is testing.

Another great reason to include all these pieces of information in the name of the test is that the name is usually the only thing that shows up when an automated build pipeline fails. You'll see the names of the failed tests in the log of the build that failed, but you won't see any comments or the code of the tests. If the names are good enough, you might not need to read the code of the tests or debug them; you may understand the cause of the failure simply by reading the log of the failed build. This can save precious debugging and reading time.

A good test name also serves to contribute to the idea of executable documentation—if you can ask a developer who is new to the team to read the tests so they can understand how a specific component or application works, that's a good sign of readability. If they can't make sense of the application or the component's behavior from the tests alone, it might be a red flag for readability.

9.2 Magic values and naming variables

Have you heard the term "magic values"? It sounds awesome, but it's the opposite of that. It should really be "witchcraft values" to convey the negative effects of using them. What are they, you ask? They are hardcoded, undocumented, or poorly understood constants or variables. The reference to magic indicates that these values work, but you have no idea why.

Consider the following test.

Listing 9.3 A test with magic values

```
describe('password verifier', () => {
  test('on weekends, throws exceptions', () => {
    expect(() => verifyPassword('jhGGu78!', [], 0))
      .toThrowError("It's the weekend!");
  });
});
```
Magic values

This test contains three magic values. Can a person who didn't write the test and doesn't know the API being tested easily understand what the 0 value means? How about the [] array? The first parameter to that function kind of looks like a password, but even that has a magical quality to it. Let's discuss:

- The 0 could mean so many things. As the reader, I might have to search around in the code, or jump into the signature of the called function, to understand that this specifies the day of the week.

- The [] forces me to look at the signature of the called function to understand that the function expects a password verification rule array, which means the test verifies the case with no rules.

- jhGGu78! seems to be an obvious password value, but the big question I'll have as a reader is, why this specific value? What's important about this specific password? It's obviously important to use this value and not any other for this test, because it seems so damned specific. In reality it isn't, but the reader won't know this. They'll likely end up using this password in other tests just to be safe. Magic values tend to propagate themselves in tests.

The following listing shows the same test with the magic values fixed.

Listing 9.4   Fixing magic values

```
describe("verifier2 - dummy object", () => {
  test("on weekends, throws exceptions", () => {
    const SUNDAY = 0, NO_RULES = [];
    expect(() => verifyPassword2("anything", NO_RULES, SUNDAY))
      .toThrowError("It's the weekend!");
  });
});
```

By putting magic values into meaningfully named variables, we can remove the questions people will have when reading our test. For the password value, I've decided to simply change the direct value to explain to the reader what is *not* important about this test.

Variable names and values are just as much about explaining to the reader what they should *not* care about as they are about explaining what *is* important.

9.3   *Separating asserts from actions*

For the sake of readability and all that is holy, avoid writing assertions and the method call in the same statement. The following listing shows what I mean.

Listing 9.5   Separating asserts from actions

```
expect(verifier.verify("any value")[0]).toContain("fake reason");
```
Bad example

```
const result = verifier.verify("any value");     Good
expect(result[0]).toContain("fake reason");      example
```

See the difference between the two examples? The first example is much harder to read and understand in the context of a real test because of the length of the line and the nesting of the act and assert parts.

It's also much easier to debug the second example than the first one, if you wanted to focus on the result value after the call. Don't skimp on this small tip. The people after you will whisper a small thank you when your test doesn't make them feel stupid for not understanding it.

9.4   *Setting up and tearing down*

Setup and teardown methods in unit tests can be abused to the point where the tests or the setup and teardown methods are unreadable. The situation is usually worse in the setup method than in the teardown method.

The following listing shows one possible abuse that is very common: using the setup (or `beforeEach` function) for setting up mocks or stubs.

Listing 9.6   Using a setup (`beforeEach`) function for mock setup

```
describe("password verifier", () => {
  let mockLog;
  beforeEach(() => {                                          Setting up
    mockLog = Substitute.for<IComplicatedLogger>();    ◁───  a mock
  });

  test("verify, with logger & passing, calls logger with PASS",() => {
    const verifier = new PasswordVerifier2([], mockLog);
    verifier.verify("anything");

    mockLog.received().info(
      Arg.is((x) => x.includes("PASSED")),
      "verify"
    );
  });
});
```

Using the mock → (points to `const verifier` and `mockLog.received().info(`)

If you set up mocks and stubs in a setup method, that means they don't get set up in the actual test. That, in turn, means that whoever is reading your test may not even realize that there are mock objects in use, or what the test expects from them.

The test in listing 9.6 uses the `mockLog` variable, which is initialized in the `beforeEach` function (a setup method). Imagine you have dozens or more of these tests in the file. The setup function is at the beginning of the file, and you are stuck reading a test way down in the file. You come across the `mockLog` variable and you have to start asking questions such as, "Where is this initialized? How will it behave in the test?" and more.

Another problem that can arise if multiple mocks and stubs are used in various tests in the same file is that the setup function becomes a dumping group for all the various states used by your tests. It becomes a big mess, a soup of many parameters, some used by one test and others used somewhere else. It becomes difficult to manage and understand such a setup.

It's much more readable to initialize mock objects directly in the test, with all their expectations. The following listing is an example of initializing the mock in each test.

Listing 9.7   Avoiding a setup function

```
describe("password verifier", () => {
  test("verify, with logger & passing,calls logger with PASS",() => {
    const mockLog = Substitute.for<IComplicatedLogger>();     ◁———  Initializing
                                                                     the mock
                                                                     in the test
    const verifier = new PasswordVerifier2([], mockLog);
    verifier.verify("anything");

    mockLog.received().info(
      Arg.is((x) => x.includes("PASSED")),
      "verify"
    );
  });
});
```

When I look at this test, everything is clear as day. I can see when the mock is created, its behavior, and anything else I need to know.

If you're worried about maintainability, you can refactor the creation of the mock into a helper function that each test would call. That way, you're avoiding the generic setup function and are instead calling the same helper function from multiple tests. As the following listing shows, you keep the readability and gain more maintainability.

Listing 9.8   Using a helper function

```
describe("password verifier", () => {
  test("verify, with logger & passing,calls logger with PASS",() => {
    const mockLog = makeMockLogger();                         ◁———
                                                                     Using a helper
                                                                     function to
    const verifier = new PasswordVerifier2([], mockLog);             initialize the
    verifier.verify("anything");                                     mock

    mockLog.received().info(
      Arg.is((x) => x.includes("PASSED")),
      "verify"
    );
  });
});
```

And yes, if you follow this logic, you can see that I'm perfectly OK with you not having *any* setup functions in your tests. I've often written full test suites that don't have a setup function, instead calling helper methods from each test, for the sake of maintainability. The tests were still readable and maintainable.

Summary

- When naming a test, include the name of the unit of work under test, the current test scenario, and the expected behavior of the unit of work.
- Don't leave magic values in your tests. Either wrap them in variables with meaningful names, or put the description into the value itself, if it's a string.

- Separate assertions from actions. Merging the two shortens the code but makes it significantly harder to understand.
- Try not to use test setups at all (such as `beforeEach` methods). Introduce helper methods to simplify the test's arrange part, and use those helper methods in each test.

10

Developing
a testing strategy

This chapter covers

- Testing level pros and cons
- Common antipatterns in test levels
- The test recipe strategy
- Delivery-blocking and non-blocking tests
- Delivery vs. discovery pipelines
- Test parallelization

Unit tests represent just one of the types of tests you could and should write. In this chapter, we'll discuss how unit testing fits into an organizational testing strategy. As soon as we start to look at other types of tests, we start asking some really important questions:

- At what *level* do we want to test various features? (UI, backend, API, unit, etc.)

- How do we decide at which level to test a feature? Do we test it multiple times on many levels?

- Should we have more functional end-to-end tests or more unit tests?

- How can we optimize the speed of tests without sacrificing trust in them?
- Who should write each type of test?

The answers to these questions, and many more, are what I'd call a *testing strategy*.

The first step in our journey is to frame the scope of the testing strategy in terms of test types.

10.1 Common test types and levels

Different industries might have different test types and levels. Figure 10.1, which we first discussed in chapter 7, is a rather generic set of test types that I feel fits 90% of the organizations I consult with, if not more. The higher the level of the tests, the more real dependencies they use, which gives us confidence in the overall system's correctness. The downside is that such tests are slower and flakier.

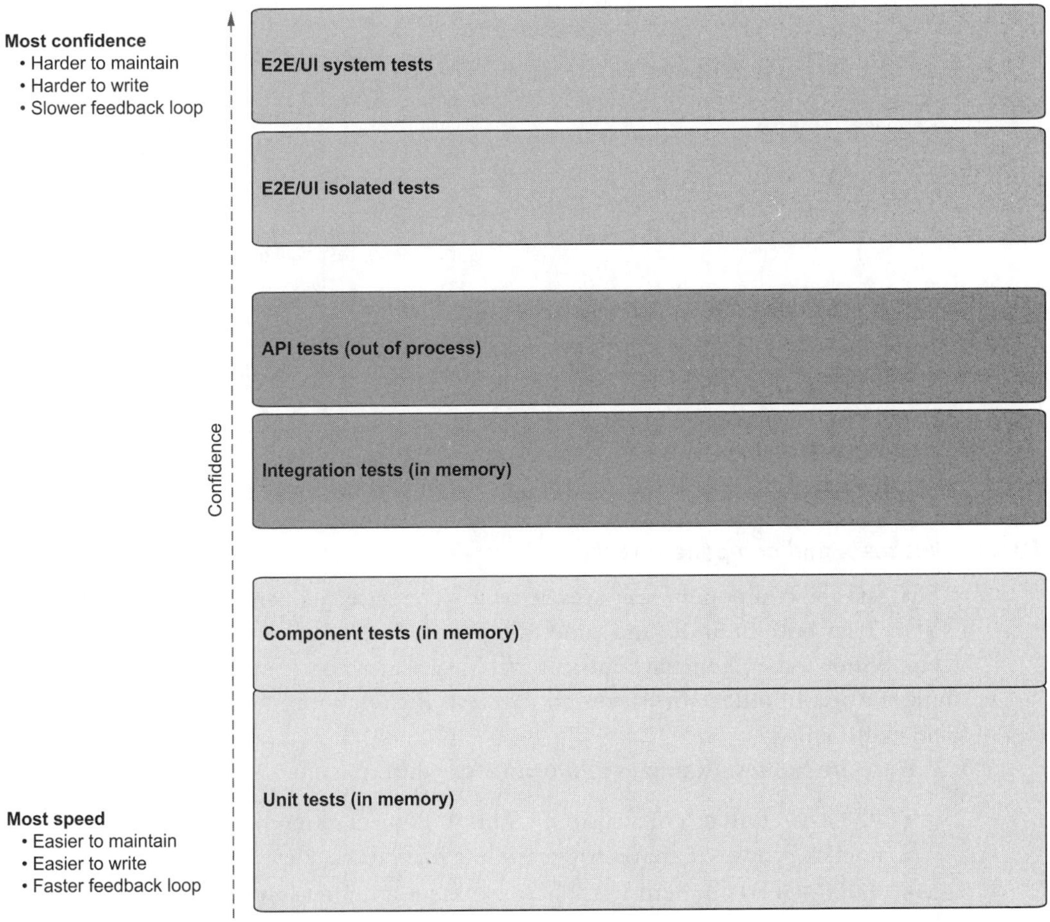

Figure 10.1   Common software test levels

Nice diagram, but what do we do with it? We use it when we design a framework for decision making about which test to write. There are several criteria (things that make our jobs easier or harder) I like to pinpoint; these help me decide which test type to use.

10.1.1 Criteria for judging a test

When we're faced with more than two options to choose from, one of the best ways I've found to help me decide is to figure out what my *obvious values* are for the problem at hand. These obvious values are the things we can all pretty much agree are useful or should be avoided when making the choice. Table 10.1 lists my obvious values for tests.

Table 10.1   Generic test scorecard

Criterion	Rating scale	Notes
Complexity	1–5	How complicated a test is to write, read, or debug. Lower is better.
Flakiness	1–5	How likely a test is to fail because of things it does not control—code from other groups, networks, databases, configuration, and more. Lower is better.
Confidence when passes	1–5	How much confidence is generated in our minds and hearts when a test passes. Higher is better.
Maintainability	1–5	How often the test needs to change, and how easy it is to change. Higher is better.
Execution speed	1–5	How quickly does the test finish? Higher is better.

All values are scaled from 1 to 5. As you'll see, each level in figure 10.1 has pros and cons in each of these criteria.

10.1.2 Unit tests and component tests

Unit tests and component tests are the types of tests we've been discussing in this book so far. They both fit under the same category, with the only differentiation being that component tests might have more functions, classes, or components as part of the unit of work. In other words, component tests include more "stuff" between the entry and exit points.

Here are two test examples to illustrate the difference:

- *Test A*—A unit test of a custom UI button object in memory. You can instantiate it, click it, and see that it triggers some form of click event.
- *Test B*—A component test that instantiates a higher-level form component and includes the button as part of its structure. The test verifies the higher-level form, with the button playing a small role as part of the higher-level scenario.

Both tests are still unit tests, in memory, and we have full control over all the things being used; there are no dependencies on files, databases, networks, configuration, or other things we don't control. Test A is a lower-level unit test, and test B is a component test, or a higher-level unit test.

The reason this differentiation needs to be made is because I often get asked what I would call a test with a different level of abstraction. The answer is that whether a test falls into the unit/component test category is based on the dependencies it does or doesn't have, not on the abstraction level it uses. Table 10.2 shows the scorecard for the unit/component test layer.

Table 10.2 Unit/component test scorecard

Complexity	1/5	These are the least complex of all test types due to the smaller scope and the fact that we can control everything in the test.
Flakiness	1/5	These are the least flaky of all test types, since we can control everything in the test.
Confidence when passes	1/5	It feels nice when a unit test passes, but we're not really confident that our *application* works. We just know that a small piece of it does.
Maintainability	5/5	These are the easiest to maintain out of all test types, since it's relatively simple to read and to reason about.
Execution speed	5/5	These are the fastest of all test types, since everything runs in memory without any hard dependencies on files, network, or databases.

10.1.3 Integration tests

Integration tests look almost exactly like regular unit tests, but some of the dependencies are not stubbed out. For example, we might use a real configuration, a real database, a real filesystem, or all three. But to invoke the test, we still instantiate an object from our production code in memory and invoke an entry point function directly on that object. Table 10.3 shows the scorecard for integration tests.

Table 10.3 Integration test scorecard

Complexity	2/5	These tests are slightly or greatly more complex, depending on the number of dependencies that we do not fake in the test.
Flakiness	2–3/5	These tests are slightly or much flakier depending on how many real dependencies we use.
Confidence when passes	2–3/5	It feels much better when an integration test passes because we are verifying that the code uses something we do not control, like a database or a config file.
Maintainability	3–4/5	These tests are more complex than a unit test because of the dependencies.
Execution speed	3–4/5	These tests are slightly or much slower than a unit test because of the dependency on the filesystem, network, database, or threads.

10.1.4 *API tests*

In previous lower levels of tests, we haven't needed to deploy the application under test or make it properly run to test it. At the API test level, we finally need to deploy, at least in part, the application under test and invoke it through the network. Unlike unit, component, and integration tests, which can be categorized as in-memory tests, API tests are out-of-process tests. We are no longer instantiating the unit under test directly in memory. This means we're adding a new dependency into the mix: a network, as well as the deployment of some network service. Table 10.4 shows the scorecard for API tests.

Table 10.4 API test scorecard

Complexity	3/5	These tests are slightly or greatly more complex, depending on the deployment complexity, configuration, and API setup needed. Sometimes we need to include the API schema in the test, which takes extra work and thinking.
Flakiness	3–4/5	The network adds more flakiness to the mix.
Confidence when passes	3–4/5	It feels even better when an API test passes. We can trust that others can call our API with confidence after deployment.
Maintainability	2–3/5	The network adds more setup complexity and needs more care when changing a test or adding/changing APIs.
Execution speed	2–3/5	The network slows the tests down considerably.

10.1.5 *E2E/UI isolated tests*

At the level of isolated end-to-end (E2E) and user interface (UI) tests, we are testing our application from the point of view of a user. I use the word *isolated* to specify that we are testing *only* our own application or service, without deploying any dependency applications or services that our application might need. Such tests fake third-party authentication mechanisms, the APIs of other applications that are required to be deployed on the same server, and any code that is not specifically a part of the main application under test (including apps from the same organization's other departments—those would be faked as well).

Table 10.5 shows the scorecard for E2E/UI isolated tests.

Table 10.5 E2E/UI isolated test scorecard

Complexity	4/5	These tests are much more complex than previous tests, since we are dealing with user flows, UI-based changes, and capturing or scraping the UI for integration and assertions. Waiting and timeouts abound.
Flakiness	4/5	There are lots of reasons the test may slow down, time out, or not work due to the many dependencies involved.
Confidence when passes	4/5	It's a huge relief when this type of test passes. We gain a lot of confidence in our application.

Table 10.5 E2E/UI isolated test scorecard *(continued)*

Maintainability	1–2/5	More dependencies add more setup complexity and require more care when changing a test or adding or changing workflows. Tests are long and usually have multiple steps.
Execution speed	1–2/5	These tests can be very slow as we navigate user interfaces, sometimes including logins, caching, multipage navigation, etc.

10.1.6 *E2E/UI system tests*

At the level of system E2E and UI tests *nothing* is fake. This is as close to a production deployment as we can get: all dependency applications and services are real, but they might be differently configured to allow for our testing scenarios. Table 10.6 shows the scorecard for E2E/UI system tests.

Table 10.6 E2E/UI system test scorecard

Complexity	5/5	These are the most complex tests to set up and write due to the number of dependencies.
Flakiness	5/5	These tests can fail for any of thousands of different reasons, and often for multiple reasons.
Confidence when passes	5/5	These tests give us the highest confidence because of all the code that gets tested when the tests execute.
Maintainability	1/5	These tests are hard to maintain, due to the many dependencies and long workflows.
Execution speed	1/5	These tests are very slow because they use the UI and real dependencies. They can take minutes to hours for a single test.

10.2 *Test-level antipatterns*

Test-level antipatterns are not technical but organizational in nature. You've likely seen them firsthand. As a consultant, I can tell you that they are very prevalent.

10.2.1 *The end-to-end-only antipattern*

A very common strategy that an organization will have is using mostly, if not only, E2E tests (both isolated and system tests). Figure 10.2 shows what this looks like in the diagram of test levels and types.

Why is this an antipattern? Tests at this level are very slow, hard to maintain, hard to debug, and very flaky. These costs remain the same, while the value you get from each new E2E test diminishes.

DIMINISHING RETURNS FROM E2E TESTS

The first E2E test you write will bring you the most confidence because of how many other paths of code are included as part of that scenario, and because of the glue—the code orchestrating the work between your application and other systems—that gets invoked as part of that test.

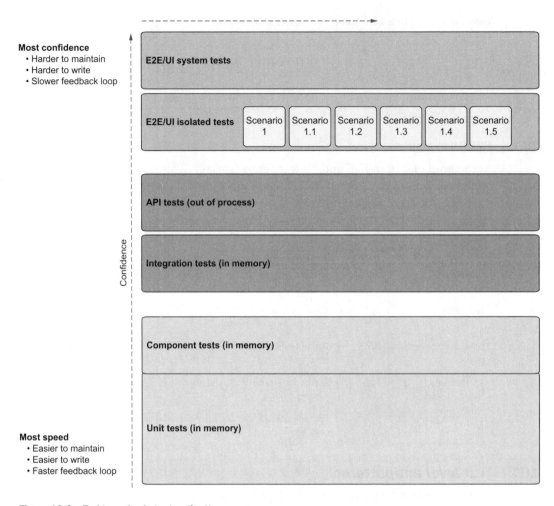

Figure 10.2   End-to-end-only test antipattern

But what about the second E2E test? It will usually be a variation on the first test, which means it might only bring a small fraction of the same value. Maybe there's a difference in a combo box and other UI elements, but all the dependencies, such as the database and third-party systems, remain the same.

The amount of extra confidence you get from the *second* E2E test is also only a fraction of the extra confidence you got from the first E2E test. However, the cost of debugging, changing, reading, and running that test is not a fraction; it is basically the same as for the previous test. You're incurring a lot of extra work for a very small bit of extra confidence, which is why I like to say that E2E tests have quickly diminishing returns.

If I want variation on the first test, it would be much more pragmatic to test at a lower level than the previous test. I already know most, if not all, of the glue between layers works, from the first test. There's no need to pay the tax of another E2E test if I can prove the next scenario at a lower level and pay a much smaller fee for pretty much the same bit of confidence.

THE BUILD WHISPERER

With E2E tests, not only do we have diminishing returns, we create a new bottleneck in the organization. Because high-level tests are often flaky, they break for many different reasons, some of which are not relevant to the test. You then need special people in the organization (usually QA leads) to sit down and analyze each of the many failing tests, and to hunt down the cause and determine if it's actually a problem or a minor issue.

I call these poor souls *build whisperers*. When the build is red, which it is most of the time, build whisperers are the ones who must come in, parse the data, and knowingly say, after hours of inspection, "Yes, it looks red, but it's actually green."

Usually, the organization will drive build whisperers into a corner, demanding that they say the build is green because "We have to get this release out the door." They are the gatekeepers of the release, and that is a thankless, stressful, and often manual and frustrating job. Whisperers usually burn out within a year or two, and they get chewed up and spit out into the next organization, where they do the same thankless job all over again. You'll often see build whisperers when this antipattern of many high-level E2E tests exists.

AVOIDING BUILD WHISPERERS

There is a way to resolve this mess, and that's to create and cultivate robust, automated test pipelines that can automatically judge whether a build is green or not, even if you have flaky tests. Netflix has openly blogged about creating their own tool for measuring how a build is doing statistically in the wild, so that it can be automatically approved for full release deployment (http://mng.bz/BAA1). This is doable, but it takes time and culture to achieve such a pipeline. I write more about these types of pipelines in my blog at https://pipelinedriven.org.

A "THROW IT OVER THE WALL" MENTALITY

Another reason having only E2E tests hurts organizations is that the people in charge of maintaining and monitoring these tests are people in the QA department. This means that the organization's developers might not care about or even know the results of these builds, and they are not invested in fixing or caring for these tests. They don't own them.

This "throw it over the wall" mentality can cause lots of miscommunication and quality issues because one part of the organization is not connected to the consequences of its actions, and the other side is suffering the consequences without being able to control the source of the issue. Is it any wonder that, in many organizations, developers and QA people don't get along? The system around them is often designed to make them mortal enemies instead of collaborators.

WHEN THIS ANTIPATTERN HAPPENS

These are some reasons why I see this happen:

- *Separation of duties*—Separate QA and development departments with separate pipelines (automated build jobs and dashboards) exist in many organizations. When a QA department has its own pipeline, it is likely to write more tests of the same kind. Also, a QA department tends to write only a specific type of test—the ones they're used to and are expected to write (sometimes based on company policy).
- *An "if it works, don't change it" mentality*—A group might start with E2E tests and see that they like the results. They continue to add all their new tests in the same way, because it's what they know, and it has proven to be useful. When the time it takes to run tests gets too long, it's already too late to change direction (which relates to the next point).
- *Sunk-costs fallacy*—"We have lots of these types of tests, and if we changed them or replaced them with lower-level tests, it would mean we've wasted all that time and effort on tests that we are removing." This is a fallacy, because maintaining, debugging, and understanding test failures costs a fortune in human time. If anything, it costs *less* to delete such tests (keeping only a few basic scenarios) and get that time back.

SHOULD YOU AVOID E2E TESTS COMPLETELY?

No, we can't avoid E2E tests. One of the good things they offer is *confidence* that the application works. It's a completely different level of confidence compared to unit tests, because they test the integration of the full system, with all of its subsystems and components, from the point of view of a user. When they pass, the feeling you get is huge relief that the major scenarios you expect your users to encounter actually work.

So don't avoid them entirely. Instead, I highly recommend *minimizing* the number of E2E tests. We'll talk about what that minimum is in section 10.3.3.

10.2.2 *The low-level-only test antipattern*

The opposite of having only E2E tests is to have low-level tests only. Unit tests provide fast feedback, but they don't provide the amount of confidence needed to fully trust that your application works as a single integrated unit (see figure 10.3).

In this antipattern, the organization's automated tests are mostly or exclusively low-level tests, such as unit tests or component tests. There may be hints of integration tests, but there are no E2E tests in sight.

The biggest issue with this is that the confidence level you get when these types of tests pass is simply not enough to feel confident that your application works. That means people will run the tests and then continue to do manual debugging and testing to get the final sense of confidence needed to release something. Unless what you're shipping is a code library that's meant to be used in the way your unit tests are

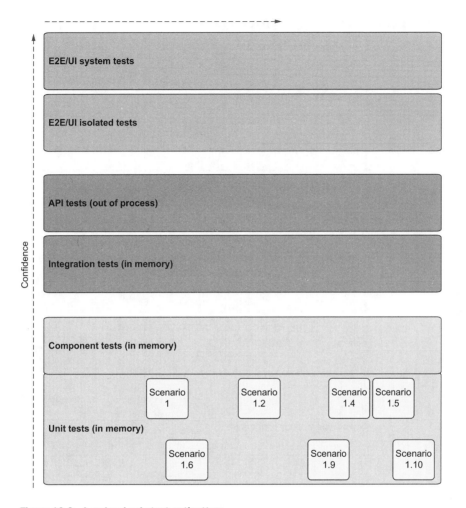

Figure 10.3 Low-level-only test antipattern

using it, this won't be enough. Yes, the tests will run quickly, but you'll still spend lots of time manually testing and verifying.

This antipattern often happens when your developers are only used to writing low-level tests, if they don't feel comfortable writing high-level tests, or if they expect the QA people to write those types of tests.

Does that mean you should avoid unit tests? Obviously not. But I highly recommend that you have *not only* unit tests but also higher-level tests. We'll discuss this recommendation in section 10.3.

10.2.3 *Disconnected low-level and high-level tests*

This pattern might seem healthy at first, but it really isn't. It might look a bit like figure 10.4.

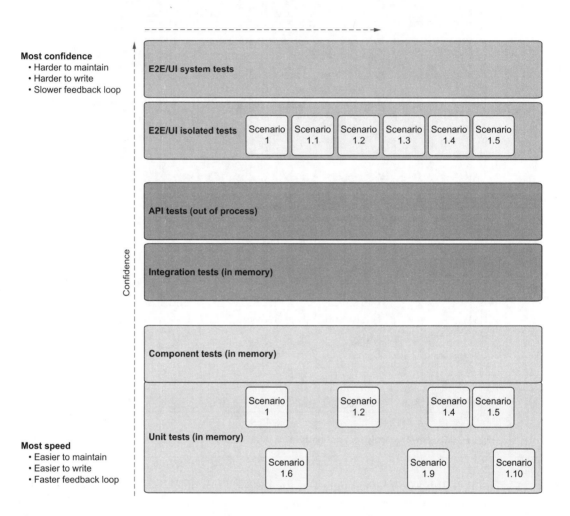

Figure 10.4   Disconnected low-level and high-level tests

Yes, you want to have both low-level tests (for speed) and high-level tests (for confidence). But when you see something like this in an organization, you will likely encounter one or more of these anti-behaviors:

- Many of the tests repeat in multiple levels.
- The people who write the low-level tests are not the same people who write the high-level tests. This means they don't care about each other's test results, and

they'll likely have different pipelines execute the different test types. When one pipeline is red, the other group might not even know nor care that those tests are failing.

- We suffer the worst of both worlds: at the top level, we suffer from the long test times, difficult maintainability, build whisperers, and flakiness; at the bottom level, we suffer from lack of confidence. And because there is often a lack of communication, we don't get the speed benefit of the low-level tests because they repeat at the top anyway. We also don't get the top-level confidence because of how flaky such a large number of tests is.

This pattern often happens when we have separate test and a development organizations with different goals and metrics, as well as different jobs and pipelines, permissions, and even code repositories. The larger the company, the more likely this is to happen.

10.3   Test recipes as a strategy

My proposed strategy to achieve balance in the types of tests used by the organization is to use *test recipes*. The idea is to have an informal plan for how a particular feature is going to be tested. This plan should include not only the main scenario (also known as the *happy path*), but also all its significant variations (also known as *edge cases*), as shown in figure 10.5. A well-outlined test recipe gives a clear picture of what test level is appropriate for each scenario.

10.3.1   How to write a test recipe

It's best to have at least two people create a test recipe—hopefully one with a developer's point of view and one with a tester's point of view. If there is no test department, two developers, or a developer with a senior developer will suffice. Mapping each scenario to a specific level in the test hierarchy can be a highly subjective task, so two pairs of eyes will help keep each other's implicit assumptions in check.

The recipes themselves can be stored as extra text in a TODO list or as part of the feature story on the tracking board for the task. You don't need a separate tool for planning tests.

The best time to create a test recipe is just before you start working on the feature. This way, the test recipe becomes part of the definition of "done" for the feature, meaning the feature is not complete until the full test recipe is passing.

Of course, a recipe can change as time goes by. The team can add or remove scenarios from it. A recipe is not a rigid artifact but a continuous work in progress, just like everything else in software development.

A test recipe represents the list of scenarios that will give its creators "pretty good confidence" that the feature works. As a rule of thumb, I like to have a 1 to 5 or 1 to 10 ratio between levels of tests. For any high-level, E2E test, I might have 5 tests at a lower level. Or, if you think bottom-up, say you have 100 unit tests. You usually won't need to have more than 10 integration tests and 1 E2E test.

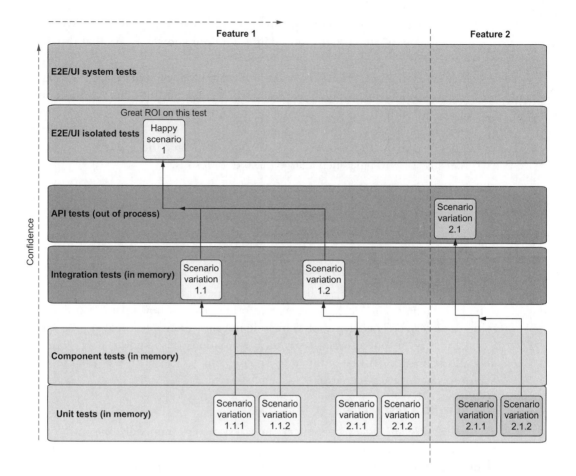

Figure 10.5   A test recipe is a test plan, outlining at which level a particular feature should be tested.

Don't treat test recipes as something formal, though. A test recipe is not a binding commitment or a list of test cases in a test-planning piece of software. Don't use it as a public report, a user story, or any other kind of promise to a stakeholder. At its core, a recipe is a simple list of 5 to 20 lines of text detailing simple scenarios to be tested in an automated fashion and at what level. The list can be changed, added to, or subtracted from. Consider it a comment. I usually like to just put it right in the user story or feature in Jira or whatever program I'm using.

Here's an example of what one might look like:

```
User profile feature testing recipe

E2E - Login, go to profile screen, update email, log out, log in with new
        email, verify profile screen updated

API - Call UpdateProfile API with more complicated data
```

```
Unit test - Check profile update logic with bad email
Unit test - Profile update logic with same email
Unit test - Profile serialization/deserialization
```

10.3.2 When do I write and use a test recipe?

Just before you start coding a feature or a user story, sit down with another person and try to come up with various scenarios to be tested. Discuss at which level that scenario should be best tested. This meeting will usually be no longer than 5 to 15 minutes, and after it, coding begins, including the writing of the tests. (If you're doing TDD, you'll start with the tests.)

In organizations where there are automation or QA roles, the developer will write the lower-level tests, and the QA will focus on writing the higher-level tests, while coding of the feature is taking place. Both people are working at the same time. One does not wait for the other to finish their work before starting to write their tests.

If you are working with feature toggles, they should also be checked as part of the tests, so that if a feature is off, its tests will not run.

10.3.3 Rules for a test recipe

There are several rules to follow when writing a test recipe:

- *Faster*—Prefer writing tests at lower levels, unless a high-level test is the only way for you to gain confidence that the feature works.
- *Confidence*—The recipe is done when you can tell yourself, "If all these tests passed, I'll feel pretty good about this feature working." If you can't say that, write more scenarios that will allow you to say that.
- *Revise*—Feel free to add or remove tests from the list as you code. Just make sure you notify the other person you worked with on the recipe.
- *Just in time*—Write this recipe just before starting to code, when you know who is going to code it.
- *Pair*—Don't write it alone if you can help it. People think in different ways, and it's important to talk through the scenarios and learn from each other about testing ideas and mindset.
- *Don't repeat yourself from other features*—If this scenario is already covered by an existing test (perhaps an E2E test from a previous feature), there is no need to repeat this scenario at that level.
- *Don't repeat yourself from other layers*—Try not to repeat the same scenario at multiple levels. If you're checking a successful login at the E2E level, lower-level tests should only check variations of that scenario (logging in with different providers, unsuccessful login results, etc.).
- *More, faster*—A good rule of thumb is to end up with a ratio of at least one to five between levels (for one E2E test, you might end up with five or more lower-level tests).

- *Pragmatic*—Don't feel the need to write tests at all levels for a given feature. Some features or user stories might only require unit tests. Others, only API or E2E tests. The basic idea is that, if all the scenarios in the recipe pass, you should feel confidence, regardless of what level they are tested at. If that's not the case, move the scenarios around to different levels until you feel more confident, without sacrificing too much speed or maintenance burden.

By following these rules, you'll get the benefit of fast feedback, because most of your tests will be low level, while not sacrificing confidence because the few most important scenarios are still covered by high-level tests. The test recipe approach also allows you to avoid most of the repetition between tests by positioning scenario variations at levels lower than the main scenario. Finally, if QA people are involved in writing test recipes too, you'll form a new communication channel between people within your organization, which helps improve mutual understanding of your software project.

10.4   *Managing delivery pipelines*

What about performance tests? Security tests? Load tests? What about lots of other tests that might take ages to run? Where and when should we run them? Which layer are they? Should they be part of our automated pipeline?

Lots of organizations run those tests as part of the integration automated pipeline that runs for each release or pull request. However, this causes huge delays in feedback, and the feedback is often "failed," even though the failure is not essential for a release to go out for these types of tests.

We can divide these types of tests into two main groups:

- *Delivery-blocking tests*—These are tests that provide a go or no-go for the change that is about to be released and deployed. Unit, E2E, system, and security tests all fall into this category. Their feedback is binary: they either pass and announce that the change didn't introduce any bugs, or they fail and indicate that the code needs to be fixed before it's released.
- *Good-to-know tests*—These are tests created for the purpose of discovery and continuous monitoring of key performance indicator (KPI) metrics. Examples include code analysis and complexity scanning, high-load performance testing, and other long-running nonfunctional tests that provide nonbinary feedback. If these tests fail, we might add new work items to our next sprints, but we would still be OK releasing our software.

10.4.1   *Delivery vs. discovery pipelines*

We don't want our good-to-know tests to take valuable feedback time from our delivery process, so we'll also have two types of pipelines:

- *Delivery pipeline*—Used for delivery-blocking tests. When the pipeline is green, we should be confident that we can automatically release the code to production. Tests in this pipeline should provide relatively fast feedback.

- *Discovery pipeline*—Used for good-to-know tests. This pipeline runs in parallel with the delivery pipeline, but continuously, and it's not taken into account as a release criterion. Since there's no need to wait for its feedback, tests in this pipeline can take a long time. If errors are found, they might become new work items in the next sprints for the team, but releases are not blocked.

Figure 10.6 illustrates the features of these two kinds of pipelines.

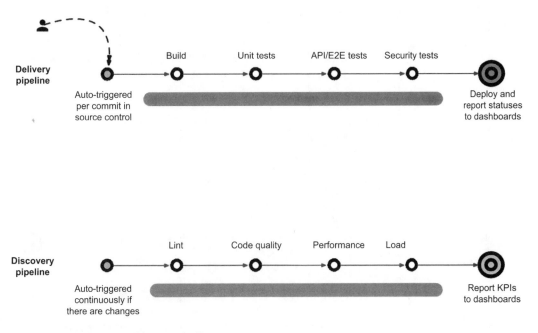

Figure 10.6   Delivery vs. discovery pipelines

The point of the delivery pipeline is to provide a go/no-go check that also deploys our code if all seems green, perhaps even to production. The point of the discovery pipeline is to provide refactoring objectives for the team, such as dealing with code complexity that has become too high. It can also show whether those refactoring efforts are effective over time. The discovery pipeline does not deploy anything except for the purpose of running specialized tests or analyzing code and its various KPI metrics. It ends with numbers on a dashboard.

Speed is a big factor in getting teams to be more engaged, and splitting tests into discovery and delivery pipelines is yet another technique to keep in your arsenal.

10.4.2 *Test layer parallelization*

Since fast feedback is very important, a common pattern you can and should employ in many scenarios is to run different test layers in parallel to speed up the pipeline feedback, as shown in figure 10.7. You can even use parallel environments that are created dynamically and destroyed at the end of the test.

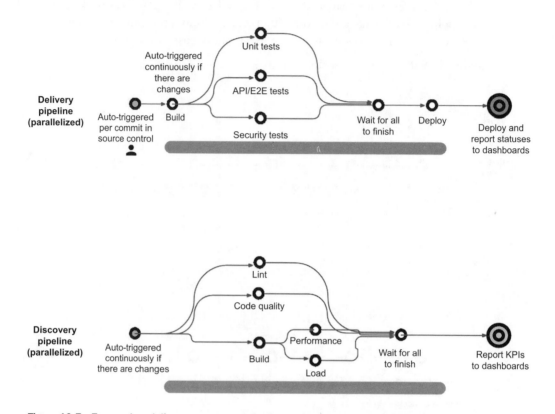

Figure 10.7   To speed up delivery, you can run pipelines, and even stages in pipelines, in parallel.

This approach benefits greatly from having access to dynamic environments. Throwing money at environments and automated parallel tests is almost always much more effective than throwing money at more people to do more manual tests, or simply having people wait longer to get feedback because the environment is being used right now.

Manual testing is unsustainable because such manual work only increases over time and becomes more and more frail and error prone. At the same time, simply waiting longer for pipeline feedback results in a huge waste of time for everyone. The waiting time, multiplied by the number of people waiting and the number of builds per day, results in a monthly investment that can be much larger than investing in dynamic environments and automation. Grab an Excel file and show your manager a simple formula to get that budget.

You can parallelize not only stages inside a pipeline; you can go further and run individual tests in parallel too. For example, if you're stuck with a large number of

E2E tests, you can break them up into parallel test suites. That shaves a lot of time off your feedback loop.

Don't do nightly builds

It's best to run your delivery pipeline after every code commit, instead of at a certain time. Running tests with each code change gives you more granular and faster feedback than the crude nightly build that simply accumulates all changes from the previous day. But if, for some reason, you absolutely have to run your pipeline on a timely basis, at least run them continuously instead of once a day.

If your delivery pipeline build takes a long time, don't wait for a magical trigger or schedule to run it. Imagine, as a developer, needing to wait until tomorrow to know if you broke something. With tests running continuously, you would still need to wait, but at least it would only be a couple of hours instead of a full day. Isn't that more productive?

Also, don't just run the build on demand. The feedback loop will be faster if you run the build automatically as soon as the previous one finishes, assuming there are code changes since the previous build, of course.

Summary

- There are multiple levels of tests: unit, component, and integration tests that run in memory; and API, isolated end-to-end (E2E), and system E2E tests that run out of process.
- Each test can be judged by five criteria: complexity, flakiness, confidence when it passes, maintainability, and execution speed.
- Unit and component tests are best in terms of maintainability, execution speed, and lack of complexity and flakiness, but they're worst in terms of the confidence they provide. Integration and API tests are the middle ground in the trade-off between confidence and the other metrics. E2E tests take the opposite approach from unit tests: they provide the best confidence but at the expense of maintainability, speed, complexity, and flakiness.
- The *end-to-end-only antipattern* is when your build consists solely of E2E tests. The marginal value of each additional E2E test is low, while the maintenance costs of all tests are the same. You'll get the most return on your efforts if you have just a few E2E tests covering the most important functionality.
- The *low-level-only antipattern* is when your build consists solely of unit and component tests. Lower-level tests can't provide enough confidence that your functionality as a whole works, and they must be supplemented with higher-level tests.
- *Disconnected low-level and high-level tests* is an antipattern because it's a strong sign that your tests are written by two groups of people who don't communicate with each other. Such tests often duplicate each other and carry high maintenance costs.

- *A test recipe* is a simple list of 5 to 20 lines of text, detailing which simple scenarios should be tested in an automated fashion and at what level. A test recipe should give you confidence that, if all outlined tests pass, the feature works as intended.

- Split your build pipeline into *delivery* and *discovery* pipelines. The delivery pipeline should be used for delivery-blocking tests, which, if they fail, stop delivery of the code under test. The discovery pipeline is used for good-to-know tests and runs in parallel with the delivery pipeline.

- You can parallelize not just pipelines but also stages inside those pipelines, and even groups of tests inside stages too.

Integrating unit testing into the organization

As a consultant, I've helped several companies, big and small, integrate continuous delivery processes and various engineering practices, such as test-driven development and unit testing, into their organizational culture. Sometimes this has failed, but those companies that succeeded had several things in common. In any type of organization, changing people's habits is more psychological than technical. People don't like change, and change is usually accompanied with plenty of FUD (fear, uncertainty, and doubt) to go around. It won't be a walk in the park for most people, as you'll see in this chapter.

11.1 Steps to becoming an agent of change

If you're going to be the agent of change in your organization, you should first accept that role. People will view you as the person responsible (and sometimes accountable) for what's happening, whether or not you want them to, and there's no use in hiding. In fact, hiding can cause things to go terribly wrong.

As you start to implement or push for changes, people will start asking tough questions related to what they care about. How much time will this "waste"? What does this mean for me as a QA engineer? How do we know it works? Be prepared to answer. The answers to the most common questions are discussed in section 11.5. You'll find that convincing others inside the organization before you start making changes will help you immensely when you need to make tough decisions and answer those questions.

Finally, someone will have to stay at the helm, making sure the changes don't die for lack of momentum. That's you. There are ways to keep things alive, as you'll see in the next sections.

11.1.1 *Be prepared for the tough questions*

Do your research. Read the questions and answers at the end of this chapter, and look at the related resources. Read forums, mailing lists, and blogs, and consult with your peers. If you can answer your own tough questions, there's a good chance you can answer someone else's.

11.1.2 *Convince insiders: Champions and blockers*

Few things make you feel as lonely in an organization as the decision to go against the current. If you're the only one who thinks what you're doing is a good idea, there's little reason for anyone to make an effort to implement what you're advocating. Consider who can help and hurt your efforts: the champions and blockers.

CHAMPIONS

As you start pushing for change, identify the people you think are most likely to help in your quest. They'll be your *champions*. They're usually early adopters, or people who are open minded enough to try the things you're advocating. They may already be half convinced but are looking for an impetus to start the change. They may have even tried it and failed on their own.

Approach them before anyone else and ask for their opinions on what you're about to do. They may tell you some things that you hadn't considered, including

- Teams that might be good candidates to start with
- Places where people are more accepting of such changes
- What (and who) to watch out for in your quest

By approaching them, you're helping to ensure that they're part of the process. People who feel part of the process usually try to help make it work. Make them your champions: ask them if they can help you and be the ones people can come to with questions. Prepare them for such events.

BLOCKERS

Next, identify the *blockers*. These are the people in the organization who are most likely to resist the changes you're making. For example, a manager might object to adding unit tests, claiming that they'll add too much time to the development effort and increase the amount of code that needs to be maintained. Make them part of the process instead of resisters of it by giving them (at least those who are willing and able) an active role in the process.

The reasons why people might resist changes vary. Answers to some of the possible objections are covered in section 11.4 on *influence forces*. Some will be worried about job security, and some will just feel too comfortable with the way things currently are. Approaching potential blockers and detailing all the things they could have done better is often not constructive, as I've found out the hard way. People don't like to be told that their baby is ugly.

Instead, ask blockers to help you in the process by being in charge of defining coding standards for unit tests, for example, or by doing code and test reviews with peers every other day. Or make them part of the team that chooses the course materials or outside consultants. You'll give them a new responsibility that will help them feel relied on and relevant in the organization. They need to be part of the change or they'll almost certainly undermine it.

11.1.3   Identify possible starting points

Identify where in the organization you can start implementing changes. Most successful implementations take a steady route. Start with a pilot project in a small team, and see what happens. If all goes well, move on to other teams and other projects.

Here are some tips that will help you along the way:

- Choose smaller teams.
- Create subteams.
- Consider project feasibility.
- Use code and test reviews as teaching tools.

These tips can take you a long way in a mostly hostile environment.

CHOOSE SMALLER TEAMS

Identifying possible teams to start with is usually easy. You'll generally want a small team working on a low-profile project with low risks. If the risk is minimal, it's easier to convince people to try your proposed changes.

One caveat is that the team needs to have members who are open to changing the way they work and to learning new skills. Ironically, the people with less experience on a team are usually most likely to be open to change, and people with more experience tend to be more entrenched in their way of doing things. If you can find a team with an experienced leader who's open to change, but that also includes less-experienced developers, it's likely that team will offer little resistance. Go to the team and ask their opinion on holding a pilot project. They'll tell you if this is (or is not) the right place to start.

CREATE SUBTEAMS

Another possible candidate for a pilot test is to form a subteam within an existing team. Almost every team will have a "black hole" component that needs to be maintained, and while it does many things right, it also has many bugs. Adding features for such a component is a tough task, and this kind of pain can drive people to experiment with a pilot project.

CONSIDER PROJECT FEASIBILITY

For a pilot project, make sure you're not biting off more than you can chew. It takes more experience to run more difficult projects, so you might want to have at least two options—a complicated project and an easier project—so that you can choose between them.

USE CODE AND TEST REVIEWS AS TEACHING TOOLS

If you're the technical lead on a small team (up to eight people), one of the best ways of teaching is instituting code reviews that also include test reviews. The idea is that as you review other people's code and tests, you teach them what you look for in the tests and your way of thinking about writing tests or approaching TDD. Here are some tips:

- Do the reviews in person, not through remote software. The personal connection lets much more information pass between you in nonverbal ways, so learning happens better and faster.
- In the first couple of weeks, review every line of code that gets checked in. This will help you avoid the "we didn't think this code needs reviewing" problem.
- Add a third person to your code reviews—one who will sit on the side and learn how you review the code. This will allow them to later do code reviews themselves and teach others, so that you won't become a bottleneck for the team as the only person capable of doing reviews. The idea is to develop others' ability to do code reviews and accept more responsibility.

If you want to learn more about this technique, I wrote about it in my blog for technical leaders: "What Should a Good Code Review Look and Feel Like?" at https://5whys .com/blog/what-should-a-good-code-review-look-and-feel-like.html.

11.2 *Ways to succeed*

There are two main ways an organization or team can start changing a process: from the bottom-up or the top-down (and sometimes both). The two ways are very different, as you'll see, and either could be the right approach for your team or company. There's no one right way.

As you proceed, you'll need to learn how to convince management that *your* efforts should also be *their* efforts, or when it would be wise to bring in someone from outside to help. Making progress visible is important, as is setting clear goals that can be measured. Identifying and avoiding obstacles should also be high on your list. There are many battles that can be fought, and you need to choose the right ones.

11.2.1 *Guerrilla implementation (bottom-up)*

Guerrilla-style implementation is all about starting out with a team, getting results, and only then convincing other people that the practices are worthwhile. Usually the driver for guerrilla implementation is a team who's tired of doing things the prescribed way. They set out to do things differently; they study on their own and make changes happen. When the team shows results, other people in the organization may decide to start implementing similar changes in their own teams.

In some cases, guerrilla-style implementation is a process *adopted* first by developers and then by management. At other times, it's a process *advocated* for first by developers and then by management. The difference is that you can accomplish the first covertly, without the higher powers knowing about it. The latter is done in conjunction with management. It's up to you to figure out which approach will work better. Sometimes the only way to change things is by covert operations. Avoid this if you can, but if there's no other way, and you're sure the change is needed, you can just do it.

Don't take this as a recommendation to make a career-limiting move. Developers do things without permission all the time: debugging code, reading email, writing code comments, creating flow diagrams, and so on. These are all tasks that developers do as a regular part of the job. The same goes for unit testing. Most developers already write tests of some sort (automated or not). The idea is to redirect the time spent on tests into something that will provide benefits in the long term.

11.2.2 *Convincing management (top-down)*

The top-down move usually starts in one of two ways. A manager or a developer will initiate the process and start the rest of the organization moving in that direction, piece by piece. Or a mid-level manager may see a presentation, read a book (such as this one), or talk to a colleague about the benefits of specific changes to the way they work. Such a manager will usually initiate the process by giving a presentation to people in other teams or even using their authority to make the change happen.

11.2.3 *Experiments as door openers*

Here's a powerful way to get started with unit testing in a large organization (it could also fit other types of transformation or new skills). Declare an experiment that will last two to three months. It will apply to only one pre-picked team and relate to only one or two components in a real application. Make sure it's not too risky. If it fails, the company won't go under or lose a major client. It also shouldn't be useless: the experiment must provide real value and not just serve as a playground. It has to be something you'll end up pushing into your codebase and use in production eventually; it shouldn't be a write-and-forget piece of code.

The word "experiment" conveys that the change is temporary, and if it doesn't work out, the team can go back to the way they were before. Also, the effort is timeboxed, so we know when the experiment is finished.

Such an approach helps people feel more at ease with big changes, because it reduces the risk to the organization, the number of people affected (and thus the number of people objecting), and the number of objections relating to fear of changing things "forever."

Here's another hint: when faced with multiple options for an experiment, or if you get objections pushing for another way of working, ask, "Which idea do we want to experiment with *first?*"

WALK THE WALK

Be prepared that your idea might not be selected from among all the options for an experiment. When push comes to shove, you have to hold experiments based on what the consensus of leadership decides, whether you like it or not.

The nice thing about going with other people's experiments is that, like with yours, they are time-boxed and temporary! The best outcome might be that another approach fixes what you were trying to fix, and you might want to keep someone else's experiment going. However, if you hate the experiment, just remember that it's temporary, and you can push for the next experiment.

METRICS AND EXPERIMENTS

Be sure to record a baseline set of metrics before and after the experiment. These metrics should be related to things you're trying to change, such as eliminating waiting times for a build, reducing the lead time for a product to go out the door, or reducing the number of bugs found in production.

To dive deeper into the various metrics you might use, take a look at my talk "Lies, Damned Lies, and Metrics," which you can find in my blog at https://pipelinedriven .org/article/video-lies-damned-lies-and-metrics.

11.2.4 Get an outside champion

I highly recommend getting an outside person to help with the change. An outside consultant coming in to help with unit testing and related matters has advantages over someone who works in the company:

- *Freedom to speak*—A consultant can say things that people inside the company may not be willing to hear from someone who works there ("The code integrity is bad," "Your tests are unreadable," and so on).
- *Experience*—A consultant will have more experience dealing with resistance from the inside, coming up with good answers to tough questions, and knowing which buttons to push to get things going.
- *Dedicated time*—For a consultant, this is their job. Unlike other employees in the company who have better things to do than push for change (like writing software), the consultant does this full time and is dedicated to this purpose.

I've often seen a change break down because an overworked champion doesn't have the time to dedicate to the process.

11.2.5 *Make progress visible*

It's important to keep the progress and status of the change visible. Hang white-boards or posters on walls in corridors or in the food-related areas where people congregate. The data displayed should be related to the goals you're trying to achieve. For example:

- Show the number of passing or failing tests in the last nightly build.
- Keep a chart showing which teams are already running an automated build process.
- Put up a Scrum burndown chart of iteration progress or a test-code-coverage report (as shown in figure 11.1) if that's what you have your goals set to. (You can learn more about Scrum at www.controlchaos.com.)
- Put up contact details for yourself and all the champions, so someone can answer any questions that arise.

Darjeeling > vs-plugin v4 (NCover) > ⌄ #5.0.119.0 (18 Feb 10 12:27)

| Overview | Changes (1) | Tests | Build Log | Build Parameters | Dependencies | Artifacts | Code Coverage |

NCoverExplorer Coverage Report - Darjeeling :: vs-plugin v4 (NCover)
Report generated on: Thu 18-Feb-2010 at 13:08:54
NCoverExplorer version: 1.3.6.36
Filtering / Sorting: None / CoveragePercentageDescending

Project Statistics: Files: 607   **NCLOC:** 16797
Classes: 869
Functions: 3901   Unvisited: 2470
Seq Pts: 15490   Unvisited: 10201

Project	Acceptable	Unvisited Functions	Function Coverage
Darjeeling :: vs-plugin v4 (NCover)	80.0 %	2470	36.7 %

Modules	Acceptable	Unvisited Functions	Function Coverage
JetBrains.TeamCity.EventTrackers.dll	80.0 %	10	84.6 %
JetBrains.TeamCity.WebLinkListener.dll	80.0 %	11	76.6 %
JetBrains.TeamCity.Network.Login.dll	80.0 %	35	61.1 %
JetBrains.TeamCity.Common.dll	80.0 %	2	60.0 %
JetBrains.TeamCity.Connect.dll	80.0 %	214	51.6 %
JetBrains.TeamCity.SVN.dll	80.0 %	215	59.6 %
JetBrains.TeamCity.Perforce.dll	80.0 %	151	64.0 %
JetBrains.TeamCity.Network.Utils.dll	80.0 %	12	52.0 %
JetBrains.TeamCity.Utils.dll	80.0 %	533	33.2 %
JetBrains.TeamCity.TestsView.dll	80.0 %	142	16.5 %
JetBrains.TeamCity.Login.dll	80.0 %	35	16.7 %
JetBrains.TeamCity.RemoteRun.dll	80.0 %	797	15.3 %
JetBrains.TeamCity.Package.dll	80.0 %	313	3.4 %

Module	Acceptable	Unvisited Functions	Function Coverage
JetBrains.TeamCity.EventTrackers.dll	80.0 %	10	84.6 %
Namespace / Classes			
JetBrains.TeamCity.EventTrackers.Impl		9	85.5 %
PersonalChangesTrackerBase		0	100.0 %
ListenerInfo		0	100.0 %
T......C......C...........Th....d		0	100.0 %

Figure 11.1   An example of a test-code-coverage report in TeamCity with NCover

- Set up a big-screen display that's always showing, in big bold graphics, the status of the builds, what's currently running, and what's failing. Put that in a visible place where all developers can see—in a well-trafficked corridor, for example, or at the top of the team room's main wall.

Your aim in using these charts is to connect with two groups:

- *The group undergoing the change*—People in this group will gain a greater feeling of accomplishment and pride as the charts (which are open to everyone) are updated, and they'll feel more compelled to complete the process because it's visible to others. They'll also be able to keep track of how they're doing compared to other groups. They may push harder, knowing that another group implemented specific practices more quickly.
- *Those in the organization who aren't part of the process*—You're raising interest and curiosity among these people, triggering conversations and buzz, and creating a current that they can join if they choose.

11.2.6 *Aim for specific goals, metrics, and KPIs*

Without goals, the change will be hard to measure and to communicate to others. It will be a vague "something" that can easily be shut down at the first sign of trouble.

LAGGING INDICATORS

At the organizational level, unit tests are generally part of a bigger set of goals, usually related to continuous delivery. If that's the case for you, I highly recommend using the four common DevOps metrics:

- *Deployment frequency*—How often an organization successfully releases to production.
- *Lead time for changes*—The time it takes a feature request to get into production. Note that many places incorrectly publish this as the amount of time it takes a commit to get into production, which is only a part of the journey that a feature goes through, from an organizational standpoint. If you're measuring from commit time, you're closer to measuring the "cycle time" of a feature from commit up to a specific point. Lead time is made up of multiple cycle times.
- *Escaped bugs/change failure rate*—The number of failures found in production per some unit, usually release, deployment, or time. You can also use the percentage of deployments causing a failure in production.
- *Time to restore service*—How long it takes an organization to recover from a failure in production.

These four are what we'd call *lagging indicators*, and they're very hard to fake (although they're pretty easy to measure in most places). They are great in making sure we do not lie to ourselves about the results of experiments.

LEADING INDICATORS

Often we'd like faster feedback to ensure that we're going the right way. That's where *leading indicators* come in. Leading indicators are things we can control on a day-to-day basis—code coverage, number of tests, build run time, and more. They are easier to fake, but combined with lagging indicators, they can often provide us with early signs that we might be going the right way.

Figure 11.2 shows a sample structure and ideas for lagging and leading indicators you can use in your organization. You can find a high-resolution image with color at https://pipelinedriven.org/article/a-metrics-framework-for-continuous-delivery.

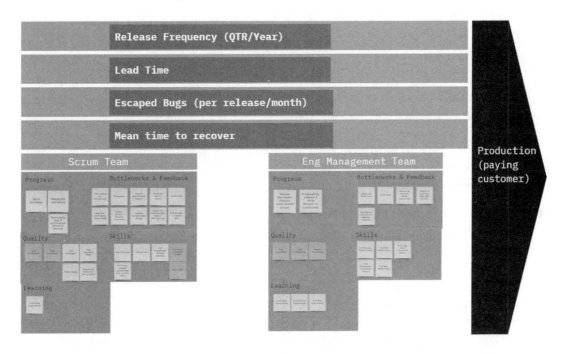

Figure 11.2   An example of a metrics framework for use in continuous delivery

INDICATOR CATEGORIES AND GROUPS

I usually break up leading indicators into two groups:

- *Team level*—Metrics that an individual team can control
- *Engineering management level*—Metrics that require cross-team collaboration or aggregate metrics across multiple teams

I also like to categorize them based on what they will be used to solve:

- *Progress*—Used to solve visibility and decision making on the plan
- *Bottlenecks and feedback*—As the name implies
- *Quality*—Escaped bugs in production

- *Skills*—Track that we are slowly removing knowledge barriers inside teams or across teams
- *Learning*—Acting like we're a learning organization

QUALITATIVE METRICS

The metrics are mostly quantitative (i.e., they are numbers that can be measured), but a few are qualitative, in that you ask people how they feel or think about something. The ones I use are

- How confident you are that the tests can and will find bugs in the code if they arise (from 1 to 5)? Take the average of the responses from the team members or across multiple teams.
- Does the code do what it is supposed to do (from 1 to 5)?

These are surveys you can ask at each retrospective meeting, and they take five minutes to answer.

TREND LINES ARE YOUR FRIEND

For all leading and lagging indicators, you want to see *trend lines*, not just snapshots of numbers. Lines over time is how you see if you're getting better or worse.

Don't fall into the trap of having a nice dashboard with large numbers on it. Numbers without context are not good or bad. Trend lines tell you if you're better this week than you were last week.

11.2.7 *Realize that there will be hurdles*

There are always hurdles. Most will come from within the organizational structure, and some will be technical. The technical ones are easier to fix, because it's a matter of finding the right solution. The organizational ones need care and attention and a psychological approach.

It's important not to surrender to a feeling of temporary failure when an iteration goes bad, tests go slower than expected, and so on. It's sometimes hard to get going, and you'll need to persist for at least a couple of months to start feeling comfortable with the new process and to iron out all the kinks. Have management commit to continuing for at least three months even if things don't go as planned. It's important to get their agreement up front. You don't want to be running around trying to convince people in the middle of a stressful first month.

Also, absorb this short realization, shared by Tim Ottinger on Twitter (@Tottinge): "If your tests don't catch all defects, they still make it easier to fix the defects they didn't catch. It is a profound truth."

Now that we've looked at ways of ensuring things go right, let's look at some things that can lead to failure.

11.3 *Ways to fail*

In the preface to this book, I talked about one project I was involved with that failed, partly because unit testing wasn't implemented correctly. That's one way a project can fail. I'll discuss several others here, along with one that cost me that project, and some things that can be done about them.

11.3.1 *Lack of a driving force*

In the places where I've seen change fail, the lack of a driving force was the most powerful factor in play. Being a consistent driving force of change has its price. It will take time away from your normal job to teach others, help them, and wage internal political wars for change. You need to be willing to surrender time for these tasks, or the change won't happen. Bringing in an outside person, as mentioned in section 11.2.4, will help you in your quest for a consistent driving force.

11.3.2 *Lack of political support*

If your boss explicitly tells you not to make the change, there isn't a whole lot you can do, besides trying to convince management to see what you see. But sometimes the lack of support is much more subtle than that, and the trick is to realize that you're facing opposition.

For example, you may be told, "Sure, go ahead and implement those tests. We're adding 10% to your time to do this." Anything below 30% isn't realistic for beginning a unit testing effort. This is one way a manager may try to stop a trend—by choking it out of existence.

You need to recognize that you're facing opposition, but once you know what to look for, it's easy to identify. When you tell them that their limitations aren't realistic, you'll be told, "So don't do it."

11.3.3 *Ad hoc implementations and first impressions*

If you're planning to implement unit testing without prior knowledge of how to write good unit tests, do yourself one big favor: involve someone who has experience and follow good practices (such as those outlined in this book).

I've seen developers jump into the deep water without a proper understanding of what to do or where to start, and that's not a good place to be. Not only will it take a huge amount of time to learn how to make changes that are acceptable for your situation, but you'll also lose a lot of credibility along the way for starting out with a bad implementation. This can lead to the pilot project being shut down.

If you read this book's preface, you'll know that this happened to me. You have only a couple of months to get things up to speed and convince the higher-ups that you're achieving results with experiments. Make that time count, and remove any risks that you can. If you don't know how to write good tests, read a book or get a consultant. If you don't know how to make your code testable, do the same. Don't waste time reinventing testing methods.

11.3.4 *Lack of team support*

If your team doesn't support your efforts, it will be nearly impossible to succeed, because you'll have a hard time consolidating your extra work on the new process with your regular work. You should strive to have your team be part of the new process or at least not interfere with it.

Talk to your team members about the changes. Getting their support one by one is sometimes a good way to start, but talking to them as a group about your efforts—and answering their hard questions—can also prove valuable. Whatever you do, don't take the team's support for granted. Make sure you know what you're getting into; these are the people you have to work with on a daily basis.

11.4 *Influence factors*

I've written and covered influencing behaviors as a full chapter in my book *Elastic Leadership* (Manning, 2016). If you find this topic interesting, I recommend picking that one up, or reading more about it at 5whys.com.

One of the things I find even more fascinating than unit tests is people and why they behave the way they do. It can be very frustrating to try to get someone to start doing something (like TDD, for example), and regardless of your best efforts, they just won't do it. You may have already tried reasoning with them, but you see they don't do anything in response to your little talk.

In the book *Influencer: The Power to Change Anything* (McGraw-Hill, 2007) by Kerry Patterson, Joseph Grenny, David Maxfield, Ron McMillan, and Al Switzler, you'll find the following mantra (paraphrased):

> *For every behavior that you see, the world is perfectly designed for that behavior to happen. That means that there are other factors besides the person wanting to do something or being able to do it that influence their behavior. Yet we rarely look beyond those two factors.*

The book exposes us to six influence factors:

- *Personal ability*—Does the person have all the skills or knowledge to perform what is required?
- *Personal motivation*—Does the person take satisfaction from the right behavior or dislike the wrong behavior? Do they have the self-control to engage in the behavior when it's hardest to do so?
- *Social ability*—Do you or others provide the help, information, and resources required by that person, particularly at critical times?
- *Social motivation*—Are the people around them actively encouraging the right behavior and discouraging the wrong behavior? Are you or others modeling the right behavior in an effective way?
- *Structural (environmental) ability*—Are there aspects in the environment (building, budget, and so on) that make the behavior convenient, easy, and safe? Are there enough cues and reminders to stay on course?

- *Structural motivation*—Are there clear and meaningful rewards (such as pay, bonuses, or incentives) when you or others behave the right or wrong way? Do short-term rewards match the desired long-term results and behaviors you want to reinforce or want to avoid?

Consider this a short checklist for starting to understand why things aren't going your way. Then consider another important fact: there might be more than one factor in play. For the behavior to change, you should change all the factors in play. If you change just one, the behavior won't change.

Table 11.1 is an example of an imaginary checklist about someone not performing TDD. (Keep in mind that this will differ for each person in each organization.)

Table 11.1 Influence factors checklist

Influence factor	Question to ask	Example answer
Personal ability	Does the person have all the skills or knowledge to perform what is required?	Yes. They went through a three-day TDD course with Roy Osherove.
Personal motivation	Does the person take satisfaction from the right behavior or dislike the wrong behavior? Do they have the self-control to engage in the behavior when it's hardest to do so?	I spoke with them, and they like doing TDD.
Social ability	Do you or others provide the help, information, and resources required by that person, particularly at critical times?	Yes.
Social motivation	Are the people around them actively encouraging the right behavior and discouraging the wrong behavior? Are you or others modeling the right behavior in an effective way?	As much as possible.
Structural (environmental) ability	Are there aspects in the environment (building, budget, and so on) that make the behavior convenient, easy, and safe? Are there enough cues and reminders to stay on course?	They don't have a budget for a build machine.*
Structural motivation	Are there clear and meaningful rewards (such as pay, bonuses, or incentives) when you or others behave the right or wrong way? Do short-term rewards match the desired long-term results and behaviors you want to reinforce or want to avoid?	When they try to spend time unit testing, their managers tell them they're wasting time. If they ship early and crappy, they get a bonus.*

I put asterisks next to the items in the right column that require work. Here I've identified two issues that need to be resolved. Solving only the build machine budget problem won't change the behavior. They have to get a build machine *and* deter their managers from giving a bonus on shipping crappy stuff quickly.

I write much more on this in *Notes to a Software Team Leader* (Team Agile Publishing, 2014), a book about running a technical team. You can find it at 5whys.com.

11.5   *Tough questions and answers*

This section covers some questions I've come across in various places. They usually arise from the premise that implementing unit testing can hurt someone personally—a manager concerned about their deadlines or a QA employee concerned about their relevance. Once you understand where a question is coming from, it's important to address the issue, directly or indirectly. Otherwise, there will always be subtle resistance.

11.5.1   *How much time will unit testing add to the current process?*

Team leaders, project managers, and clients are the ones who usually ask how much time unit testing will add to the process. They're the people at the front lines in terms of timing.

Let's begin with some facts. Studies have shown that raising the overall code quality in a project can increase productivity and shorten schedules. How does this match up with the fact that writing tests makes coding slower? Through maintainability and the ease of fixing bugs, mostly.

> **NOTE**   For studies on code quality and productivity, see *Programming Productivity* (McGraw-Hill College, 1986) and *Software Assessments, Benchmarks, and Best Practices* (Addison-Wesley Professional, 2000), both by Capers Jones.

When asking about time, team leaders may really be asking, "What should I tell my project manager when we go way past our due date?" They may actually think the process is useful but be looking for ammunition for the upcoming battle. They may also be asking the question not in terms of the whole product but in terms of specific feature sets or functionality. A project manager or customer who asks about timing, on the other hand, will usually be talking in terms of full product releases.

Because different people care about different scopes, your answers may vary. For example, unit testing can double the time it takes to implement a specific feature, but the overall release date for the product may actually be reduced. To understand this, let's look at a real example I was involved with.

A TALE OF TWO FEATURES

A large company I consulted with wanted to implement unit testing in their process, beginning with a pilot project. The pilot consisted of a group of developers adding a new feature to a large existing application. The company's main livelihood was in creating this large billing application and customizing parts of it for various clients. The company had thousands of developers around the world.

The following measures were taken to test the pilot's success:

- The time the team spent on each of the development stages
- The overall time for the project to be released to the client
- The number of bugs found by the client after the release

The same statistics were collected for a similar feature created by a different team for a different client. The two features were nearly the same size, and the teams were roughly at the same skill and experience level. Both tasks were customization efforts—one with unit tests, the other without. Table 11.2 shows the differences in time.

Table 11.2   Team progress and output measured with and without tests

Stage	Team without tests	Team with tests
Implementation (coding)	7 days	14 days
Integration	7 days	2 days
Testing and bug fixing	Testing, 3 days Fixing, 3 days Testing, 3 days Fixing, 2 days Testing, 1 day Total: 12 days	Testing, 3 days Fixing, 1 day Testing, 1 day Fixing, 1 day Testing, 1 day Total: 7 days
Overall release time	26 days	23 days
Bugs found in production	71	11

Overall, the time it took to release with tests was less than without tests. Still, the managers on the team with unit tests didn't initially believe the pilot would be a success, because they only looked at the implementation (coding) statistic (the first row in table 11.2) as the criteria for success, instead of the bottom line. It took twice the amount of time to code the feature (because unit tests require you to write more code). Despite this, the extra time was more than compensated for when the QA team found fewer bugs to deal with.

That's why it's important to emphasize that although unit testing can increase the amount of time it takes to implement a feature, the overall time requirements balance out over the product's release cycle because of increased quality and maintainability.

11.5.2   *Will my QA job be at risk because of unit testing?*

Unit testing doesn't eliminate QA-related jobs. QA engineers will receive the application with full unit test suites, which means they can make sure all the unit tests pass before they start their own testing process. Having unit tests in place will actually make their job more interesting. Instead of doing UI debugging (where every second button click results in an exception of some sort), they'll be able to focus on finding more logical (applicative) bugs in real-world scenarios. Unit tests provide the first layer of defense against bugs, and QA work provides the second layer—the user acceptance layer. As with security, the application always needs to have more than one layer of protection. Allowing the QA process to focus on the larger issues can produce better applications.

In some places, QA engineers write code, and they can help write unit tests for the application. That happens in conjunction with the work of the application developers and not instead of it. Both developers and QA engineers can write unit tests.

11.5.3 Is there proof that unit testing helps?

There aren't any specific studies on whether unit testing helps achieve better code quality that I can point to. Most related studies talk about adopting specific agile methods, with unit testing being just one of them. Some empirical evidence can be gleaned from the web, of companies and colleagues having great results and never wanting to go back to a codebase without tests. A few studies on TDD can be found at The QA Lead here: http://mng.bz/dddo.

11.5.4 Why is the QA department still finding bugs?

You may not have a QA department anymore, but this is still a very prevalent practice. Either way, you'll still be finding bugs. Please use tests at multiple levels, as described in chapter 10, to gain confidence across many layers of your application. Unit tests give you fast feedback and easy maintainability, but they leave some confidence behind, which can only be gained through some levels of integration tests.

11.5.5 We have lots of code without tests: Where do we start?

Studies conducted in the 1970s and 1980s showed that, typically, 80% of bugs are found in 20% of the code. The trick is to find the code that has the most problems. More often than not, any team can tell you which components are the most problematic. Start there. You can always add some metrics related to the number of bugs per class.

> #### Sources for the 80/20 figure
> Studies that show 80% of the bugs are in 20% of the code include the following: Albert Endres, "An analysis of errors and their causes in system programs," *IEEE Transactions on Software Engineering* 2 (June 1975), 140–49; Lee L. Gremillion, "Determinants of program repair maintenance requirements," *Communications of the ACM* 27, no. 8 (August 1984), 826–32; Barry W. Boehm, "Industrial software metrics top 10 list," *IEEE Software* 4, no. 9 (September 1987), 84–85 (reprinted in an IEEE newsletter and available online at http://mng.bz/rjjJ); and Shull and others, "What we have learned about fighting defects," *Proceedings of the 8th International Symposium on Software Metrics* (2002), 249–58.

Testing legacy code requires a different approach than when writing new code with tests. See chapter 12 for more details.

11.5.6 *What if we develop a combination of software and hardware?*

You can use unit tests even if you develop a combination of software and hardware. Look into the test layers mentioned in the previous chapter to make sure you cover both software and hardware. Hardware testing usually requires the use of simulators and emulators at various levels, but it is a common practice to have a suite of tests both for low-level embedded and high-level code.

11.5.7 *How can we know we don't have bugs in our tests?*

You need to make sure your tests fail when they should and pass when they should. TDD is a great way to make sure you don't forget to check those things. See chapter 1 for a short walk-through of TDD.

11.5.8 *Why do I need tests if my debugger shows that my code works?*

Debuggers don't help much with multithreaded code. Also, you may be sure your code works fine, but what about other people's code? How do you know it works? How do they know your code works and that they haven't broken anything when they make changes? Remember that coding is the first step in the life of the code. Most of its life, the code will be in maintenance mode. You need to make sure it will tell people when it breaks, using unit tests.

A study held by Curtis, Krasner, and Iscoe ("A field study of the software design process for large systems," *Communications of the ACM* 31, no. 11 (November 1988), 1268–87) showed that most defects don't come from the code itself but result from miscommunication between people, requirements that keep changing, and a lack of application domain knowledge. Even if you're the world's greatest coder, chances are that if someone tells you to code the wrong thing, you'll do it. When you need to change it, you'll be glad you have tests for everything else, to make sure you don't break it.

11.5.9 *What about TDD?*

TDD is a style choice. I personally see a lot of value in TDD, and many people find it productive and beneficial, but others find that writing tests after the code is good enough for them. You can make your own choice.

Summary

- Implementing unit testing in their organization is something that many readers of this book will have to face at one time or another.
- Make sure that you don't alienate the people who can help you. Recognize champions and blockers inside the organization. Make both groups part of the change process.

- Identify possible starting points. Start with a small team or project with a limited scope to get a quick win and minimize project duration risks.
- Make the progress visible to everyone. Aim for specific goals, metrics, and KPIs.
- Take note of potential causes of failure, such as the lack of a driving force and lack of political or team support.
- Be prepared to have good answers to the questions you're likely to be asked.

Working with legacy code

I once consulted for a large development shop that produced billing software. They had over 10,000 developers and mixed .NET, Java, and C++ in products, sub-products, and intertwined projects. The software had existed in one form or another for over five years, and most of the developers were tasked with maintaining and building on top of existing functionality.

My job was to help several divisions (using all languages) learn TDD techniques. For about 90% of the developers I worked with, this never became a reality for several reasons, some of which were a result of legacy code:

- It was difficult to write tests against existing code.
- It was next to impossible to refactor the existing code (or there wasn't enough time to do it).
- Some people didn't want to change their designs.
- Tooling (or a lack of tooling) was getting in the way.
- It was difficult to determine where to begin.

Anyone who's ever tried to add tests to an existing system knows that most such systems are almost impossible to write tests for. They were usually written without proper places (called *seams*) in the software to allow extensions or replacements to existing components.

There are two problems that need to be addressed when dealing with legacy code:

- There's so much work, where should you start to add tests? Where should you focus your efforts?
- How can you safely refactor your code if it has no tests to begin with?

This chapter will tackle these tough questions associated with approaching legacy codebases by listing techniques, references, and tools that can help.

12.1 *Where do you start adding tests?*

Assuming you have existing code inside components, you'll need to create a priority list of components for which testing makes the most sense. There are several factors to consider that can affect each component's priority:

- *Logical complexity*—This refers to the amount of logic in the component, such as nested `if`s, switch cases, or recursion. Such complexity is also called *cyclomatic complexity*, and you can use various tools to check it automatically.
- *Dependency level*—This refers to the number of dependencies in the component. How many dependencies do you have to break in order to bring this class under test? Does it communicate with an outside email component, perhaps, or does it call a static log method somewhere?
- *Priority*—This is the component's general priority in the project.

You can give each component a rating for these factors, from 1 (low priority) to 10 (high priority). Table 12.1 shows classes with ratings for these factors. I call this a *test-feasibility table*.

Table 12.1   A simple test-feasibility table

Component	Logical complexity	Dependency level	Priority	Notes
Utils	6	1	5	This utility class has few dependencies but contains a lot of logic. It will be easy to test, and it provides lots of value.
Person	2	1	1	This is a data-holder class with little logic and no dependencies. There's little real value in testing this.
TextParser	8	4	6	This class has lots of logic and lots of dependencies. To top it off, it's part of a high-priority task in the project. Testing this will provide lots of value but will also be hard and time consuming.

Table 12.1 A simple test-feasibility table *(continued)*

Component	Logical complexity	Dependency level	Priority	Notes
ConfigManager	1	6	1	This class holds configuration data and reads files from disk. It has little logic but many dependencies. Testing it will provide little value to the project and will also be hard and time consuming.

From the data in table 12.1, you can create a diagram like the one shown in figure 12.1, which graphs your components by the amount of value to the project and number of dependencies. You can safely ignore items that are below your designated threshold of logic (which I usually set at 2 or 3), so Person and ConfigManager can be ignored. You're left with only the top two components in figure 12.1.

There are two basic ways to look at the graph and decide what you'd like to test first (see figure 12.2):

- Choose the one that's more complex and easier to test (top left).
- Choose the one that's more complex and harder to test (top right).

The question now is what path you should take. Should you start with the easy stuff or the hard stuff?

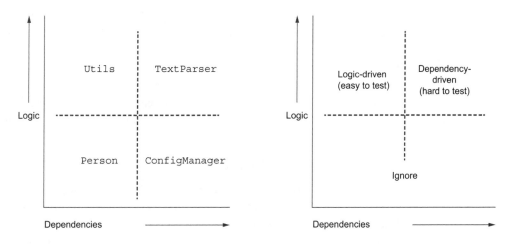

Figure 12.1 Mapping components for test feasibility

Figure 12.2 Easy, hard, and irrelevant component mapping based on logic and dependencies

12.2   *Choosing a selection strategy*

As the previous section explained, you can start with the components that are easy to test or the ones that are hard to test (because they have many dependencies). Each strategy presents different challenges.

12.2.1   *Pros and cons of the easy-first strategy*

Starting out with the components that have fewer dependencies will make writing the tests initially much quicker and easier. But there's a catch, as figure 12.3 demonstrates.

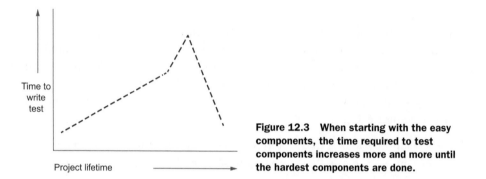

Figure 12.3   **When starting with the easy components, the time required to test components increases more and more until the hardest components are done.**

Figure 12.3 shows how long it takes to bring components under test during the life-time of the project. Initially it's easy to write tests, but as time goes by, you're left with components that are increasingly harder and harder to test, with the particularly tough ones waiting for you at the end of the project cycle, just when everyone is stressed about pushing a product out the door.

If your team is relatively new to unit testing techniques, it's worth starting with the easy components. As time goes by, the team will learn the techniques needed to deal with the more complex components and dependencies. For such a team, it may be wise to initially avoid all components over a specific number of dependencies (with four being a reasonable limit).

12.2.2   *Pros and cons of the hard-first strategy*

Starting with the more difficult components may seem like a losing proposition ini-tially, but it has an upside as long as your team has experience with unit testing tech-niques. Figure 12.4 shows the average time to write a test for a single component over the lifetime of the project, if you start testing the components with the most depen-dencies first.

With this strategy, you could be spending a day or more to get even the simplest tests going on the more complex components. But notice the quick decline in the time required to write the tests relative to the slow incline in figure 12.3. Every time you bring a component under test and refactor it to make it more testable, you may

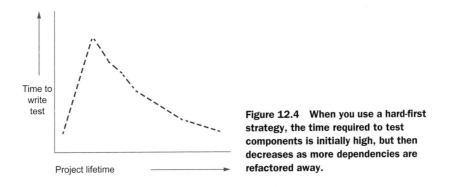

Figure 12.4   **When you use a hard-first strategy, the time required to test components is initially high, but then decreases as more dependencies are refactored away.**

also be solving testability issues for the dependencies it uses or for other components. Because that component has lots of dependencies, refactoring it can improve things for other parts of the system. That's the reason for the quick decline.

The hard-first strategy is only possible if your team has experience in unit testing techniques, because it's harder to implement. If your team does have experience, use the priority aspect of components to choose whether to start with the hard or easy components. You might want to choose a mix, but it's important that you know in advance how much effort will be involved and what the possible consequences are.

12.3   *Writing integration tests before refactoring*

If you do plan to refactor your code for testability (so you can write unit tests), a practical way to make sure you don't break anything during the refactoring phase is to write integration-style tests against your production system.

I consulted on a large legacy project, working with a developer who needed to work on an XML configuration manager. The project had no tests and was hardly testable. It was also a C++ project, so we couldn't use a tool to easily isolate components from dependencies without refactoring the code.

The developer needed to add another value attribute into the XML file and be able to read and change it through the existing configuration component. We ended up writing a couple of integration tests that used the real system to save and load configuration data and that asserted on the values the configuration component was retrieving and writing to the file. Those tests set the "original" working behavior of the configuration manager as our base of work.

Next, we wrote an integration test that showed that once the component was reading the file, it contained no attribute in memory with the name we were trying to add. We proved that the feature was missing, and we now had a test that would pass once we added the new attribute to the XML file and correctly wrote to it from the component.

Once we wrote the code that saved and loaded the extra attribute, we ran the three integration tests (two tests for the original base implementation and a new one that tried to read the new attribute). All three passed, so we knew that we hadn't broken existing functionality while adding the new functionality.

As you can see, the process is relatively simple:

- Add one or more integration tests (no mocks or stubs) to the system to prove the original system works as needed.
- Refactor or add a failing test for the feature you're trying to add to the system.
- Refactor and change the system in small chunks, and run the integration tests as often as you can, to see if you break something.

Sometimes, integration tests may seem easier to write than unit tests, because you don't need to understand the internal structure of the code or where to inject various dependencies. But making those tests run on your local system may prove annoying or time consuming because you have to make sure every little thing the system needs is in place.

The trick is to work on the parts of the system that you need to fix or add features to. Don't focus on the other parts. That way, the system grows in the right places, leaving other bridges to be crossed when you get to them.

As you continue adding more and more tests, you can refactor the system and add more unit tests to it, growing it into a more maintainable and testable system. This takes time (sometimes months and months), but it's worth it.

Chapter 7 of *Unit Testing Principles, Practices, and Patterns* by Vladimir Khorikov (Manning, 2020) contains an in-depth example of such refactoring. Refer to that book for more details.

12.3.1 *Read Michael Feathers' book on legacy code*

Working Effectively with Legacy Code by Michael Feathers (Pearson, 2004) is another valuable source that deals with the issues you'll encounter with legacy code. It shows many refactoring techniques and gotchas in depth that this book doesn't attempt to cover. It's worth its weight in gold. Get it.

12.3.2 *Use CodeScene to investigate your production code*

Another tool called CodeScene allows you to discover lots of technical debt and hidden issues in legacy code, among many other things. It is a commercial tool, and while I have not personally used it, I've heard great things. You can learn more about it at https://codescene.com/.

Summary

- Before starting to write tests for legacy code, it's important to map out the various components according to their number of dependencies, their amount of logic, and each component's general priority in the project. A component's logical complexity (or cyclomatic complexity) refers to the amount of logic in the component, such as nested `ifs`, switch cases, or recursion.
- Once you have that information, you can choose the components to work on based on how easy or how hard it will be to get them under test.

- If your team has little or no experience in unit testing, it's a good idea to start with the easy components and let the team's confidence grow as they add more and more tests to the system.
- If your team is experienced, getting the hard components under test first can help you get through the rest of the system more quickly.
- Before a large-scale refactoring, write integration tests that will sustain that refactoring mostly unchanged. After the refactoring is completed, replace most of these integration tests with smaller and more maintainable unit tests.

appendix
Monkey-patching
functions and modules

In chapter 3, I introduced various stubbing techniques that I called "accepted," in that they are usually considered safe for both the maintainability and readability of the code and the tests that they guide us to write. In this appendix, I'll describe a few of the less accepted and less safe ways in which we can fake whole modules in our tests.

A.1   *An obligatory warning*

I have good news and bad news about global patching and stubbing out functions and modules. Yes, you can do it—I'll show you several ways to accomplish this. Is it a great idea? I'm not convinced. The costs of maintaining your tests with the techniques I'll show you tend to be, from my experience, worse than maintaining code that is well parameterized or has proper seams built in.

However, there might be special times when you need to use these techniques. Such times include, but are not limited to, faking dependencies in code that you do not own and cannot change, and sometimes when using immediately executable functions or modules. Another case is when a module exposes only functions without objects, which limits the faking options quite a bit.

Try to avoid using the techniques I describe in this appendix as much as you can. If you can find a way to write your tests or refactor your code so you don't need these approaches, use that way. If all else fails, the techniques in this appendix are a necessary evil. If you must use them, try to minimize how much you use them. Your tests will suffer and will become more fragile and harder to read.

Let's dive in.

A.2 Monkey-patching functions, globals, and possible issues

Monkey-patching refers to the act of changing the behavior of a running program instance at run time. I first encountered the term when I was working in Ruby, where monkey-patching is very common. In JavaScript, it's just as easy to "patch" a function at run time.

In chapter 3 we looked at the issue of time management in our tests and code. With monkey-patching, we could look at any function, global or local, and replace it (for a specific JavaScript scope) with a different implementation. If we wanted to patch time, we could monkey-patch the global `Date.now` so that any code from that point on would be affected by this change, both production and test code.

Listing A.1 shows a test that does this for the original production code that uses `Date.now` directly. It fakes the global `Date.now` function to control time during the test.

Listing A.1 Issues in faking the global `Date.now()`

```
describe('v1 findRecentlyRebooted', () => {
  test('given 1 of 2 machines under threshold, it is found', () => {
    const originalNow = Date.now;
    const fromDate = new Date(2000,0,3);
    Date.now = () => fromDate.getTime();

    const rebootTwoDaysEarly = new Date(2000,0,1);
    const machines = [
      { lastBootTime: rebootTwoDaysEarly, name: 'ignored' },
      { lastBootTime: fromDate, name: 'found' }];

    const result = findRecentlyRebooted(machines, 1, fromDate);

    expect(result.length).toBe(1);
    expect(result[0].name).toContain('found');

    Date.now = originalNow;
  });
});
```

Saving the original `Date.now` → (points to `const originalNow = Date.now;`)

Replacing Date.now with a custom date (points to `const fromDate = new Date(2000,0,3);` / `Date.now = () => fromDate.getTime();`)

Restoring the original Date.now (points to `Date.now = originalNow;`)

In this listing, we're replacing the global `Date.now` with a custom date. Because this is a global function, other tests can be affected by it, so we clean up after ourselves at the end of the test by restoring the original `Date.now` to its rightful place.

There are several major issues in a test like this. First, these asserts throw exceptions when they fail, which means if they fail, the restoration of the original `Date.now` might never be executed, and other tests will suffer a "dirty" global time that might affect them.

It's also cumbersome to save the time function and then put it back. It's making its mark on the test and making it longer and harder to read, plus harder to write. It's easy to forget to reset the global state.

Finally, we've impaired parallelism. Jest seems to handle this well, as it creates a separate set of dependencies for each test file, but with other frameworks that might run tests in parallel, there could be a race condition. Multiple tests can change or expect the global time to have a certain value. When running in parallel, these tests can collide and create race conditions in the global state and affect each other. It's not required in our case, but if you wanted to eliminate uncertainty, Jest allows you to run the Jest command line with the extra `--runInBand` command-line parameter to avoid parallelism.

We can avoid some of these issues by resorting to the `beforeEach()` and `afterEach()` helper functions.

Listing A.2   Resorting to `beforeEach()` and `afterEach()`

```
describe('v2 findRecentlyRebooted', () => {          Saving the
  let originalNow;                                    original Date.now
  beforeEach(() => originalNow = Date.now);
  afterEach(() => Date.now = originalNow);            Restoring the
                                                      original Date.now

  test('given 1 of 2 machines under threshold, it is found', () => {
    const fromDate = new Date(2000,0,3);
    Date.now = () => fromDate.getTime();

    const rebootTwoDaysEarly = new Date(2000,0,1);
    const machines = [
      { lastBootTime: rebootTwoDaysEarly, name: 'ignored' },
      { lastBootTime: fromDate, name: 'found' }];

    const result = findRecentlyRebooted(machines, 1, fromDate);

    expect(result.length).toBe(1);
    expect(result[0].name).toContain('found');
  });
});
```

Listing A.2 solves some of our issues but not all of them. The good part is that we don't need to remember to save and reset `Date.now` anymore, because `beforeEach()` and `afterEach()` will take care of it. It's also now easier to read the tests.

But we still have a potential major issue with parallel tests. Jest is smart enough to run parallel tests only per file, which means the tests in this spec file will run linearly, but this behavior is not guaranteed for tests in other files. Any one of the parallel tests might have their own `beforeEach()` and `afterEach()` that reset global state and might affect our tests without realizing it.

I'm not a fan of faking global objects (i.e., "singletons" in most typed languages) when I can help it. There are always strings attached—extra coding, extra maintenance, extra test fragility, or affecting other tests indirectly and worrying about cleaning up all the time are some reasons why. Most of the time, the code comes out better when I factor seams into the design of the code under test instead of around it in an implicit manner, such as what we just did.

Especially when considering that more and more frameworks might start to copy Jest's features and run tests in parallel, global fakes become more and more dangerous.

A.2.1 Monkey-patching a function the Jest way

To make the picture more complete, Jest also supports the idea of monkey-patching through the use of two functions that work in tandem: `spyOn` and `mockImplementation`. Here's `spyOn`:

```
Date.now = jest.spyOn(Date, 'now')
```

`spyOn` takes as parameters the scope and the function that requires tracking. Note that we need to use a string as a parameter here, which is not really refactoring-friendly—it's easy to miss if we rename that function.

A.2.2 Jest spies

The word "spy" has a slightly more interesting shade of grey to it than the terms we've encountered so far in this book, which is why I don't like to use it too much (or at all) if I can help it. Unfortunately, this word is a major part of Jest's API, so let's make sure we understand it.

xUnit Test Patterns (Addison-Wesley, 2007), by Gerard Meszaros, says this in its discussion of spies: "Use a Test Double to capture the indirect output calls made to another component by the system under test (SUT) for later verification by the test." The only difference between a spy and a fake or test double is that a spy is calling the *real* implementation of the function underneath, and it only tracks the inputs to and outputs from that function, which we can later verify through the test. Fakes and test doubles don't use the real implementation of a function.

My refined definition of a *spy* is pretty close: The act of wrapping a *unit of work* with an invisible tracking layer on the *entry points* and *exit points* without changing the underlying functionality, for the purpose of tracking its inputs and outputs during testing.

A.2.3 spyOn with mockImplementation()

This "tracking without changing functionality" behavior that is inherent to spies also explains why just using `spyOn` won't be enough for us to fake `Date.now`. It's only meant for tracking, not faking.

To actually *fake* the `Date.now` function and turn it into a *stub*, we'll use the confusingly named `mockImplementation` to replace the underlying unit of work's functionality:

```
jest.spyOn(Date, 'now').mockImplementation(() => /*return stub time*/);
```

> ### Too much "mock"
>
> If I were in a position to decide on a new name for `mockImplementation`, I'd name it `fakeImplementation`, because it can easily be used to create either stubs that return data or mocks that verify the data being sent into them as parameters. The word "mock" is used far too often in our industry to signify anything that isn't real, when the distinction could help us make less brittle tests. "Mock" in the name immediately implies that this is something we'll verify against later on, at least when I look at it, and given how I treat the ideas of mocks versus stubs in this book.
>
> Jest is littered with overuse of the word "mock," especially when comparing its API to an isolation framework such as Sinon.js, which uses naming that is less surprising and avoids using "mock" where it's not necessary.

Here's how the `spyOn` and `mockImplementation` combo looks in our code.

Listing A.3   Using `jest.SpyOn()` to monkey-patch `Date.now()`

```
describe('v4 findRecentlyRebooted with jest spyOn', () => {
  afterEach(() => jest.restoreAllMocks());

  test('given 1 of 2 machines under threshold, it is found', () => {
    const fromDate = new Date(2000,0,3);
    Date.now = jest.spyOn(Date, 'now')
      .mockImplementation(() => fromDate.getTime());

    const rebootTwoDaysEarly = new Date(2000,0,1);
    const machines = [
      { lastBootTime: rebootTwoDaysEarly, name: 'ignored' },
      { lastBootTime: fromDate, name: 'found' }];
```

You can see that the last piece of the puzzle in the code is inside `afterEach()`. We use another function called `jest.restoreAllMocks`, which is Jest's way of resetting any global state that has been spied on to its original implementation with no extra fake layers around it.

Note that even though we are using a spy, we're not verifying that the function was actually called. Doing that would mean we're using it as a mock object, which we are not. We're merely using it as a stub. With Jest, we have to go through a "spy" to stub stuff out.

All of the advantages and disadvantages I've listed before still apply here. I prefer using parameters when it makes sense, instead of using global functions or variables.

A.3   *Ignoring a whole module with Jest is simple*

Of all the techniques mentioned in this appendix, this is the safest because it does not deal with the internal workings of the unit under test. It just ignores things in a broad manner.

If we don't care about the module at all during our tests, and we just want to get it out of the way of our scenario without getting any fake data back from it, a simple call to `jest.mock('module path')` at the top of the test file will do just fine, without too much fuss.

The next section helps if you want to simulate custom data in each test from a fake module, which makes us go through more hoops.

A.4   Faking module behavior in each test

Faking a module basically means faking a global object that gets loaded whenever `import` or `require` is used for the first time by the code under test. Depending on the test framework we're using, the module might be cached internally or through the standard Node.js `require.cache` mechanism. Since this only happens once, when our test imports the system under test, we have a bit of an issue when we're trying to fake different behavior or data for different tests in the same file.

To fake custom behavior for our fake module, we need to take care of the following in our tests: clean up the required module from memory, replace it, re-require it, and get the code under test to use the new module instead of the original one by requiring our code under test again. That's quite a bit. I call this pattern Clear-Fake-Require-Act (CFRA):

1　*Clear*—Before each test, clear all the cached or required modules in the test runner's memory.
2　During the arrange part of the test:
　a　*Fake*—Fake the module that will be required by the `require` action invoked by the test code.
　b　*Require*—Require the code under test just before invoking it.
3　*Act*—Invoke the entry point.

If we forget any of these steps, or perform them in the wrong order, or not at the right point in the test's life cycle, there'll be a lot of question marks when we execute the test and things seem not to be faking correctly. Worse, they might *sometimes* work correctly. Shudder.

Let's look at a real example, starting with the following code.

Listing A.4   Code under test with a dependency

```
const { getAllMachines } = require('./my-data-module');        The dependency
                                                               to fake
const daysFrom = (from, to) => {
  const ms = from.getTime() - new Date(to).getTime();
  const diff = (ms / 1000) / 60 / 60 / 24; // secs * min * hrs
  console.log(diff);
  return diff;
};
```

```
const findRecentlyRebooted = (maxDays, fromDate) => {
  const machines = getAllMachines();
  return machines.filter(machine => {
    const daysDiff = daysFrom(fromDate, machine.lastBootTime);
    console.log(`${daysDiff} vs ${maxDays}`);
    return daysDiff < maxDays;
  });
};
```

The first line contains the dependency we need to break in our test. It's the `getAll-Machines` function, being destructured from `my-data-module`. Because we are using the function detached from its parent module, we can't just fake functions on the parent module and expect our tests to pass. We have to get the *destructured* function to get a fake function during the destructuring process, and that's where the tricky part comes in.

A.4.1   *Stubbing a module with vanilla require.cache*

Before we use Jest and other frameworks to fake a whole module, let's see how we can achieve this effect and explore what's going on in the various frameworks.

You can use the CFRA pattern without using any framework by using `require.cache` directly.

Listing A.5   Stubbing with `require.cache`

```
const assert = require('assert');
const { check } = require('./custom-test-framework');

const dataModulePath = require.resolve('../my-data-module');

const fakeDataFromModule = fakeData => {
  delete require.cache[dataModulePath];          ⟵┘ Clear
  require.cache[dataModulePath] = {              ⟵┐ Fake
    id: dataModulePath,
    filename: dataModulePath,
    loaded: true,
    exports: {
      getAllMachines: () => fakeData
    }
  };
  require(dataModulePath);
};

const requireAndCall_findRecentlyRebooted = (maxDays, fromDate) => {
  const { findRecentlyRebooted } = require('../machine-scanner4');   ⟵┘ Require
  return findRecentlyRebooted(maxDays, fromDate);    ⟵┐ Act
};


check('given 1 of 2 machines under the threshold, it is found', () => {
  const rebootTwoDaysEarly = new Date(2000,0,1);
  const fromDate = new Date(2000,0,3);
```

```
fakeDataFromModule([
  { lastBootTime: rebootTwoDaysEarly, name: 'ignored' },
  { lastBootTime: fromDate, name: 'found' }
]);

const result = requireAndCall_findRecentlyRebooted(1, fromDate);
assert(result.length === 1);
assert(result[0].name.includes('found'));
});
```

Unfortunately, this code will not work with Jest, because Jest ignores `require.cache` and implements its own caching algorithm internally. To execute this test, run it directly through the Node.js command line. You'll see that I've implemented my own little `check()` function, so that I don't use Jest's API. This test will work just fine when using a framework such as Jasmine.

Remember this line in our code under test?

```
const { getAllMachines } = require('./my-data-module');
```

Our tests need to *execute* this destructuring every time we want to return a fake value. That means we'll need to execute a require or import of the unit under test from our test code, not at the top of the file, but somewhere in the middle of our test execution. You can see where this happens in the following part of listing A.5:

```
const requireAndCall_findRecentlyRebooted = (maxDays, fromDate) => {
  const { findRecentlyRebooted } = require('../machine-scanner4');
  return findRecentlyRebooted(maxDays, fromDate);
};
```

It is because of this destructuring code pattern that modules are not just objects with properties, for which normal monkey-patching techniques can be used. We need to jump through more hoops.

Let's map the four CFRA steps to the code in listing A.5:

- *Clear*—This is part of the `fakeDataFromModule` function, which is invoked during the test.
- *Fake*—we are telling `require.cache`'s dictionary entry to return a custom object that seems to represent what a module looks like, but which has a custom implementation that returns `fakeData`.
- *Require*—We are requiring the code under test as part of the `requireAndCall_findRecentlyRebooted()` function, which is invoked during the test.
- *ACT*—This is part of the same `requireAndCall_findRecentlyRebooted()` function that is invoked by the test.

Notice that we do not use `beforeEach()` for this test. We are doing everything directly from the test, because each test will fake its own data from the module.

A.4.2   *Stubbing custom module data with Jest is complicated*

We've seen the "vanilla" way of stubbing custom module data. That's not usually how you'd do it if you're using Jest, though. Jest contains several confusingly and very closely named functions that deal with clearing and faking modules, including mock, doMock, genMockFromModule, resetAllMocks, clearAllMocks, restoreAllMocks, resetModules and more. Yay!

The code I'll recommend here feels the cleanest and simplest of all of Jest's APIs in terms of readability and maintainability. I do cover other variations on it in the GitHub repository at https://github.com/royosherove/aout3-samples and under the "other-variations" folder at http://mng.bz/Jddo.

This is the common pattern for faking a module with Jest:

1   Require the module you'd like to fake in your own tests.
2   Stub out the module above the tests with jest.mock(modulename).
3   In each test, tell Jest to override the behavior of one of the functions in that module by using [modulename].function.mockImplementation() or mockImplementation-Once().

The following is what it might look like.

Listing A.6   Stubbing a module with Jest

```
const dataModule = require('../my-data-module');
const { findRecentlyRebooted } = require('../machine-scanner4');

const fakeDataFromModule = (fakeData) =>
    dataModule.getAllMachines.mockImplementation(() => fakeData);

jest.mock('../my-data-module');

describe('findRecentlyRebooted', () => {
  beforeEach(jest.resetAllMocks); //<- the cleanest way

  test('given no machines, returns empty results', () => {
    fakeDataFromModule([]);
    const someDate = new Date(2000,0,1);

    const result = findRecentlyRebooted(0, someDate);

    expect(result.length).toBe(0);
  });

  test('given 1 of 2 machines under threshold, it is found', () => {
    const fromDate = new Date(2000,0,3);
    const rebootTwoDaysEarly = new Date(2000,0,1);
    fakeDataFromModule([
      { lastBootTime: rebootTwoDaysEarly, name: 'ignored' },
      { lastBootTime: fromDate, name: 'found' }
    ]);
    const result = findRecentlyRebooted(1, fromDate);
```

```
    expect(result.length).toBe(1);
    expect(result[0].name).toContain('found');
});
```

Here's how you can approach each part of CFRA with Jest.

Clear	`jest.resetAllMocks`
Fake	`jest.mock()+` `[fake].mockImplementation()`
Require	Regularly at the top of the file
Act	Regularly

The `jest.mock` and `jest.resetAllMocks` methods are all about faking the module and resetting the fake implementation to an empty one. Note that the module is still fake after `resetAllMocks`. Only its behavior is reset to the default fake implementation. Calling it without telling it what to return will yield weird errors.

With the `FromModule` method, we replace the default implementation with a function that returns our hardcoded values in each test.

We could have used `mockImplementationOnce()` to do mocking, instead of the `fakeDataFromModule()` method, but I find that this can create very brittle tests. With stubs, we normally shouldn't care how many times they return the fake values. If we did care how many times they were called, we would use them as *mock* objects, and that's the subject of chapter 4.

A.4.3   *Avoid Jest's manual mocks*

Jest contains the idea of *manual mocks*, but don't use them if you can help it. This technique requires you to put a special __mocks__ folder in your tests that contain hardcoded fake module code, with a naming convention based on the module's name. This will work, but the maintainability costs are too high when you want to control the fake data. The readability costs are too high as well, as it increases scroll fatigue to an unneeded level, requiring us to switch between multiple files to understand a test. You can read more about manual mocks in the Jest documentation: https://jestjs.io/docs/en/manual-mocks.html.

A.4.4   *Stubbing a module with Sinon.js*

For comparison, and so that you can see that the pattern of CFRA repeats in other frameworks, here's an implementation of the same test with Sinon.js—a framework dedicated to creating stubs.

Listing A.7   Stubbing a module with Sinon.js

```
const sinon = require('sinon');
let dataModule;
```

```
const fakeDataFromModule = fakeData => {
  sinon.stub(dataModule, 'getAllMachines')
    .returns(fakeData);
};

const resetAndRequireModules = () => {
  jest.resetModules();
  dataModule = require('../my-data-module');
};

const requireAndCall_findRecentlyRebooted = (maxDays, someDate) => {
  const { findRecentlyRebooted } = require('../machine-scanner4');
  return findRecentlyRebooted(maxDays, someDate);
};

describe('4  sinon sandbox findRecentlyRebooted', () => {
  beforeEach(resetAndRequireModules);

  test('given no machines, returns empty results', () => {
    const someDate = new Date('01 01 2000');
    fakeDataFromModule([]);

    const result = requireAndCall_findRecentlyRebooted(2, someDate);

    expect(result.length).toBe(0);
  });
});
```

Let's map the relevant parts with Sinon.

Clear	Before each test: `jest.resetModules + re-require fake module`

Fake	Before each test:
	`sinon.stub(module,'function')`
	`.returns(fakeData)`

Require (module under test)	Before invoking the entry point
Act	After re-requiring the module under test

A.4.5 *Stubbing a module with testdouble*

Testdouble is another isolation framework that can easily be used to stub things out. Due to the refactoring already done in previous tests, the code changes are minimal.

Listing A.8 Stubbing a module with testdouble

```
let td;

const resetAndRequireModules = () => {
  jest.resetModules();
  td = require('testdouble');
  require('testdouble-jest')(td, jest);
};
```

```
const fakeDataFromModule = fakeData => {
  td.replace('../my-data-module', {
    getAllMachines: () => fakeData
  });
};

const requireAndCall_findRecentlyRebooted = (maxDays, fromDate) => {
  const { findRecentlyRebooted } = require('../machine-scanner4');
  return findRecentlyRebooted(maxDays, fromDate);
};
```

Here are the important parts with testdouble.

Clear	Before each test:
	`jest.resetModules + require('testdouble');`
	`require('testdouble-jest')`
	`                    (td, jest);`

Fake	Before each test: `Td.replace(module, fake object)`
Require (module under test)	Before invoking the entry point
Act	After re-requiring the module under test

The test implementation is exactly the same as with the Sinon example. We're also using `testdouble-jest`, as it connects to the Jest module replacement facility. This is not needed if we're using a different test framework.

These techniques *will* work, but I recommend staying away from them unless there's absolutely no other way. There is almost always another way, and you can see many of those in chapter 3.

index